C0-APJ-268

# Foodways:

## *Culinary Traditions of Aransas County*

Karl—

Enjoy all the stories and art and recipes of your new home!

Kay Betz

# Foodways:

## *Culinary Traditions of Aransas County*

Edited by

**Vickie Moon Merchant, Ph.D.**

**and**

**Kay Betz, Ph.D**

Copyright© 2019 The History Center for Aransas County

All rights reserved.

ISBN – 13:

9781093757798

ISBN – 10

1093757795

The Friends of the History Center wish to thank the Margaret Sue Rust Foundation for their financial support of the
"Foodways: Culinary Traditions of Aransas County Exhibit" and the publication of
"Foodways: Culinary Traditions of Aransas County".

# Contents

BATHING AT ROCKPORT. TEXAS

we are just having a fine time tell
Sunday she ought to be here.

From the Collection of Jim Moloney

# INTRODUCTION

## WELCOME!

### To Rockport, Fulton and Lamar

❖❖❖❖❖❖

*Best Fishing, Swimming and Boating on the Texas Coast*

❖❖❖❖❖

Your Pleasure is our business, and upon the service we render depends future visits from you, and we are always ready to do everything possible to make your stay with us the most enjoyable you have ever had on the Texas Coast. Let your wishes or needs be known. We'll do our best to please! As an added courtesy we are co-operating with the Rockport Pilot in bringing this newspaper to our guests each week. On this page, and elsewhere in the paper, you will find information that will be of assistance to you in making all your vacation hours count, including suggestions on where to go and what to do.

Rockport, Fulton, Lamar and adjacent areas along the 15-mile coastline of Live Oak and Lamar Peninsulas form the most ideal "family playground" on the Texas Coast. Here stretches fifteen miles of tree-lined beaches and natural beauty that comes from blending of skies, water and trees, bathed in a semi-tropic sunshine and tempered by cooling Gulf breezes. Here one can enjoy the activity of fishing, boating and swimming, or just loaf in an Eden-like atmosphere, so different from the usual highly commercialized tourist resort.

## There's Fun For All in This Vacation Land

### .-BAIT-.
BAIT SHRIMP

LIVE            DEAD
75c             15c
Hundred         Pound

SKIFFS—TOW-OUTS
COLD DRINKS & CANDY
—½ MILE ON SHORE SOUTH OF ROCKPORT—

### SHIPYARD POINT
"FISHING AT ITS BEST"
HANK WIGINTON, Owner

### ROCKPORT PAVILION
DINE -:- DANCE -:- SWIM
—Menu—

FISH DINNER, With Salad and Cocktail ............ 60c
FISH DINNER, With Salad .......................... 50c
FRIED SHRIMP ..................................... 50c
1 DEVILED CRAB ................................... 50c
STEAK DINNER ................................ 75c & 50c
CHICKEN DINNER .............................. 50c & 25c
BARBECUED CRAB ................................... 60c
SHRIMP COCKTAIL .................................. 50c
HAMBURGERS -:- SANDWICHES -:- SALADS

MISS ALLYN BUNKER, Proprietor

### OLEANDER COURT
Tourist Homes . . . .

TRULY MODERN . . . .
ELECTRIC REFRIGERATION
HUNTERS' AND FISHERMEN'S
PARADISE

Mrs. B. W. HAMBLIN, Manager
JACK F. HORTON, Owner
Rockport    Hwy. 35, Bus. Rt.    P. 261

# Acknowledgements

This book was developed to accompany "Foodways: The Culinary Traditions of Aransas County," an exhibit presented by the Friends of the History Center for Aransas County in the summer of 2017. Kay Betz and Vickie Merchant co-curated the exhibit with the assistance of a Culinary Exhibit Committee -- Lucretia Wright, Leah Oliva, Karey Swartwout, Janet Taylor, Kam Wagert and Maureen Winkelman.

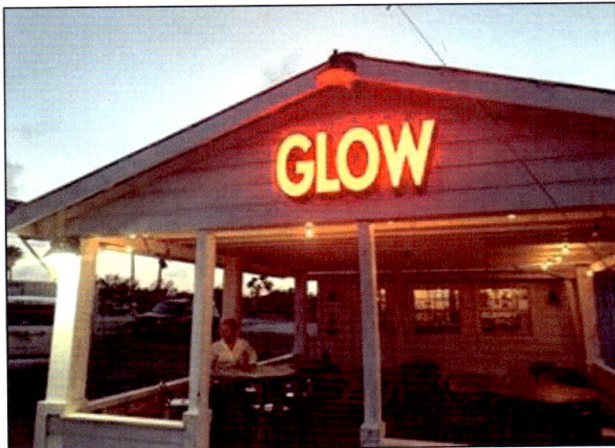

The exhibit was inspired by the pioneering work of Karey Swartwout, the owner of "GLOW" Restaurant, who researched and wrote about many local culinary practices in Aransas County in a column called "Coastal Flavors" for the *Corpus Christi Caller Times* during 2012.

Karey has revived many early local culinary traditions, including the use of local game and seafood, fresh, seasonal local ingredients, and forgotten ingredients such as mesquite beans. YouTube videos associated with her column were part of media content for this exhibit. "How to Make Your Own Sea Salt" documents regional salt harvesting practices in the area. "Fishing for Flounder" observes Flower, a local Vietnamese woman, cleaning fresh-caught fish.

The Margaret Sue Rust Foundation, a long-standing supporter of the History Center's initiatives and sustainability, funded the Foodways Exhibit and publication of this book. Its Board Member, Susie Bracht Black, has been a steady source of creative inspiration, practical advice, and strategic perspective.

Monica Burdette, a local Commissioner for the Texas Historical Commission, also a chef and cookbook author, was another member of an informal "Kitchen Cabinet." Her remarks for the exhibit's opening are included as our "Foreward." A noted Texas cookbook author, Terry Thompson-Anderson, was also key to helping us develop this book, as well

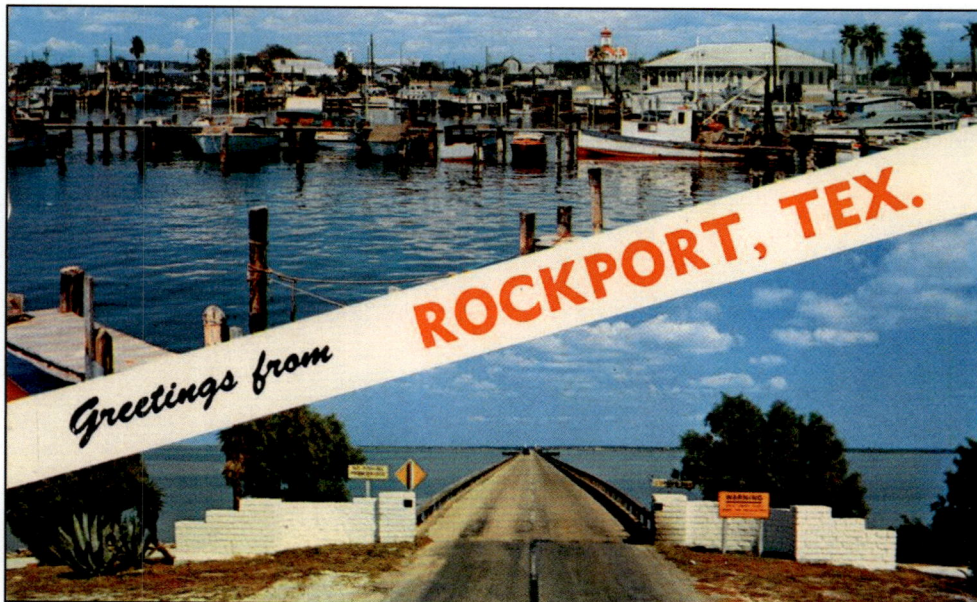

Greetings from ROCKPORT, TEX.

Courtesy of Gordon Stanley

4

as allowing us to include her remarks from an accompanying program as our "Introduction."

Interviews with area residents added greatly to the exhibit and book content. We thank Dan Agler, Kay Barnebey, Sandy Bellaire, Tom Betz, Susie Bracht Black, Leslie "Bubba" Casterline, Stephanie Casterline-LeMons, Tony and Alicia Dominguez, Jeff and Melody Easterday, Jessie Ellis, Susan Forrest, James Richard and Laura Fox, Lisa Baer Frederick, Katy Jones-Gulsby, John and Debbie Jackson, N.F. Jackson, The S. F. Jackson Family, Lloyd and Elsa Lopez Mathews, Harriet and Bob McCarty, Gary Merchant, Melissa Cosby Pina, Mike and Diane Probst, Carla Krueger Rinche, David and Gail Roaten, Sara Sanchez Roe and Charles Roe, III, Steve and Sherol Russell, Abraham Sanchez, Jr., Richard Schendel, Theresa Roe Smith, the family of Felix and Candelaria Solis, David and Karey Swartwout, Tommy Thompson and Yvette Munoz Webb. Thanks also to Veronica Camehl and Kay Betz for capturing the candid photos at the exhibit's opening.

For images contained within the book, we thank Jim Moloney, "Turf" Overturf, Gordon Stanley, Janet Taylor and Kam Wagert, Texas Maritime Museum,

Courtesy of Gordon Stanley

Corpus Christi LaRetama Library, the DeGolyer Library, Southern Methodist University, Texas: Photographs, Manuscripts, and Imprints, Corpus Christi Museum of Science and History, The Rockport Pilot, Ty Husak and Melissa Cosby… among others. We also appreciate other research that informed the exhibit and book, conducted by the Aransas County Historical Commission, the Visionaries in Preservation Program, Kathryn Morrow, Louise S. O'Connor and Sue Hastings, co-author of *Aransas: The Life of a Texas Coastal County*.

In an homage to the late Guy Clark, local songwriter, our guests sang "Homegrown Tomatoes" accompanied by Steve Russell, Jessie Ellis and Richard Schendel at the exhibit's opening.

Additionally, Friends of the History Center's board members, John Bemrose, Leah Oliva, Janet Gaskamp, David Swartwout, Lisa Kaye Knoblett, Robin Jones, Robert Lawrence, Carla Krueger Rinche, Lloyd Mathews, and Maureen Winkelman who worked tirelessly throughout the process.

Becky Sanders, The History Center's Administrative Assistant, was extremely important in this book's graphic design and production. The cover was designed by Evan Morgan, a graphic designer residing in Austin. Further, The Friends would like to thank Aransas Pathways, of which the History Center is a part, for their continuing support since its inception. Pathways is a leader in preserving many of Aransas County's natural resources and especially Judge Burt Mills and Aransas County Commissioners: Leslie "Bubba" Casterline, Jack Chaney, Brian Olson, Betty Stiles and Project Manager John Strothman, who have been ardent supporters of the programs and initiatives of The History Center for Aransas County.

The exhibit, "Foodways: Culinary Traditions of Aransas County," can be found under *Past Exhibits*, www.thehistorycenterforaransascounty.org

# Dedication

The Culinary Heritage of Aransas County is founded in the Bounty of Nature. Native American tribes roamed from the coastline to inland areas, living off the plentiful turtles, fish and seafood in our bays and wild game such as bison, deer and birds.

Early settlers were lured here to create communities with promises of fertile land for agriculture and other lucrative financial opportunities. The cattle on the prairies led to ranching interests and the establishment of cattle packeries, which made fortunes for people like George Fulton, Thomas Mathis and John Mathis, as well as Youngs Coleman and Thomas Coleman. Salt operations to preserve the meat from the cattle and other food stuffs followed.

Once the cattle trade declined, new packeries exploited the abundant migrating green sea turtles.

JAN. 1927 ROCKPORT, TEXAS.

21 WILD DUCKS.

From the Collection of Jim Moloney

Fishing, shrimping, oystering and other seafood-related business prospered, helping our community to grow and flourish. Grocery stores, purveyors, ship chandlers, restaurants, cafes and diners fed local residents and generations of tourists, second-home buyers and retirees, who grew to love the area's recreational opportunities and food.

In the seventies and eighties, a group of ardent nature lovers, wildlife enthusiasts and artists helped create conservation and environmental groups such as the Coastal Conservation Association and Ducks Unlimited to stop over-fishing and harvesting, and, instead, protect and restore our county's abundance of natural resources. These Stewards of Nature still work throughout our community to ensure that our Foodways are preserved for future generations.

This book is dedicated to all those who came before us -- the successive waves of hard-working and inventive families, who fed their families, local residents and visitors, and to the small business men and women, who settled in Aransas County over the years, building a vibrant community around the bounty of nature.

Ranchers, truck farmers, boat builders, net

GOOD FISHING    HALF DAY'S CATCH BY RUFUS AND CHAS. CLEVELAND
ROCKPORT, TEXAS

From the Collection of Jim Moloney

makers, packery workers, shrimpers, oyster and fisher men and women, hotel cooks and waiters, café staff, dairy workers, dry good and grocery store workers, mothers and fathers cooking for their family – all built a hard-working, food loving, neighbor-helping-neighbor culture that we still enjoy today.

Pare cling stone peaches, put in syrup, boil until can be pierced with a fork, skim out, place in a jar, pour the boiling syrup over them. Have enough syrup to cover and keep the fruit well under.  For the syrup, one quart of the best cider vinegar to three pints of sugar, boil and skim, pour over fruit boiling hot.  Repeat each day until the fruit is the color of the syrup and the syrup like thin molasses. Add a few cloves and pieces of cinnamon back to the syrup while boiling.

-Mrs. J. M. Hoopes

# Foreword

By Monica Burdette

Along the sparkling waters of the Gulf of Mexico, after heading north about 150 miles from the southern tip at Brownsville, the Texas coastline takes a right turn and leisurely veers east towards Houston and Beaumont. Nestled in this "Coastal Bend" is charming and historic Aransas County.

From its earliest days, much of Aransas County's history involves food in one way or another. Around the time Aransas County was established in 1871, much of the area was devoted to cattle ranching, making the ports of Rockport and Fulton key locations for shipping cattle. Before refrigeration came to the Coastal Bend, meat was canned and cured to preserve it.

OTHER GAME THAN FEATHERED.

FAIR LUCK.

Numerous meat packeries sprang up in the area to fill this need. The installation of an ice plant and refrigeration later made it possible to ship fresh meat. The 1880s ushered in the oyster and fish industries in Aransas County—industries still flourishing today. In the 1890s, the turtle packing industry was also a thriving business. Since the 1930s, Aransas County continues to be one of the leading shrimp producing areas of Texas.

Hunting has also long been a revered tradition in Aransas County. Over many centuries, families have enjoyed feasting on white tail deer, feral hogs, turkeys, quail, and doves harvested in the area. The shallow bays and estuaries offer such exceptional opportunities for superior duck and goose hunting that some hunting clubs go back more than 100 years.

14

From the Collection of the Corpus Christi Public Libraries

Even with these impressive credentials, the most compelling feature of Aransas County is the abundance of sea life in the saltwater surrounding it. Anglers not only have easy access to numerous bays and estuaries for world-class shallow-water fishing, but also a front door to phenomenal deep-sea sport fishing in the Gulf of Mexico. Fish that make great eating and are commonly found in our bays are Speckled Trout, Redfish, Flounder, and Black Drum. For the more adventurous, a few miles into the Gulf one can catch Tuna, Dolphin Fish (mahi mahi), several species of Snapper, Spanish Mackerel, and King Mackerel, to name a few.

Ever since there were established communities in this area, there were "eateries" which served local seafood, as well as other fare. Having spent a great deal of time in Aransas County for the past four decades, I have seen the steady rise in the quality and variety of cuisine offered by local restaurants. Today, not only do they serve fantastic coastal seafood, they also display a wide variety of ethnic and cultural influences that have affected the Coastal Bend. The Rockport/Fulton area boasts restaurants featuring good old American, Mexican, Chinese, Vietnamese, Japanese, Italian, and Cajun.

We can enjoy seafood, gourmet cuisine, barbeque, steaks, tacos, hamburgers, sandwiches, ice cream, pizza, and donuts. There is even a barbecue place that roasts coffee beans! There are both "by the bay" as well as inland dining spots. One can find fine dining restaurants with extensive wine lists, as well as quaint family-owned places where you can BYOB. And the best part is that shorts and sandals are allowed in all!

Although I didn't own property in Aransas County until 2005, I have a long personal history in the area. In the early 1970s, as the bride of a young Army officer stationed at Fort Sam Houston in San Antonio, I spent almost every weekend fishing the bays of Aransas County with my husband.

I later ventured into the culinary arts field, attending cooking schools in Europe and the USA. I was chef for 26 years at my family's own ranch and lodging establishment, even producing my own cookbook.

Now that we are permanent residents of Rockport, my husband Ray maintains a Coast Guard Captain's License, which allows him to take fishing charters into the bountiful bays and Gulf. Needless to say, we have become "fish snobs"—only eating freshly caught fish! One of the things I like most about living in the Coastal Bend is that we can take my husband's catch of the day to any number of restaurants that will cook our own fresh fish for us.

This book lovingly showcases the culinary history and diversity of Aransas County and the many elements that contributed to its making. I know you will "savor" exploring the "delectable" array of photographs of people, places and things featured in this book. So, enjoy, buen provecho, Hǎo wèikǒu, chúc ngon miệng, Shokuyoku o sosoru, buon appetito, bon appetit, and chalo khaane!

Serving as a Commissioner on the Texas Historical Commission, preserving important historical elements of Texas communities is a priority for me. I take great pride in filling this small role in helping to preserve a part of Aransas County history.

**Monica P. Burdette** is from Rockport, Texas—the location of Fulton Mansion, one of the Texas Historical Commission's 21 State Historic Sites. Burdette retired to Rockport with her husband Ray after 26 years of managing her family-owned El Canelo Ranch and The Inn at El Canelo located in Kenedy County, just south of the King Ranch. She is a descendent of Francisco Yturria of Brownsville and a fifth-generation landowner of part of his holdings. Burdette served several terms on the Board of Directors of The Museum of South Texas History (MoSTH— previously known as the Hidalgo County

Historical Museum) in Edinburg, where she served as Board Secretary. She chaired a MoSTH committee which produced a cookbook: *Mesquite Country: Tastes and Traditions from the Tip of Texas*, which won the McIlhenny Award—an annual award for best community cookbook in America.

Other activities include Burdette's conservation efforts and nature tourism promotion. She has allowed important nature-related projects and research on El Canelo Ranch.

---

## Laguna Madre Speckled Trout
### By Monica Burdette

1 cup prepared Hidden Valley Ranch dressing (made from mix)

¼ cup finely chopped cilantro

1 Tablespoon chopped shallot

3 cloves garlic, peeled, smashed and minced

2 medium jalapeno peppers, seeds and membrane removed, finely minced.

Juice of 1 Key lime

6 medium speckled trout fillets

1 Tablespoon butter

2 Tablespoons Panko breadcrumbs

1 Tablespoon freshly grated Parmesan cheese

Preheat oven to 400°. Line a baking sheet with aluminum foil and spray with cooking spray; set aside. In medium bowl, mix together prepared HVR dressing, cilantro, shallot, garlic, jalapeno, and lime juice. Set aside. Place trout fillets on prepared baking sheet; blot fish with paper towels to remove excess moisture. Spread generously with HVR mixture. Bake in oven 10 minutes. Meanwhile, melt butter in small frying pan over medium heat. Add Panko breadcrumbs and stir until lightly toasted; remove from heat. Wait 5 minutes and stir in Parmesan; set aside. When fish has cooked 10 minutes, sprinkle Panko/Parmesan mixtures on top and return to oven. Cook 5 minutes or until fish flakes easily when tested with a fork.  Makes 6 servings.

# Medaillon de Venaison au Poivre Vert

by Monica Burdette

3 lbs. whole venison backstrap

2 tablespoon butter

3 tablespoon canned green peppercorns

Salt, to taste

2 tablespoon olive oil

1/3 cup brandy

1 cup heavy cream

Preheat oven to 200º.  Trim backstrap of any fat, tendons, or connective tissue; place in a glass-baking dish. Rinse peppercorns in cold water. If firm, roughly crush with a mortar and pestle.  Press peppercorns onto entire surface of backstrap. Cover tightly with plastic wrap and refrigerate several hours. Heat oil and butter over HIGH heat in a large frying pan.  Leaving peppercorns on meat, sauté meat quickly on all sides until just browned. Do not overcook. Pour brandy over the meat and deglaze pan, scraping bottom of pan with a metal spatula.  CAREFULLY ignite brandy with a long-tipped lighter; allow flame to subside on its own.  Immediately transfer meat to a warm dish; loosely cover with foil and place in a preheated oven to keep warm.

Pour cream into frying pan; bring to a boil.  Lower heat and simmer until volume is reduced by at least half. Sauce should be golden and the consistency of thin gravy.  Adjust seasonings as needed. Slice venison into ¼" slices. Arrange medallions overlapping on warm serving platter.  Pour sauce over medallions. Garnish with parsley sprigs. Serve immediately.  Makes about 8 modest servings.

Note:  Traditional "au poivre" dishes use black peppercorns, but I really like the flavor of green peppercorns. Substitute black peppercorns, if desired.  Also, substitute nilgai or other big game backstrap in this recipe, if desired.

### Refrigerator Rolls

| | |
|---|---|
| ¾ c. hot water | ½ c. sugar |
| 1 Tbsp. salt | 3 Tbsp. margarine |
| 1 c. warm water | 2 pkg. dry yeast |
| 1 egg, beaten | 5 ¼ c unsifted flour |

Mix hot water, sugar, salt, margarine; cool to lukewarm.  Measure warm water into a large bowl; sprinkle in yeast; stir until dissolved.  Stir in lukewarm mixture, egg, 3 c. flour.  Beat til smooth.  Add rest of the flour, mixing well.  Place dough in greased bowl; brush top with soft margarine.  Cover tightly with waxed paper or foil. Refrigerate until doubled in bulk or until needed (up to four days.). To use, punch mixture down, cut off amount of dough required and form into favorite shapes. Cover.  Let rise in warm place until doubled in bulk about 1 hour.  Brush with melted margarine. Bake at 400 degrees about 10-15 minutes or until done.

Mrs. Fayenell Harrell

# Doves in Sherry Sauce

by Georgia Stillwell

15 dove breasts

½ cup half & half

¾ cup flour, seasoned with salt, pepper & garlic powder

2 tablespoon butter

1 (14.5 oz.) can petite diced tomatoes, undrained

1 (4oz.) jar, marinated mushrooms

1 tablespoon Worcestershire sauce

1 cup water

1 cup sherry, divided (3/4 C. + ¼ C.)

1 (1 oz.) pkg. onion soup mix

Debone dove breasts, if desired, with a sharp filet knife. Place breasts in a single layer in a large pan; pour half and half over breasts, turning to coat all sides. Let set about 30 minutes while you assemble the rest of the ingredients. Place seasoned flour in shallow bowl; set aside. Melt butter in large frying pan or Dutch oven over medium-high heat. Remove the dove breasts from half & half and dredge in seasoned flour; sauté breasts in melted butter.

In medium bowl, mix together tomatoes, onion soup mix, mushrooms, Worcestershire, water, and ¾ cup sherry. Pour over breasts in frying pan. Bring to a boil; lower heat, cover and simmer one hour or until meat pulls away from the bone. Add reserved ¼ cup sherry; cook 15 minutes. Serve with rice. Makes about 6 servings

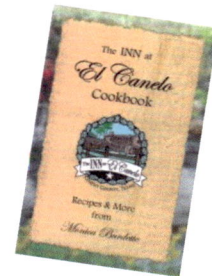

# Is There a Gulf Coast Cuisine?

By Terry Thompson-Anderson

Two essentials control the basis of life for all living things on the earth – food and water. So crucial are these that the history of the world has been dictated by the quest for both and access to a sustainable supply of them.

Over the span of the recorded and researched history of mankind's eating patterns, eating styles have evolved to reflect each region on the planet. Today we refer to this myriad of eating styles as ethnic and regional cuisines. And they often vary drastically from region to region. Behind this evolution of eating habits is a principle, which the French named *terroir*. It's a simple, yet at the same time convoluted concept meaning essentially *a sense of place*. Terroir encompasses geography, topography, climate, and soil conditions. Recently, a more complex component

Courtesy of Haak Vineyards and Winery

has been added to the genre of terroir – that of culture and its influence on things grown in a particular region. The word originated in the French wine industry many years ago to clarify what made wines – even those made from the very same grapes – taste differently in each area of the country in which the grapes were grown. Terroir determines which species of plants and animals will grow – and thrive – in a particular region, and, surprisingly, how the edible species will taste! The same breed of lamb raised in the Normandy region of France, where the fertile terroir lends itself to the proliferation of vast pastures of wild thyme, will taste quite differently than that same lamb raised in the Texas Hill Country on native grasses.

Likewise, the meat of a white-tailed deer that roams the cool mountains of Colorado will vary in taste from one that ranges on the sandy soils of the Texas Gulf Coast. Same with a Charolaise steer from Southwest France where the breed originated, and the King Ranch, which successfully introduced them to Texas. And, yes, nutria, from the bayous of South Louisiana does taste different, though not necessarily better than, one from the Texas coastal wetlands.

Over many centuries Texas has borrowed elements from all over the world in the evolution of its own many cuisines. Wines produced from Texas-grown fruit are a good example. Starting from a slow and often painful growth, winemakers in the Texas wine industry have finally begun to seek out the varietals of grapes, which closely pair with the terroir and eating habits of the Lone Star State. Those varietals have proven to be the biggest, boldest, and most noteworthy from around the world – both red and white. These are the wines that have the body and structure to stand up to our flavor-packed, two-fisted, and often-spicy style of eating. And guess what? Those varietals come from regions where the terroir is very much the same as in different regions of Texas – and the eating styles in those areas also closely resemble ours.

In the beginning, Texas winemakers planted the most popular grapes from California and tried to emulate California's wines – those Rutherford Bench-style Cabernet Sauvignons, Pinot Noir, with their need for gently warm days and cool nights, and the big, oaky, buttery Chardonnays. But those grapes failed to thrive in Texas; the resulting wines produced from them were more often than not, pretty dismal. They bore no resemblance to those produced in California from California-grown grapes. The early Texas winemakers had not studied the issue of terroir and its effect on things grown in different terroirs. So, research had to be done to select grapes from the regions of the world with similar geography, topography, climate, soil conditions, and similar cultures – the terroir.

When Texas winemakers began to plant these new-found grapes, they discovered that they grew prolifically and produced fine wines.

Texas now boasts a massive list of wine varietals that are not produced successfully anywhere else in the U.S. AND, in the results of the research, they discovered that there were areas in coastal

Southeast and South Central Texas, which have otherwise abundant, fertile growing conditions, where European *vinus vinifera* grapes would simply not grow. There is no other wine-growing region in the world with a matching terroir. The climate is too hot 24 hours a day, year 'round, and too humid – conditions which led to bug-borne infestations of bacteria, which literally killed the vines planted in these areas from the roots up, the most notable being *Pierce's Disease*. This disease emanates from a grasshopper, the Glassy-winged Sharpshooter which is prolific in South Texas.

Again, thousands of acres of European grape vines were lost in the effort to grow European grapes in an unsuitable terroir.

Courtesy of Terry Thompson-Anderson

Then along came a pioneer researcher, who owned some property in Santa Fe, Texas; yes, the Santa Fe that's roughly 6 miles from Galveston, on which he wanted to plant a vineyard and establish a winery. He was told he was crazy by winemakers from around the state, but Raymond Haak had done his homework. He discovered a humble native American grapevine at a local nursery, which had been growing in the region for eons, but mostly ignored. So, he planted his vineyard with these native Blanc du Bois grapes and they thrived beyond his expectations, producing groundbreaking white wines that could be made in either dry or sweet styles. Then he went on to experiment with a red, native American grape known as Black Spanish, or Lenoir, with the same outstanding results. Raymond had always loved Madeira, that sultry, ever-so-slightly sweet fortified wine that provides the perfect end to a fine meal.

Raymond traveled to the island of Madeira and to Portugal to study the process of making Madeira. Somewhere in his "winemaking" mind,

Courtesy of Haak Vineyards & Winery

26

he saw a connection to his Lenoir grapes. When he returned to Santa Fe, he constructed an authentic *estufa*. This is a heated chamber, in which

Madeira is traditionally aged in the barrel for six months. And he produced Madeira from his Lenoir grapes; the wine world was set on its ears, besting famous European producers, and even some from Madeira, in prestigious competitions all over the world.

Raymond's Madeira was "grandfathered" two days before a law was passed in Madeira and Portugal that made it illegal to label a wine "Madeira" that was not grown and produced in those two regions. So, Texas now claims the only "Madeira" grown and produced in the United States. And the grapes had long been a native plant in our Coastal terroir.

Within the state of Texas, there are ten recognized ecological regions defined by their terroir. The most well-known include El Paso, where the cuisine reflects the region's Spanish/Mexican heritage established when the Spanish built missions in the region in the late 1500s, as well as the Native Americans, who originally inhabited the area for thousands of years.

Eating styles in the Panhandle Plains region, where many of the state's best wine grapes grow, are centered around beef from the legendary ranches that originated there when the enterprising owners of vast parcels of land rounded up the thousands of feral cattle, which were the generations of offspring of the cattle that had been brought by the Spanish to feed the missions they established. When the missions were abandoned, or assimilated into local communities, most of the cattle became feral and adapted to the harsh conditions of the West Texas terroir – evolving into the state's beloved Longhorn cattle.

The Central Texas Hill Country's cuisine reflects the strong influences of the early German and Czech settlers, who produced sausages and mouth-watering pastries, like kolaches and klobasnikis, in the style of their homeland – using the ingredients native to the hill country region.

The roots of San Antonio's style of eating certainly lie in its strong Tex-Mex heritage, which added such iconic dishes as tacos, enchiladas, tamales, and queso to the culinary offerings of Texas. And let's not forget that one of America's most well-loved concoctions was solely – and provably - born out of San Antonio's Tex-Mex terroir – that classic "bowl o' red" we call Chili.

East Texas became known for its fine barbecue, which began in the region's Black churches where large cuts of beef or even whole split steers were cooked over low embers for hours to be enjoyed by church members on Sunday afternoons after services. The church ladies would prepare what we know as traditional side dishes served with barbecue – like potato salad, cabbage slaws, and homemade pickles. Eventually, the reputation of the outstanding flavor quality of the "barbecue" became so widespread in the region that the churches began to sell the meat and sides to others to benefit their church coffers.

One remaining region of Texas has nurtured a style of eating over hundreds of years that is often taken for granted, although millions of visitors have traveled there each year since the 1800s to sample the offerings of its smorgasbord of culinary specialties.

So, is there a bonafide Gulf Coast cuisine? The answer is a resounding "You Betcha' " – and, as we know, it includes its own unique wines. It's always been here and has evolved into one of the Lone Star State's most noteworthy cuisines. Why? Because our *terroir* is one of the most outstanding in the state. The Texas Gulf Coast is within the Migratory Flyway used by thousands of birds, which winter on our coast, giving us access to tasty ducks and geese. And, our terroir includes the Gulf of Mexico and its hundreds of species of seasonal birds, fish, and shellfish.

Aransas County has an eating style that began thousands of years ago when the region was inhabited by the Karankawa and Atakapa-(uh-TAK-uh-paw) Ishak Indians. Both tribes were hunters and gatherers and they would roam the area seasonally in their search for food. In the winter, they moved inland to hunt deer and feast on Native pecans. In the heart of winter, they enjoyed ducks, geese, and local turtles.

In the spring and summer, they fished the coastal waters for oysters, fish, and crabs and supplemented their diet with local roots.

Around 450 to 500 years ago, Spanish explorers began to arrive in the region, introducing pigs and cattle. As they established missions over South Texas, the pigs and cattle were used to feed those missions, but over the centuries many of the animals escaped or were left behind when the missions were abandoned. The pigs became feral, adapting to the wild coastal terroir. Today we know them as wild boar hogs. Hunters know them as a great hunt with tasty meat as a reward. Farmers and ranchers call them other names because of their terrible destruction of pastureland and crop fields. All these foods remain in our local cuisine. Plus, a saucy Mexican/ Spanish note was added to the tune of the Coastal terroir.

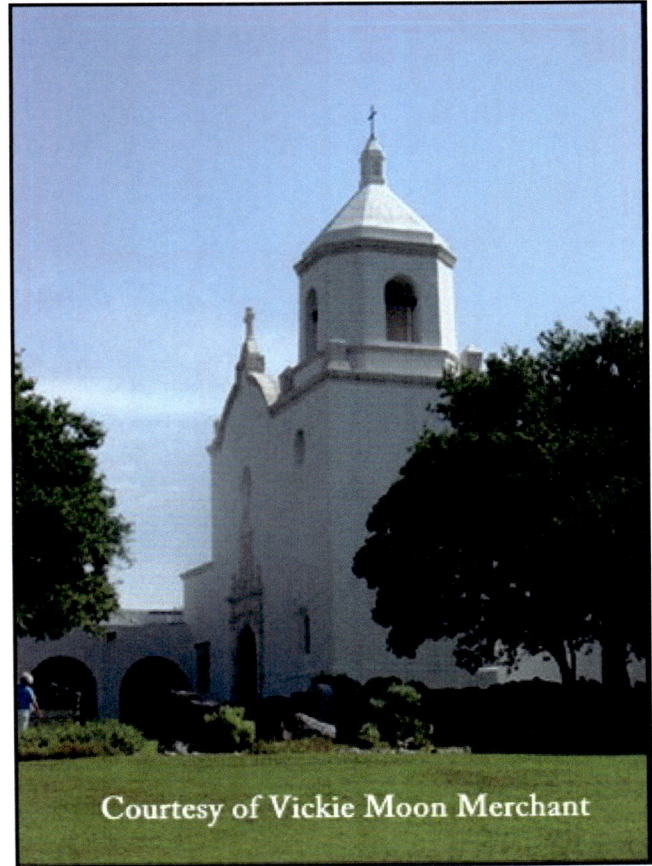

Courtesy of Vickie Moon Merchant

Courtesy of the Texas Maritime Museum

The City of Rockport was established in 1871 as a port for cattle slaughtering, packing, and shipping. Many large cattle ranches were also established in the area, including one of some 115,000 acres owned by the Coleman, Fulton, and Mathis families, three of the region's early founding families. Although the packing plants shut down when transport lines withdrew shipping to the port, Rockport had been established as a center for beef. In the 1880s, boatbuilding and commercial fishing began to develop in Rockport. Around 1925 a shrimping industry was established, followed by oystering.

After the fall of Vietnam in 1975, hundreds of skilled Vietnamese fishermen made their homes on the Texas Gulf Coast, adding greatly to the local economies, and, importantly, fusing the unique native cuisine of their homeland with our native foods and introducing new foods, which have thrived in our terroir.

Today the region between Palacios and Rockport is home to one of the largest shrimping fleets in America. Our local fish markets offer the bounty of all - freshly caught fish, shrimp, oysters, and crabs both to our local restaurants and directly to consumers or anglers, can revel in the excitement of catching their own. In addition, our local markets brim with local, seasonal vegetables and fruits from the nearby Rio Grande Valley. Although access to all these foods has become easier, they've always been in our backyard and on our tables.

So, let's imagine a grand buffet to which we would invite residents as well as those not fortunate enough to live on our Texas Gulf Coast. The menu for our buffet would include the foods, which comprise our "Taken-for-Granted" cuisine. It might read something like:

### *Coastal Waters Grand Buffet*

### Appetizers

Chilled Boiled Gulf Shrimp with Spicy Red Cocktail Sauce

Seafood Campechano

Oysters on the Half-shell over ice with Horseradish-Chili Sauce

Half-shell Baked Oysters with Browned Butter Topping

Chipotle Shrimp Tacos with Cilantro-

Lime Slaw and Avocado Salsa Verde

Crabmeat au Gratin

Crab Fingers

Turtle Soup with Madeira

Torn Mixed Local Greens with Toasted Pecans and
Local Satsuma orange segments dressed with a tangy
blackberry vinaigrette

Nopalito Salad with Escabeche, Avocado, Lime, and
Queso Fresca

## Entrée

Vietnamese Salt and Pepper Shrimp on Rice Noodles

Fried Shrimp and Oysters

Whole, Crab-stuffed Broiled Flounder Draped
with Lemon Butter
Pan-seared, lightly-floured Grouper filets with Crab and
Mexican Mint Marigold Cream Sauce

Grilled Redfish on the Half-shell

Vietnamese Crispy Fish with Lemongrass and Cilantro

Slow-smoked leg of Wild Boar served with Blackberry
and Arbol Chili Sauce

Roast Venison Backstrap with Ancho Chili and
Local Honey Reduction

Grilled, Bone-in Beef Ribeye Steak
Roast Mallard Duck with Smothered Local Greens
and Turnips

Local Vegetables Grilled with Mathis, Texas,

Olive Oil

## Dessert Course

Fresh Strawberry Shortcake with
Whipped Crème Fraiche

And, of course,
many well-chilled bottles of Haak Winery Blanc du Bois
and Madeira for after the feast.

*Surely, no one would leave this buffet doubting that
there is a Texas Gulf Coast cuisine – and it's always
been here!*

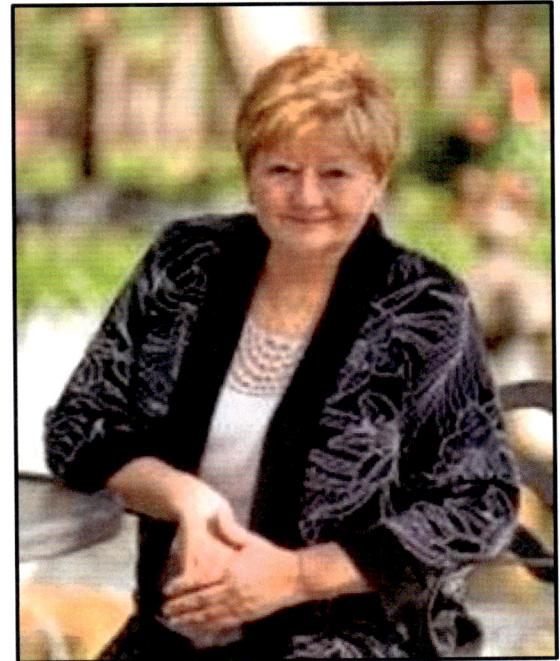

**Terry Thompson-Anderson** grew up a Texas gal in Houston. She received a degree in English from the University of Houston, but eventually food and wine became a consuming passion, leading her to pursue culinary studies at L'Academie de Cuisine in Bethesda, MD. Terry did an apprenticeship with the doyenne of Southern foods, Nathalie Dupree, and also pursued studies with James Beard, Chef Paul Prudhomme, and Karen McNeil, author of *The Wine Bible*, at the CIA's Greystone campus in Napa Valley. She owned Café Raintree, a cozy bistro in Bay St. Louis, Mississippi. While living in Mississippi, she served as President of the Gulf Coast Writer's Association. Terry is a charter member of The International Association of Culinary Professionals and a member of the San Antonio Chapter of Les Dames d'Escoffier. She returned to Houston in 1990, following a personal tragedy, and became the Executive Chef for the Halliburton Corporation, managing food and beverage service at their executive lodges in Texas and the Florida Keys, a position she held for 14 years.

Terry is the author of nine books, beginning with the best-selling *Cajun-Creole Cooking* (Putnam-Penguin, 1986). Her eighth book, *Texas on the Table: People, Places & Recipes Celebrating the Flavors of the Lone Star State*, a tribute to the Texas terroir, was released by the University of Texas Press in October 2014 and was a finalist in the 2015 James Beard Cookbook Awards. Her ninth book, also published by the University of Texas Press, *Breakfast in Texas*, was released in April 2017. Her tenth book is now in the works.

Terry lived in Rockport, Texas for several years, but had to move after Hurricane Harvey. She writes for *Edible Austin* magazine and Garden & Gun's *The Local Palate*, published in Charleston,

S.C., and pursues other writing and consulting projects, along with promoting Texas wine and food. She is an avid gardener and tends a large herb garden.

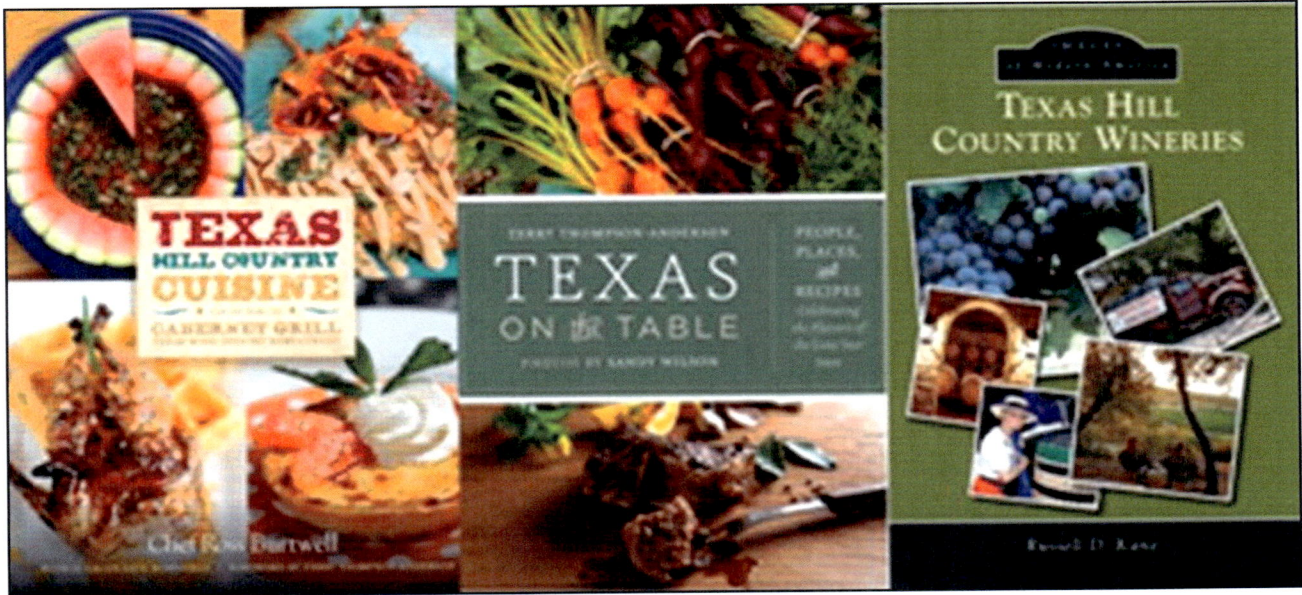

# Mesquite Smoked Oysters

## by Terry Thompson-Anderson

In Texas, we put just about anything on the barbecue grill. If it can't be grilled, smoked, or barbecued, it's probably not worth eating! I love oysters, so I just had to try them over mesquite coals. Mmmmm. They were keepers.

24 sucked oysters on the half-shell and their liquor, bottom shells reserved

½ cup unsalted butter, melted

Dash of mesquite liquid smoke

1-1/2 tablespoons minced sun-dried tomatoes

2 teaspoons freshly squeezed lime juice

Salt to taste

2 medium garlic cloves, minced

1/8 teaspoon ground cumin

2 teaspoons minced fresh cilantro

1 teaspoon Worcestershire sauce

¼ teaspoon freshly ground black pepper

Prepare a mesquite charcoal fire in a smoker pit with a lid. Position grilling rack 10-12 inches above coals. Let the fire burn down until coals are covered with a layer of white ash. Drain the liquor from the oysters into a heavy bottomed one-quart saucepan. Add remaining ingredients, except salt, and cook, stirring once or twice until heated through. Add salt to taste. Arrange the oysters in the reserved shells on a perforated grilling rack. Spoon a portion of the sauce over each oyster. Place the oysters on the rack of the pit and close the lid. Smoke just until the oysters are opaque, about 15 to 20 minutes. Serve hot. Serves 4.

# Browned Butter Oysters

## by Terry Thompson-Anderson

If you're an oyster lover like I am, then you're always seeking out new and different ways to serve them. I created this dish as a first course. I cook and serve the oysters in Chinese soup spoons on a long rectangular plate. In the center of the plate, I put a little mound of Beet Salad with Peppered Bacon and Goat Cheese with two of the oysters on each side. It's a colorful and visually interesting dish – and the flavors, as they play off one another, are stellar. The oysters can be assembled a few hours before serving, arranged on a baking sheet and refrigerated until you're ready to broil and serve them.

Makes 12 oysters.

12 Texas Gulf oysters and their liquor

1 teaspoon Tabasco

1 heaping tablespoon minced flat-leaf parsley

½ cup unseasoned breadcrumbs

Lemon wedges as garnish

1-1/2 sticks unsalted butter

1-1/2 teaspoons minced lemon zest

½ teaspoon kosher salt

3 tablespoons grated Romano cheese

Preheat broiler and position oven rack 6 inches below heat source. Arrange 12 Chinese soup spoons on a baking sheet. Place one oyster in each spoon along with a little of the oyster liquor. Set aside.

Combine the butter, Tabasco, lemon zest, parsley, and salt in a small saucepan; cook to melt the butter. Stir in the breadcrumbs and cheese, blending well. Divide the buttery crumb mixture between the oysters, topping each oyster with a little pile of it. Place the baking sheet under the preheated broiler and cook for 4 minutes, or until topping is golden brown and bubbly. Serve at once with lemon wedges.

# St. Charles Bay Crab Cakes and Poached Eggs on Fried Green Tomatoes with Orange-Ginger Hollandaise Sauce

by Terry Thompson-Anderson

I created this regal brunch dish one weekend when my husband and I were spending the weekend in our RV in Rockport. We had invited some friends from Houston to drive over for brunch on Sunday. We set out some crab traps when we arrived on Friday afternoon and had a nice container of freshly picked crab meat from our catch. I picked up a couple of green tomatoes at the outdoor market in town and this dish emerged from those fresh ingredients.

**Make Ahead:**

The crab cakes can be made ahead and even frozen. Thaw and reheat in a low oven before serving. The tomatoes can be fried up to an hour ahead of time and reheated in a low oven. The eggs can be poached for 2 minutes, transferred to a bowl of ice water and poached for an additional minute right before serving. The Orange-Ginger Hollandaise Sauce can be made right before you finish poaching the eggs, and kept warm over hot, not simmering water. Whisk well before using.

Serves 8. All the recipes for each part of this dish are listed below.

| | |
|---|---|
| 8 Crab Cakes | 8 Fried Green Tomato slices |
| 8 poached eggs | Orange-Ginger Hollandaise Sauce |

Green portions of 2 green onions, sliced very thin on the bias, as garnish.

**Crab Cakes:**

1 pound jumbo lump crabmeat

1 teaspoon Worcestershire sauce

1 tablespoon minced flat-leaf parsley

1 tablespoon Chef Paul's Seafood Magic Seasoning

1 cup mayonesa (lime-flavored mayonnaise)

3 green onions, chopped, including green tops

1 stick unsalted butter and ½ Cup canola oil for sautéing

1 large egg

1 tablespoon Creole mustard

2/3 cup finely crushed Ritz crackers

Juice of ½ lemon

½ cup finely chopped green bell pepper

Begin making the crab cakes by very carefully picking through the crabmeat to remove any bits of shell or cartilage, taking care not to break up those beautiful lumps! Set aside. In a large bowl, combine the eggs, Worcestershire sauce, mustard, parsley, lemon juice, Seafood Magic, and mayonnaise. Whisk to blend well. Add the green onions, bell pepper and crushed crackers; stir to incorporate. Gently fold in the crabmeat, distributing all ingredients evenly. Form the crab mixture into 8 cakes, patting them tightly in your hands. Place on a parchment-lined baking sheet, cover loosely with parchment and refrigerate until ready to sauté.

To sauté the crab cakes, melt the butter in a heavy-bottomed skillet over medium heat; stir in the canola oil to blend well. Add the crab cakes, taking care not to crowd the pan. Sauté in batches, if needed. Fry the cakes for about 3-5 minutes per side, turning once, or until golden brown and firmly cooked. Keep warm in a low oven. Note: The crab cakes can be made ahead of time and re-heated in the oven until warmed through.

**Fried Green Tomatoes:**

      3 large green tomatoes, sliced into ½-inch thick slices

      2 cups all-purpose flour

      2 teaspoons each kosher salt and freshly ground black pepper

      ¼ teaspoon cayenne pepper

      2 large eggs, well beaten with 1 cup whole buttermilk, not low fat

      Canola oil for pan-frying

      1 cup panko breadcrumbs tossed with 1 Cup yellow cornmeal

      1-1/2 tablespoons Chef Paul's Vegetable Magic seasoning

To make the Fried Green Tomatoes, place the sliced tomatoes on a plate lined with paper towels to drain off excess moisture. Toss together the flour, salt and pepper and cayenne in a shallow baking dish, blending well. Heat 1/2-inch of canola oil in a heavy-bottomed, preferably cast iron, skillet over medium heat. When ready to fry the tomatoes, dredge them first in the seasoned flour, coating well and shaking off all excess, then in the egg wash, coating well. Give the tomato slices a final dredge in the panko/cornmeal mixture, patting the panko into both sides of the slices. Gently shake off excess. Fry the tomato slices in the hot oil for about 2-3 minutes per side, turning once, or until golden brown. Drain on a wire rack set over a baking sheet. Keep warm.

## Poached Eggs:

Poaching the perfect egg is easy if you know a few simple guidelines. First, start with fresh eggs at room temperature. The white of an egg becomes looser as the egg ages and it will not poach well. Fill a deep skillet about 1/3 full of water. Add 1 tablespoon of vinegar per quart of water. Do not add salt to the water. Salt will toughen the egg whites.

Bring the water to a simmer and break an egg into the water. Cook the egg for 3 minutes, or just until the white is firm. Remove egg carefully with a slotted spoon. If any of the white has made thread-like strings on the edges, use a large round cutter to cut the egg into a perfect round shape. If poaching several eggs at one time, poach them for 2 minutes, then remove the eggs into an ice-water bath. Leave the poaching water simmering. When the eggs are needed, simply spoon out as many as you need and poach them for the final 1 minute. Serve hot.

## Orange-Ginger Hollandaise Sauce:

1 tablespoon dry white wine

½ cup freshly squeezed orange juice

1 medium shallot, minced

1 fresh thyme sprig

Juice of ½ lemon

Scant ¼ teaspoon cayenne pepper

1 teaspoon minced orange zest

1tablespoon minced pickled (Sushi) ginger

1 teaspoon whole coriander seeds, minced

4 egg yolks

½ teaspoon Kosher salt

1 cup (2 sticks) hot melted unsalted butter

1 tablespoon Creole mustard, or substitute another whole-grain mustard

To make the Orange-Ginger Hollandaise, combine the white wine, orange zest and juice, ginger, shallot, toasted coriander seeds, and thyme sprig in a small, heavy-bottomed saucepan over medium heat. Cook the mixture, stirring often, until the liquid is well-infused with the flavors and reduced by half. Strain the mixture through a fine-meshed wire strainer into a small bowl, pressing down to remove all liquid; set aside. Discard the solids left in the strainer. In a bowl of a food processor fitted with steel blade, combine the infusion liquid, egg yolks, lemon juice, mustard, salt, and cayenne pepper. Process until the mixture is thickened and light lemon-yellow in color, about 4 minutes. Stop and scrape down the side of the bowl. With the machine running, slowly add the hot melted butter through the feed tube until all has been added. Continue to process for another minute to form a strong emulsion. Transfer to a bowl and cover with plastic wrap to keep warm. Whisk just before serving.

To assemble the dish, place a Fried Green Tomato slice on each serving plate. Top each with a crab cake, then a poached egg. Drizzle a portion of the warm Orange-Ginger Hollandaise Sauce over each portion, allowing the sauce to ooze onto the plate a bit. Scatter a few pieces of sliced green onion over the tops and serve at once.

GULF COAST IMMIGRATION CO.
ROCKPORT, TEXAS.

47

Courtesy of Jim Moloney

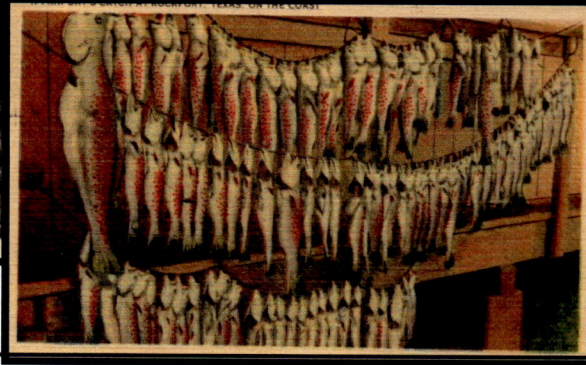

Courtesy of
the Texas
Maritime
Museum

# Bounty of Nature

Native American tribes roamed from the coastline to inland settlements, living off the plentiful turtles, fish and seafood in our bays and wild game such as bison, deer and birds.

During the 1970s and 80s, a group of ardent nature lovers, wildlife enthusiasts and artists helped create conservation and environmental groups to protect and restore our county's abundance.

Early settlers were lured here to help create communities with promises of fertile land for agriculture and other lucrative financial opportunities.

Fishing, shrimping, gathering oysters and other seafood related business also prospered; thus, helping our community to grow and flourish.

Grocers, ship chandlers, restaurants, cafes and truck farmers fed local residents, retirees and generations of tourists, who grew to love the area's recreational opportunities and food.

Grazing cattle led to ranching and the establishment of cattle packeries & turtle canneries.

# Earliest Residents of Aransas County: The Karankawa

By MM Pack

When considering the food culture of a region like the Coastal Bend, the foundations are in the flora and fauna found there. When humans first arrived on the Texas Gulf Coast, what was there for them to eat? The following will discuss the original inhabitants and foods that were consumed for millennia long before Europeans and Mexicans began to arrive during the sixteenth century. Europeans introduced corn and beans, squashes, tomatoes, and potatoes from South America; cattle, sheep, goats, and pigs from Spain, along with sugar, wheat, and oil, fruits like peaches and melons, and metal cooking vessels. With some exceptions, the indigenous foods of the earliest inhabitants are still part of Gulf Coast diets today.

There's no consensus exactly when *Homo sapiens* arrived in North America, but most archeologists think it was around 20,000 years ago. Over time, these travelers from Asia migrated down the

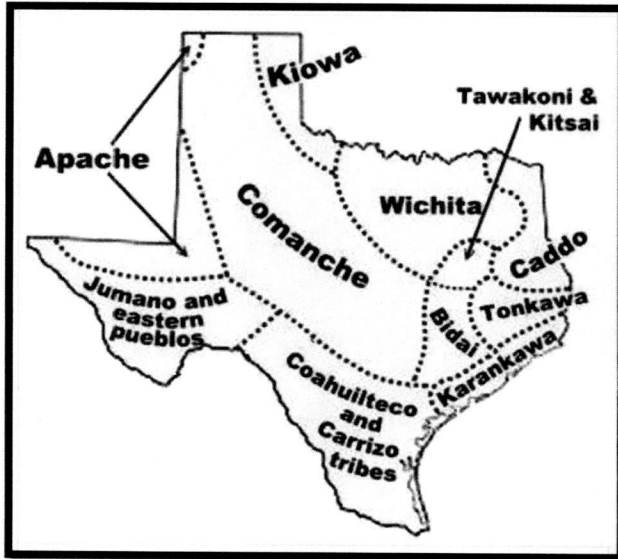

Pacific coast and spread across the continent, first appearing in the area now known as Texas around 12,000 years ago. Within Texas, eight broad regions of Native American habitats and cultures developed; together they included more than 200 distinct groups. Each area encompassed groups who were related linguistically, usually at peace with one another, and frequently in mutual alliance against other groups in adjacent areas.

Along the Gulf Coast between Galveston Bay and Corpus Christi Bay, the Karankawa region included five distinct bands, who gave themselves different names, but shared language, foodways, and other cultural elements. Moving from east down the coast, these were Capoques (Cocos), Kohanis (Cujanes), Carancaguases (Karankawas), Coapites (Guapites), and Copanes. These names may not be exactly what these peoples called themselves but were Spanish attempts at the names they

*Karankawa Indians of the Gulf Coast. Watercolour by Lino Sánchez y Tapia*

51

heard. Karankawa is the modern umbrella term for these related groups.

Karankawas were physically imposing; men were commonly more than six feet tall. Both men and women practiced facial and body tattooing and piercing, and they used a red body paint. They wore minimal clothing made from skins and woven plant material with jewelry made from cane, shells, bones, and feathers. For mosquito repellent, they smeared themselves with pungent alligator fat. Karankawas were strictly hunter/gatherers with no agricultural practices or fixed village locations. They were powerful swimmers as well as intrepid walkers and runners.

Not much is known about their religious beliefs or their language; there are records of about 400 words from French and Spanish accounts.

Karankawas possessed intimate knowledge of their environment—where to find the necessary resources for their survival and when these resources were most abundant. Following food sources, Karankawa kinship groups of 30 to 40 members migrated seasonally among the barrier islands, the bays and estuaries of the mainland coast, and up to 25 miles inland on the coastal prairies. Their portable frame houses of hides and woven mats could be taken down and set up quickly, carried on women's backs or in hollowed-log dugout canoes. They kept domesticated dogs as companions; it's generally accepted that the term Karankawa meant "dog raisers" or "dog lovers."

## Karankawa Food Sources

During much of the year, Karankawas dwelled alongside bay waters in larger fishing camps of various family groups; they were expert at catching seafood. They wove nets from plant fibers and built weirs, or dams, to trap fish and then kill them with spears. They also fished with spears and arrows from their canoes. In the 1820s, French botanist Jean Louis Berlandier noted that the Karankawa gathered fish into a small inlet and killed the largest ones with arrows, and with such skill that they often designate the species of fish which they thus want to catch."

Fish varieties they ate were catfish, flounder, black drum, redfish, speckled sea trout, croaker, and sheepshead—the same shallow-water species that modern fisherfolk catch in coastal bays today.

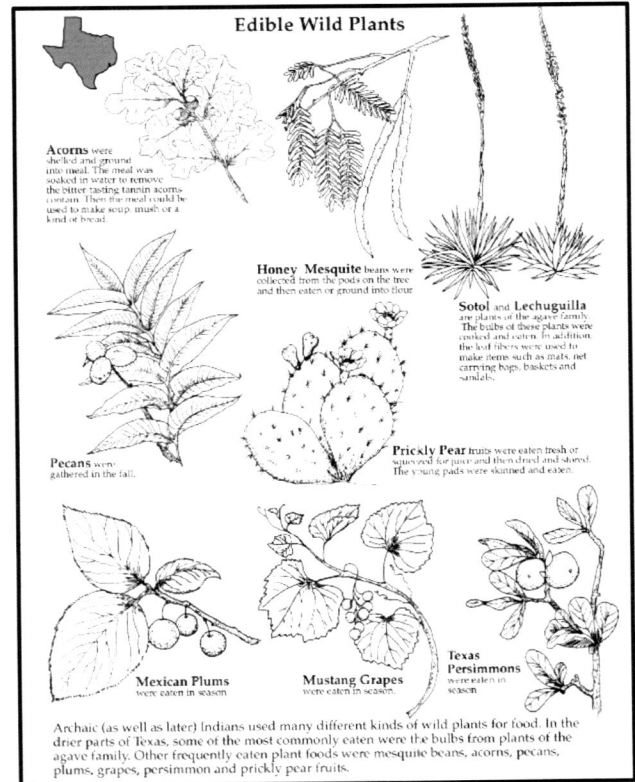

Edible Wild Plants

**Acorns** were shelled and ground into meal. The meal was soaked in water to remove the bitter tasting tannin acorns contain. Then the meal could be used to make soup, mush or a kind of bread.

**Honey Mesquite** beans were collected from the pods on the tree and then eaten or ground into flour.

**Sotol** and **Lechuguilla** are plants of the agave family. The bulbs of these plants were cooked and eaten. In addition, the leaf fibers were used to make items such as mats, net carrying bags, baskets and sandals.

**Pecans** were gathered in the fall.

**Prickly Pear** fruits were eaten fresh or squeezed for juice and then dried and stored. The young pads were skinned and eaten.

**Mexican Plums** were eaten in season.

**Mustang Grapes** were eaten in season.

**Texas Persimmons** were eaten in season.

Archaic (as well as later) Indians used many different kinds of wild plants for food. In the drier parts of Texas, some of the most commonly eaten were the bulbs from plants of the agave family. Other frequently eaten plant foods were mesquite beans, acorns, pecans, plums, grapes, persimmon and prickly pear fruits.

Courtesy of Texas Parks and Wildlife

Karankawa consumed the crabs, oysters, mussels, and clams that we still love. The jury is out whether they had nets fine enough to catch bay shrimp. They ate turtles and their eggs, as well as alligators.

When Karankawa groups went inland in smaller groups, they hunted with spears and bows and arrows for wild turkeys, quail, and ducks. They stalked whitetail deer and javelinas (peccaries) and they hunted smaller game like rabbits, raccoons, armadillos, possums, and squirrels. Bison periodically wandered as far south as the Texas Coastal Plain. These were bountiful in lean times, Karankawas consumed whatever protein they could find—mice and rats, ants and other insects, lizards, and even deer dung. They spent tremendous amounts of physical energy and they got their calories where they could.

Karankawas took advantage of wild fruits in the summer and fall. Today, people still gather the same wild blackberries and dewberries and mustang grapes in June. In November, Karankawas

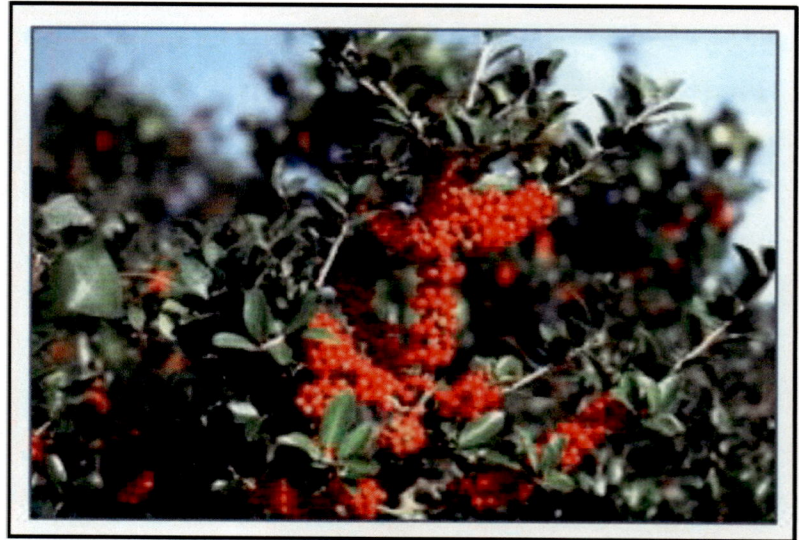

sought the little native black persimmons that grow along the coast and throughout South Texas.

Pecans, native to South Texas and Northern Mexico, were an important seasonal food source. Karankawas gathered wild pecans where the trees grew on the banks of rivers and creeks. The nuts were a valuable trading commodity among various nomadic groups and were eventually spread up the Mississippi Valley and into the Southern states.

The seedpods of the mesquite tree were a nutritional source for Karankawas and their neighbors to the south, the Coahuiltecans. Mesquite is sweet, and the seedpods, or beans, were pounded into powder and cooked in water to make a kind of mush or a drink. While mesquite hasn't been so popular with modern inhabitants, it's currently having a bit of a renaissance as an alternative sweetener and flour.

Karankawas also gathered wild greens that Mexicans call *quelites*—portulaca, lambs' quarters, and amaranth among them. A huge source of winter nutrition was a variety of roots from rain lilies, cattails, and camas bulbs. Others, whose flowering tops can still be seen along Texas roads, are starflowers, wild onions, and purple winecups. As has been recreated and demonstrated by Dr. Alston Thomas and his anthropology students at Texas A&M, digging and processing these tough roots into edible form was slow and arduous work, predictably performed by women.

Along with many Native American groups across what is now the southern United States, Karankawas brewed a tea from yaupon (*Ilex cassine*) leaves. This "black drink" was mildly intoxicating and was consumed only by men.

In late summer, Karankawas would convene with inland tribes at dense fields of *opuntia* cactus, known as prickly pear, to feast on the nutritious and sweet red fruits now called *tunas*. In addition, they roasted the green prickly pear paddles that Mexicans call *nopales*. This seasonal feasting was accompanied by dancing and singing and general merrymaking, as well as trading among the groups.

## Cabeza de Vaca

How do we know how Karankawas lived and what they ate? For one thing, there's a good bit of archeological evidence. But we also have a detailed eyewitness account--by Alvar Nunez Cabeza de Vaca, who arrived in the New World as an accountant on the ill-fated Narvaez expedition

from Spain. In 1628, he and a few companions, including Esteban, an enslaved Moroccan believed to have been the first African on the North American mainland, survived a shipwreck on

Galveston Island and then spent the next seven years traveling among and living with the coastal and south Texas tribes.

Cabeza de Vaca was the first to document the flora, fauna, and people in coastal Texas. He described the daily lives of various groups, including much detail about the Karankawas—how they traveled, traded, and interacted. He paid great attention to food and was the first to document their diet of pecans, prickly pear tunas, berries, roots, mesquite beans, game, fish, and shellfish. He described the cooking methods they used—earth ovens, grilling and smoking over open fires, and stone boiling.

As he and his companions made their way down the Texas coastal homelands of the Karankawas, Cabeza de Vaca defined groups as the Roots People, the Fish-and-Blackberry People, and the Fig People, each named for the preponderance in their diets at the time when he was with them. Figs were his name for prickly pear fruits. Aransas County falls within his Fish-and-Blackberry Peoples region.

After making his circuitous way to Mexico City, Cabeza de Vaca eventually returned to Spain. In 1542, he published an account of his years of wandering in Texas and Northern Mexico. In describing his experiences and the lives and foodways of the peoples he encountered, he was a meticulous documenter—modern translations and analyses of his writings are extremely useful to ethnobotanists and archeologists who study the early peoples of the regions he traversed.

## Cabaza de Vaca
## Archeology and Cooking Methods

Much evidence of what early Coastal Texans ate can be found in the layers of their kitchen garbage dumps, called middens, found near campsites. Karankawa midden sites are found along the shores of all the bays, on the leeward shorelines of the barrier islands, and in hunting campsites along the Aransas and Nueces Rivers. Within the boundaries of Aransas County, there are a couple of identified fishing campsites, both on Copano Bay. Middens contain mollusk shells, animal bones, and even fish scale residue.

Ethnobotanists work with archeologists to excavate Karankawa campsites, seeking evidence of diet, cooking methods and vessels, and weapons for hunting. Horizontal layers reveal the foodways over the thousands of years that Karankawas lived on the Gulf Coast. One example is the remains of the earth ovens used to slow-roast the dense, tough roots that were so important to their diet. Earth ovens are pits dug in the ground with heated clay or stones in the bottom; food is layered on and covered with leaves, dirt, sand, and other materials, and cooked for long periods of time. Variations of earth ovens are still used in many places around the planet, including Hawaii and northern Mexico.

Perhaps the easiest cooking method available was grilling and smoking foods over open wood fires. Game, fish, mollusks, and prickly pear cactus paddles were prepared this way. Foods were also buried in the coals.

A cooking method that Cabeza de Vaca described that is corroborated by archeological evidence is stone boiling, a widespread practice across Native America. This is where stones are heated in a fire and then dropped into clay pots of water to make the water boil for cooking. But—as current residents know—there aren't any stones along the Texas Gulf Coast. The resourceful Karankawas achieved the same results by baking balls of clay until they were rock-hard, and they used them as if they were stones.

The pots Karankawas used for stone boiling and other purposes were coiled clay vessels known to archeologists as Rockport Ware; this was a thin, sandy paste pottery, sometimes decorated and sometimes plain. These pots were frequently coated with asphaltum, a sticky black substance that came from petroleum seepages in the sea floor that washes onto Gulf barrier island beaches, also known as beach tar. Some things never change. Asphaltum was also used for adhesive to attach projectile points on spears and arrows.

As Spanish, Mexican, and Anglo colonists settled along the Gulf Coast, the relationships were not always cordial. Karankawas got introduced to imported foodstuffs as they were being pushed south and west inland and into Mexico; the tribal populations steadily diminished as a result of armed conflict and disease. By the 1840s, only scattered remnants of groups remained along the coast. The last known Karankawa band was exterminated near Rio Grande City in 1858.

So, as modern Gulf Coast residents enjoy the bounty of their region—fishing, crabbing, and hunting, slurping fresh oysters, gathering native pecans and blackberries, grilling over live fire—we

can remember that our Karankawa predecessors
cooked and ate these same things 10,000 years ago,
just as they did 500 years ago when Cabeza de
Vaca first described their foods.

**MM Pack** is a food writer/historian and private chef, who divides her time between San Francisco, Austin, and the Texas Gulf Coast. She has been writing and presenting on food topics since 1998 and has been included in several anthologies and reference books, including *Cornbread Nation 1, The Best of Southern Food Writing, Scribner's Encyclopedia of Food and Culture, Oxford Encyclopedia of Food & Drink in America*, and *Culinary Biographies*: *A Dictionary of the World's Great Gastronomic Personalities*. When she isn't cooking or catching crabs in Galveston Bay, she's working on a book about crops and foods that shaped the history, society, and economy of Texas.

Courtesy of Texas Parks and Wildlife

# Sweet and Smoky Mesquite

By Karey Swartwout

"Don't mess with me, folks. I'm just doing my thing." If only mesquite could talk, just imagine what its spiny thorns would say. Mesquite trees with their feathery leaves, misshapen trunks and droopy beans have been lining our coastal landscape for centuries. Aztecs adored the mesquite and used it in everything from medicine to fishing tools. Our ranchers seem to have a love-hate relationship with mesquite, considering it to be an invasive pest. These gnarled trees can be a nuisance by soaking up water from neighboring grasses, but I bet ranchers secretly respect the mesquite's tough, stubborn character.

One of the earliest uses for mesquite was food. The beans can be used in a variety of forms. An easy way to get started is to make simple syrup. All you need are mesquite beans, sugar and water. The mild, citrusy syrup can be used over fruit salads, to flavor cookies, even as a sweetener in a cocktail. A simple cookie recipe, such as shortbread, is the perfect vehicle for mesquite bean syrup because it lets the woody essence take center stage without overpowering it with heavy ingredients.

> ## MESQUITE BEAN SYRUP
> *Makes about 2 Quarts*
>
> 5 handfuls of mesquite beans, washed and picked through
> 2 quarts water
> 1 cup sugar
>
> Combine all ingredients in a pot and bring to boil on stove. Reduce heat and simmer for 15 minutes. Strain beans and store in fridge for up to 3 weeks.

This shortbread recipe is very flexible, and you can use other seasonal flavors as you crave them. Lemongrass, rosemary and lavender are great for the summer months, and heavier flavors like cinnamon, chocolate and ginger are perfect when the weather cools down. You can even make the shortbreads savory by removing the sugar and adding parmesan cheese in its place. If you want to go whole hog with the mesquite in this recipe, lay out some beans to dry for a few weeks, then grind them up to use with the flour in the shortbreads. Once you have your shortbread, keep it in the fridge. It's a handy treat to have around when guests pop over or use it as a base for pecan pie over the autumn holidays.

## MESQUITE PECAN SHORTBREAD

*Makes about 24 cookies*

2 ounces light brown sugar

4 ounces butter

4 ounces flour (or 3 ounces flour and 1 ounce mesquite bean flour, for a stronger flavor)

2 ounces toasted chopped pecans

1 T mesquite bean syrup

pinch sea salt

Mix the brown sugar and butter until fluffy and pale. Add the mesquite bean syrup. Slowly fold in the flour, pecans and salt. Roll into logs and wrap in cling film. Refrigerate for 1 hour. Remove and slice into rounds about 1/8 inch thick. Place on parchment lined baking sheet and bake at 350°F for about 15 minutes until golden around the edges. Cool on wire rack and store in airtight container.

"THE SOUTH'S IDEAL WINTER & SUMMER RESORT"

"PALM COURTS, SOUTH'S FINEST"

"OAK SHORE APARTMENTS"

INDIVIDUAL MODERN CONCRETE COTTAGES & APTS.

WRITE, WIRE, OR PHONE FOR RESERVATIONS OR LITERATURE

GUESTS RECEIVE 2 DAYS FREE RENT
EVERY TIME THE THERMOMETER IS BELOW 32°

HUNTING IN SEASON:
DUCKS, GEESE, SNIPE,
DOVES AND QUAIL —
DEER AND TURKEYS IN
NEARBY COUNTIES.

BATHING & FISHING

OAK SHORE APARTMENTS AND PALM COURTS, ROCKPORT, TEXAS.
"ON THE SHORES OF ARKANSAS BAY"

10116

# The Bounty of the Sea and Land

A Freak of Nature Most Delightful! A Paradise for Sportsmen.
An Eldorado for Truck Farmers

Native Americans, early settlers, residents and generations of visitors have been attracted to Aransas County for the bounty in nature – local fish, forage and produce; the wild game, deer, geese, and ducks; open land for raising cattle and other livestock; a good climate for gardening and agriculture; and the seafood: fish, shrimp, turtles and oysters.

In 1829, Nicholas Fagan and his family left Ireland and migrated to Texas to be part of Power and Hewtson's colony.  After landing on the beach at Copano Bay, they proceeded northward about twenty miles to the San Antonio River.  The land was uninhabited except for a few Mexican families and the Native Americans, but to the weary travelers:

> "It was paradise! Such a beautiful country, green grass and trees in mid-winter, horses running and playing over vast prairies, deer grazing quietly or peeping curiously through the bushes, while birds were so numerous the very air seemed alive with them" (Teal, 1931).

In 1835, an Irish colonist, Herman Ehrenberg, wrote in his Memoria:

> "The name of this settlement was Power. Nothing could be more attractive than this spot, quite appropriately called by the Mexicans, the Eldorado of the West.  The southern climate displayed its colorful

luxuriance here more abundantly than elsewhere. Dark woods hung with tangled masses of wild vines edged the river bed, and the stillness of the forests was animated by the voices of myriads of living creatures. Thousands of waterfowl glided across the rippling stream, while swarms of fish darted to and fro through its waters. Southern birds, with their bright plumage, trilled their merry notes in the thick woods, which rang out with the strokes and cries of the woodpeckers. The noisy clucking of turkey hens had also an agreeable sound to our ears, for it indicated hunting grounds well-stocked with game. The dimly lit groves of the forest led on to prairies where numerous flocks of wild geese waddled quite unconcernedly among droves of horses, oxen and red deer that roamed at liberty in these open spaces; prairie dogs and large wolves also abounded" (Ehrenberg, 1843, p. 44).

Early land promoters, like the Rockport Commercial Club, promoted "cheap food and cheap water and rail transportation, with products and raw material at our door, will make Rockport the largest manufacturing city in the South. Look at the map! Mexico within a stone's throw, and the nearest port to the Panama Canal." Ads praised the Live Oak Peninsula and Aransas County, where you could buy a lot or farm tract for $150 "in the heart of the FRUIT and VEGETABLE section of South Texas…"

GOOD WATER is obtainable from WELLS in quantities sufficient for TRUCK FARMING…"

Advertisements claimed that the "Bay fishing is excellent until December and during the winter months, fine catches are also made in the Yacht Basin…The thermometer rarely climbs above 88 and seldom drops to the freezing mark in winter." And "Fishing is good all year 'round in Rockport."

The Gulf Coast Immigration Company published a photo of a "magnificent vineyard and truck garden which is netting over $600.00 per acre." This booklet also claimed that Rockport's soil, climate and environments were perfect for producing the earliest Winter Vegetables on the Texas Coast. They also reported that the Rockport climate was like that of "Southern Italy, the natural home of the Fig and the Olive." And they claimed that "the farmer in this section can make from two to four crops per year."

Another photo shows "Sweet Peppers, Egg Plant and Tomatoes with a fine meadow in the background, taken at Sparks Colony where they are making from $400 to $800 per acre on Winter Vegetables".

"Rockport is becoming noted for producing the earliest and finest Winter Vegetables along the coast, and the Taft Ranch back of us has ordered four thousand acres put in truck to supply their immense canning and preserving plant now under construction." Another photo has a "View of Mrs. H.V. Delgneau's garden in which are growing three hundred varieties of temperate and tropical fruits, vegetables and flowers, all of which are doing well."

**Homeseekers and Investors**

**Attention is invited to our Property at ROCKPORT,**

**and on LIVE OAK PENINSULA, ARANSAS COUNTY, TEXAS.**

Buy a LOT or LOT and FARM TRACT for $150,

on which to build a HOME in the heart of the

FRUIT and VEGETABLE sections of South Texas,

at a Summer and Winter Resort, where you can enjoy

a fine Climate, Driving, Boating, Bathing, Fishing

and Hunting as can be found anywhere.

One property lies at the door of the GREAT HARBOR

which the UNITED STATES GOVERNMENT is commencing at PORT ARANSAS.

When the PANAMA CANAL and the RAILROADS,

now projected, are completed, ROCKPORT

will be the best place to live, and the Greatest

Commercial City on the TEXAS COAST.

GOOD WATER is obtainable from WELLS in

Quantities sufficient for TRUCK FARMING purposes,

anywhere on our property, at a depth from

TEN or TWENTY -feet, at a cost not exceeding

$20 including pump.

IT WILL PAY TO INVEST THERE.

Write for FREE ILLUSTRATED BOOKLET

**GULF   COAST   IMMIGRATION   CO.**

"Last to Load" by Thom Evans     Courtesy of Deb Gioia

69

# Meat Packeries in Aransas County

After the Civil War, cattle outnumbered the population of Texas. Wild longhorn cattle roamed freely on land south of San Antonio. These cattle were unbranded and free to anyone tough enough to corral them. "In a state with a war-ravaged economy, those cattle began to look like money on the hoof" (Cox, 2013).

The nearest market for beef was New Orleans, Louisiana. The most expeditious way to get the cattle to market was by schooner or steamer.

By the early 1870s, the area was home to a dozen packeries. The largest was the Coleman-Fulton Pasture Co., or Taft Ranch, formed in 1871 by Youngs and Tom M. Coleman, T. H. Mathis, J. M. Mathis and George W. Fulton. Eventually, this group of cattlemen owned more than 200,000 acres, which was the second largest cattle ranch in south Texas. This firm ran not only the busiest packing plant, it was the state's largest cattle business in general (Cox, 2013). Further, it was the origin of three cities and paved the way for two others (Blackland Museum, 2018).

A facility for shipping cattle, hides, and tallow was built on a limestone ledge at the end of the current Wharf Street in Rockport. It was from the existence of this rocky limestone ledge, or rocky point, for which Rockport was named.

After consulting with old friends in Cincinnati, George Fulton found markets for beef and by-products. As the demand for beef as food increased, the packeries began packing meat in barrels - pickled, salted or dried. Steamer ships carried these barrels to New Orleans and other ports (VIP, 2009) even though pickled or salted beef was unappetizing to the general public (Cox, 2013).

In 1865, William S. Hall built the first packer. In 1866, Thomas H. Mathis built the first wharf and docking facilities. James M. Doughty erected the first cattle pens and (Allen & Hastings-Taylor, 1997). They would kill and skin the cattle on the open range and transport the hides to Mexican cash markets.

From 1868 until 1882, packeries in Aransas County flourished. These factories consisted of holding pens, a main rendering barn, a skinning building, and a pier. Carcasses were usually discarded in the bay or on a 5-acre plot in Fulton. The stench was overwhelming.

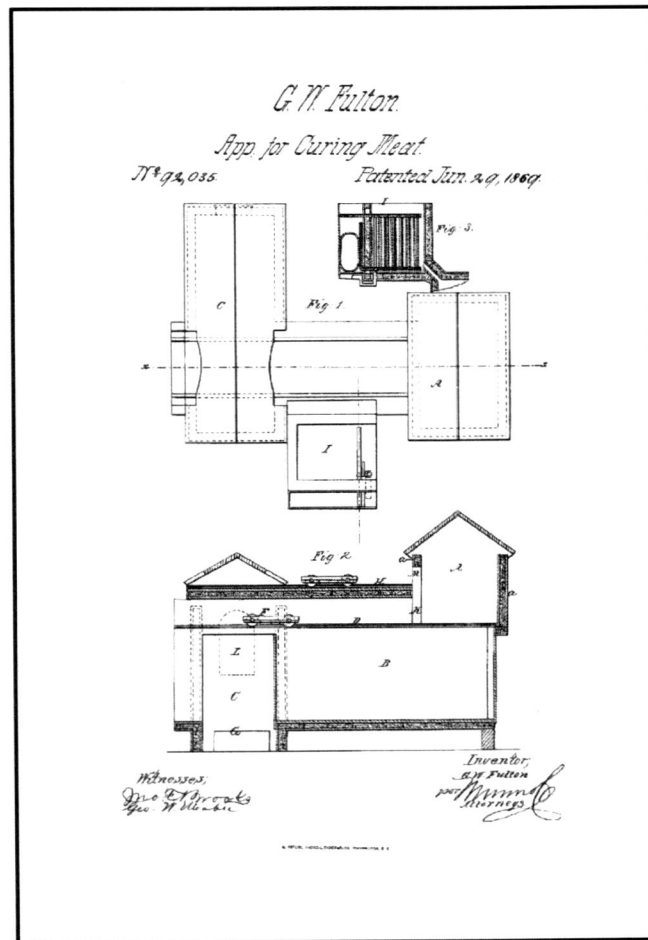

G. W. Fulton.
App. for Curing Meat.
Nº 92,055                    Patented Jun. 29, 1869.

The hides were tanned into leather, while hooves, horns, and tallow were shipped to eastern markets to make furniture, buttons, glue, candles, and soap. In a single year, over 100 million pounds of tallow, hides valued at over $2 million, 4,000 pounds of horns and twenty tons of bones would be manufactured into buttons, combs, or tool handles.

Choice sirloins were sold to local merchants, while others, cut into five or six pounds each, were supplied to the Army. A process changed the sirloins into "mess meat," or pickled beef. "Large steel vats were filled with 'three fours' formula: four pounds of brown sugar, four pounds of salt and four ounces of saltpeter" (Allen & Hastings-Taylor, 1997). The rest of the meat was cooked in steam vats rendering the fat. The

This hide puller (left) was used to strip the hide off cattle. The chain was hooked to a yoke pulled by donkeys, horses or oxen. Courtesy of Gordon Stanley

1,100-pound barrels of tallow were of more value than beef.

In 1871, E. G. Holden and Daniel L. Holden installed the first ice machine invented by G. W. Fulton in a packing house; thus, revolutionizing the industry by enabling the packery to process most of the meat instead of disposing of it. Holden became the first mechanically refrigerated slaughterhouse in America. The local packing industry declined after 1875 as railroads pushed into Texas to allow shipment of cattle directly to giant packing plants in St. Louis and Chicago. Yet, as late as 1880, the packeries located in Aransas County handled 93 percent of the Texas-packed beef production.

---

**Beef Kabob**

3 lbs. beef, cut in 2 in cubes
2 Tbsp. lemon juice
¾ c. Canned pineapple juice
1 clove garlic, minced
2 Tbsp. soy sauce
2 c. pineapple chunks, drained
Stuffed olives

Marinate beef cubes at room temperature for 2 hours in pineapple juice, soy sauce, lemon juice and garlic. Thread beef on skewers alternating it with pineapple chucks and olives. Broil for 10 minutes, basting frequently with marinade.

In 1875, John Grant Tobias painted his interpretation of the Marion Pkg. Co.

Courtesy of the Texas Maritime Museum

The shellcrete ruins of the site of the original Fulton packeries is marked with a historical marker at the corner of Fulton Beach Road (Broadway) and Chaparral in Fulton (VIP).

SITE OF
MARION PACKING CO.
THE RUINS OF THIS RENDERING VAT MARK THE LOCATION OF THE MARION PACKING CO. (SPELLED "MERIAM" IN SOME RECORDS), ONE OF THE DOZEN OR MORE MEAT PACKING PLANTS BUILT IN THE ROCKPORT-FULTON AREA IN THE 1860s AND 1870s TO PROCESS THE HUGE HERDS OF RANGE CATTLE THAT ROAMED TEXAS AFTER THE CIVIL WAR. HERE BEEF WAS DRIED, SALTED, OR PICKLED BEFORE SHIPPING. THE BY-PRODUCTS SUCH AS TALLOW, HIDES, HORNS, AND BONES WERE SENT TO EASTERN FACTORIES. LIKE MOST OF THE COASTAL PLANTS, MARION PACKING CO. FLOURISHED UNTIL ABOUT 1880, WHEN SHIPPING CATTLE TO NORTHERN MARKETS PROVED MORE PROFITABLE.

# Tapping the Sea for Salt

by Karey Swartwout

I was standing on the front porch of my new restaurant in Rockport. Just steps away from a vast ocean of salty seawater and a thought hit me. We use local seafood on our menu. Why not local salt? After a quick Google search, I grabbed a large pot and dashed out to get as much seawater as possible.

Back in the kitchen and prepping it for the oven, it occurred to me that this might not work. Why isn't anyone else doing this? What if the salt is just…blah?

Pushing the doubts out of my head, I closed the oven door and waited. Two long days later, the seawater evaporated as expected, but to my surprise, it left behind beautiful whispers of salt crystals, flowing in wavy lace-like patterns along the sides of the dish. It looks other-worldly and crumbles with the slightest touch. I slowly licked the salt off my finger-tips, and childhood memories of summer floated to the surface. Like the one of getting bowled over from a seemingly monstrous 1-

foot wave, as gallons of seawater came pouring into my little nose and mouth. The first taste of salty ocean water condensed into a tiny granular memory on the tip of my thumb.

Since opening my restaurant, I have enjoyed the joy of living by the seaside and exploring flavors that make us smile. I have had the opportunity to discover local food sources, delve into our culinary history and simply enjoy the character of this magnificent region.

Making local sea salt is so simple. Most of the effort involves hauling that big pot of water.

From the Collection of Jim Moloney

---

**Local Sea Salt**
Makes about 1 cup of sea salt.

Scoop up a few gallons of sea or bay water, ideally from a bay that opens directly onto the open sea. Fill several glass casserole dishes (not metal) with the seawater. Put them in the oven at 200° for two days or until all the water has evaporated. Scrape the salt crystals into a glass or wooden container and keep in a dry place.

Sprinkle your locally harvested sea salt on buttery roast potatoes, juicy ripe tomatoes or even handmade dark chocolate truffles.

From the Collection of Gordon Stanley

# The Fate of the Green Turtles in Aransas County

From April through November, green turtles would migrate north from Mexico and feast upon the seagrass in Aransas, Matagorda, Galveston Bays and the lower Laguna Madre. Fisherman set heavy nets near the passes within the bays. As the turtle moved into deeper water at night, they were captured.

Beginning in 1869, the Fulton packeries also began packing green sea turtles. Rockport handled almost the entire Gulf production. By 1879, C. M. Hadden opened a turtle cannery in Fulton. Buying turtles from local fisherman, Hadden increased the original cannery with a larger one just two years later. By 1886, the Fulton Cannery processed about 1,000 turtles a year into 40,000 two-pound cans of turtle meat and 800 pounds of two or three-pound cans of turtle soup.

Between 1880 and 1890, green turtle catches increased 20 times. Those not processed in Fulton were sent alive to Corpus Christi or Galveston on

GREEN-TURTLE CANNERY AT FULTON, WITH TURTLE PEN IN THE FOREGROUND.

steamer ships. Some were sent on to New York City.

Green turtles weighing between 100 and 500 pounds were trapped and kept alive in submerged 12-foot square rope and wooden pens called "kraals" until the price per pound was its highest. These 500 square foot enclosures were built beneath a pier using poles driven into the floor of the bay and connected at the top with a timber.

The workers fed fish scraps and algae to the penned turtles until they were shipped to market. To load the turtles on the ships, they would be lifted by block and tackle, attached to a swinging arm, put in shipping crates and loaded on ships waiting at the piers. Even out of the water, the turtles lived until the boat docked.

By the 1890s, Charles Stevenson, fishery agent, estimated that over 500,000 pounds of turtle meat had been processed. By the late 1890s, the turtle population had diminished; thus, ending the turtle canning industry. Soon after, the Fulton Cannery relocated to Tampico, Mexico to be closer to what remained of the green turtle population breeding grounds (U.S. Fisheries, 1906).

---

**Turtle Soup**

After turtle is killed, let bleed 12 hours, open the side, remove meat and cut in small pieces, then blanch 5 minutes in boiling water. If turtle is medium size, take off shell and put in soup kettle, cover with white broth, adding 1 teaspoon of pepper corns, 1 dozen cloves, 2 sprigs of thyme, 4 bay leaves, salt to taste; boil 1 hour. Then strain the broth, remove bones and dice the meat. Boil the broth until reduced ¾ in quantity, then add meat and boil 10 minutes. When ready to serve, add 1 tumbler of Maderira wine. When turtles cannot be obtained, get 1 pint of canned turtle meat and prepare soup same way as when using live turtle. Soup will keep for a long while if you put in stone jars, and when cold, pour hot lard over the top. Reheat when needed for use.

---

Remnants of turtle capture pens can still be found along the shores of Aransas County.

---

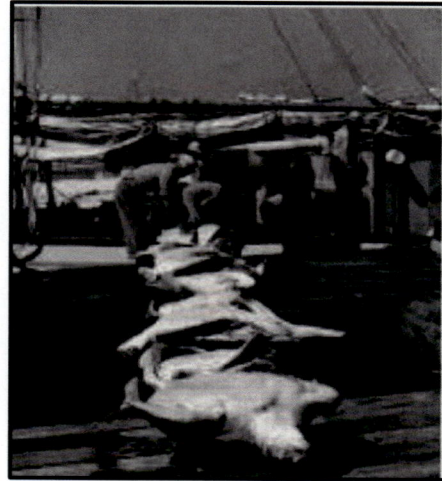

### Interesting Information:

Turtle meat is said to taste like veal, especially when fried. However, veal isn't as pricey – it's much cheaper than $25 to $50 per pound. Due to the amount of work that goes into cleaning a turtle and ecological considerations, we recommend not preparing it.

Turtle meat provides a great deal of protein and less saturated fat than beef. A cup of turtle meat contains about 220 calories, 33 grams of protein and only 2 grams of saturated fat. A cup of beef steak has about 340 calories, 37 grams of protein and 8 grams of saturated fat. Turtle meat is also high in calcium and vitamins and is even a recommended alternative medicine in some areas of the world.

Instead, drive to Port Aransas, walk out on the levee, sit and observe the water on the left side and watch the turtles swimming there.

# Commander's Palace Turtle Soup

| | | |
|---|---|---|
| 1 ½ sticks butter | 10 oz. fresh spinach | 1 ½ lbs. diced turtle meat |
| Freshly cracked pepper | 6 stalks celery, diced | 3 bell peppers, diced |
| 30 cloves garlic, minced | 2 medium onions, diced | |
| 1 tablespoon dried thyme, ground | 1 tablespoon dried oregano | |
| 4 bay leaves | 2 qts. Veal stock | 1 cup all-purpose flour |
| 1 tablespoon hot pepper sauce | 26 oz. dry sherry (750 ml bottle) | |
| 2 large lemons, juiced | ¼ cup Worcestershire sauce | |
| 6 boiled eggs, chopped | 3 cups peeled, chopped, seeded tomatoes | |
| Salt | | |

Melt ½ stick butter in a large soup pot over medium heat. Brown turtle meat. Season to taste with salt and pepper. Cook 18 to 20 minutes or until liquid is almost dry. Add onions, celery, garlic and peppers, constantly stirring. Add thyme, oregano and bay leaves. Sauté for 22 minutes. Add stock, bring to a boil and simmer for 30 minutes. Skim any fat that floats to the top.

While stock simmers, make the roux from melting the remaining butter over medium heat. Slowly add flour, constantly stirring with a wooden spoon. After flour has been added, cook until the roux smells nutty, is pale in color and has a consistence of wet sand – approximately 3 minutes. Set aside to let cool until soup is ready.

Using a whisk, stir the roux into the stock vigorously adding a little at a time to prevent lumping. Simmer for 25 minutes. Stir to prevent sticking. Add sherry; bring to a boil. Add hot sauce and Worcestershire sauce. Simmer and skim fat or foam. Add lemon juice, tomatoes and return to simmer. Add spinach and eggs, return to a simmer and adjust seasoning.

Courtesy of The Texas Maritime Museum

# Agriculture

Irish settlers brought seed corn, farm tools and food for a year when they traveled with James Power to his colony, Aransas City.

Land speculators, like the Gulf Coast Immigration Company, lured settlers into south Texas with a promise of cheap, rich land. Undeveloped land cost $1.25 an acre for a minimum of 80 acres or $100. In Texas each head of a family, male or

Egg Plants and Peppers, Over $1000 per Acre realized in this field by Mr. J. H. Sparks, Rockport, Texas

From the collection of Gordon Stanley.

female, could claim 4,605 acres.

Gulf Coast Immigration Co. described soil as deep sandy or shelly loan, rich and easily cultivated, adapted for fruit growing and market gardening. According to them, every known variety of vegetable grew in abundance.  Crops could be harvested three a year due to the climate.

In 1909, W. F. Sparks stated that he sold $800 worth of peppers and $700 of eggplant off three-fourths of an acre.

A.L. Bracht said that he shipped 19 train cars of vegetables. In the spring of 1908, 45 cars and

From the collection of Gordon Stanley

Courtesy of Four Strings Farm

the same amount of squash, green pepper, eggplant, and okra, beans and other early vegetables, but also shipped produce almost every month of the year. Home gardens were a necessity for early residents. Early settlers probably brought seeds from their previous homes. If they moved here from an area not too far away, a milk cow and chickens were brought with them. Milk cows were a necessity for families with 10 children or more.

Families earned "egg money" when they had an abundance of produce from their garden, extra eggs, and additional milk. Often extra milk would be left in milk cans alongside the road so that Wheeler's Dairy, located near Club Lake, could collect them.

Photos from the Collection of Francis Iles

At Sparks Colony off FM 1781, Apple orchards were found there in 1914. Charles Roe, Sr. planted 50 acres of produce and sold it at his store. Jim De Whitt grew cucumbers, tomatoes, peppers and squash there. Produce was sent to northern markets via the railroad. In 1916, Jim Sparks established Sparks Dairy at Sparks Colony. In 1929, the dairy was relocated to land on the current FM 1069. Milton,

Raymond and Jack, Jim's sons, worked with him at Sparks Dairy. Gardens and vineyards grew on Frandolig Island (Key Allegro).

Courtesy of Francis Iles

Families had to be self-sustaining by growing their own fruits and vegetables, hunting, or gathering seafood from the bays. Hunters arriving at Port Bay Hunting Club enjoyed the fruits of the manager's labor. Arthur R. Curry, manager of The Port Bay Hunting Club (previous page), is shown preparing his garden with the help of two mules, while others prepared a wild hog.

Even today crops are grown in the area's rich soil to supply fresh produce to local restaurants in the Farm to Table Movement.

Photos courtesy of Four Strings Farm

### Homemade Vanilla Ice Cream

2 cups heavy whipping cream
1 cup sugar
2 cups Half and Half cream
2 t. vanilla extract
ice cream maker
Kosher Salt
Ice

Combine all ingredients, stirring to dissolve sugar completely. Fill cylinder of ice cream maker no more than two-thirds full. Refrigerate mixture until ready to freeze. Freeze according to manufacturer's directions.  Serve immediately or store in covered containers in freezer.

Puree 2 cups of fresh or frozen berries for one cup of Half and Half. .

Butter is a dairy product made from churning milk or cream. The churning process separates the butterfat or solids from the buttermilk, the liquid. Usually, the butter we use comes from cow's milk or another domestic animal.
Homemade Butter

### Homemade Butter

Heavy cream          Jar with a lid

- Fill the jar half-way with cream.
- Add a lid to the jar; be sure it's a tight fit.
- Start shaking
- When the sloshing sounds stop, remove the lid, and check for whipped cream.
- Put the lid back on tightly.
- Continue to shake until the mixture separates into buttermilk and butter.
- Remove the lump of butter.
- Save the buttermilk for baking.

Courtesy of Gordon Stanley

# Abraham H. Sanchez: Truck Farmer

By Abraham Sanchez, Jr.

Rumaldo & Simona Sanchez
From the Collection of the Abraham Sanchez Family

When Abraham H. Sanchez was 5 or 6 years old, his career as a "truck farmer" began. By planting seeds or handling a weeding hoe, he became a contributing helper to his parents Rumaldo and Simona Sanchez at the farm in Ingleside, Texas. The farm produced crops such as tomatoes, cucumbers, corn, watermelons, cantaloupes, turnips, radishes, jalapeno. Operations supplied food for canning during the harvest season. These were sold at market and the proceeds carried the family over to the

From the Collection of the Abraham Sanchez, Sr. Family
The Sanchez Family Homestead painted by Steve Russell

next planting season as well as paid off accrued debt for the current year.

Upon his discharge from the Navy in 1943, Abe farmed and shrimped. By 1950, he had sold his boat and began farming full time. Abraham planted several small fields, each 3-6 acres, with a dedicated cash crop like tomatoes, cucumbers, watermelons, cantaloupes or corn. His son, Abraham Jr., age 5, ferried the tractor from field to field.

In 1952, the family moved to Lamar where Abe began share-cropping the Preston Paul land in Lamar. Compared to his previous fields, these plots were much larger. Tomatoes covered the field north of the farm house, totaling 25 acres. Corn or oats were planted in rows of two to serve as windbreaks for eight rows of tomatoes. The 2/8 pattern continued to the end of the field.

The same planting pattern was mirrored across the highway but planted with cucumber and jalapeno peppers as well as 10 acres of corn. Twenty-five acres of cotton were planted at the northern end of the fields on the west. On the south side of the farmhouse watermelon, cantaloupe, peanuts, bell pepper and potatoes grew.

From the Collection of the Abe Sanchez, Sr. family

During the farming year, the most memorable times were *chopping* and *harvest*. Chopping, or weeding and thinning the plants, occurs in the spring. This is essential for maximum production. Chopping long rows of weeds in the hot sand are not easily forgotten. During harvest, Abe, Sr. would ship truckloads of boxes of tomatoes and cucumbers to the Ingleside packing house. He also shipped pickup loads of cantaloupe, watermelon and corn to Rockport.

Based on the entries in his ledger, dozens of ears of corn at forty cents a dozen and tomatoes at $4.80 per bushel were delivered to Roe's Food Store and The Duck Inn as well as to various friends for cash or credit. He also sold to the Red & White and Weber's Grocery Store in Fulton. He would sell his produce as far south as Aransas Pass. Pickup loads of melons or cantaloupe were sold by size.

Even though these crops did not sell for much, when several pickup loads were sold each day, the nickels and dimes added up quickly.

Abe, Jr. and Tim, his brother, would stock and operate a roadside produce stand at the entrance to the farm. Each morning they would pick the ripe produce and pile it on the stand's shelves or in the shade. They would manage the stand from 9 AM until late in the day--usually around supper time! At the end of each day, the stand always seemed to need restocking and provided a reasonable income for the family.

Abraham, Sr. gave up truck farming when he tired of waiting for rain, watching too much rain

From the Collection of the Abe Sanchez, Sr. family

Susana Carpenter
Gloria Enderby
Oralia Valdez
Abraham Sanchez
Tim Sanchez
Sara Roe
Diana Garcia
Katy Miears
Wanda Brown
Cynthia Sanchez
Herb Sanchez
Denise Stanley

ruin a large portion of his planted crops and wild pigs eating the corn.

The farm had to weather sandstorms, hail, insects, and countless wild animals. It was not uncommon to have high school friends help watch the fields to eliminate wild pigs, deer and raccoons at night.

One night, a group of young men stole watermelons for a beach party. Unfortunately for them, the melons, big as they were, were not ripe yet!

None of the twelve children took the risks associated with farming or decided to take up the hoe as a tool to help earn a living. "Most of us are avid gardeners planting sweet corn, melons, cucumbers, tomatoes, jalapeno peppers and love doing it," stated Abraham Sanchez, Jr.

Today, the farmhouse has begun to crumble on itself and the farm is overrun with tall weeds and grasses. The old shade tree in the front yard toppled over in a storm a few years ago. There are even a few hilltops with a healthy growth of Live Oak trees. Here and there traces of the old Sanchez farm have almost disappeared, but not from our memories.

As adults looking back at the farming years, Abe and Katherine's children have no regrets. "We probably have false memories of *good* times spent doing any number of Dad's daily tasks for each of us. We disliked the work but loved Mom and Dad enough to do our best to carry out their wishes. Those old enough to participate in daily farming chores reminisce about the good old days when we lived on the farm".

---

### Pickled Okra

| | |
|---|---|
| Fresh okra with stems left on | Small chili peppers |
| Fresh dill heads | 1-quart vinegar |
| ½ c. canning salt | 1 ½ quart water |
| Celery seed (optional) | 1 tsp. dill seed |
| Garlic cloves | |

Wash okra and stand it in jars snuggly, but not too tight that the pods would break. To each jar, add 1 chili pepper, 1 clove garlic and 1 head fresh dill. Combine vinegar, water, salt, 1 chili pepper, 1 head fresh dill (or 1 tsp. celery seed, and 1 tsp. dill seed. Bring to a boil for 5 minutes. Pour hot liquid over okra and seal. Put jars in a large canning pot. Add enough water to cover the jars. Bring to a boil for 10 minutes. Remove and cool in a draft free place. Carrots, cauliflower, or celery may be prepared by this process.

# A Bouquet of Greens

by Karey Swartwout

Almost every week the owners from Bee Tree Farm drop by our restaurant with arms full of the most gorgeous greens you have ever seen. Wendy and Greg live in a little area called Lamar, which is a beautiful oak tree-filled town near Goose Island, a wildlife refuge. Their small farm is a sight to behold with a custom-built cistern that makes use of excess rainfall in times of drought.

The vegetables are not structured into neat rows but grow rather wildly in an organized-chaos slash Alice in Wonderland sort of way. Walking through the bushy basil plants and grapefruit trees, you almost feel as though the garden is in charge, versus the gardener. Bee Tree Farm is a magical place.

Wendy and Greg have inspired our kitchen team to use what is available, which enables us to design menus from our coastal area. It can be somewhat challenging when the cooler seasons are jam-packed and then it quiets down dramatically when the heat sets in. This time of year is my favorite when the winter greens bow down to make way for the delicate spring crop. Typically, in early March, we see lots of arugula, radish (daikon, red and black varieties), kale, red lettuce, cilantro, parsley, chive, Thai basil and grapefruit. Chervil is an herb that I love pairing with seafood, and keeping fingers crossed that it makes it out of their farm before being discovered by the deer (another challenge when gardening in the wild).

March also brings tons and tons of dill. Huge feathery branches of dill. So much dill you start to have nightmares about it. Thank goodness for the invention of pesto. Making pesto with dill is an efficient way

Courtesy of Four Strings Farm

to use up the excess and it keeps in the fridge for weeks. This zesty herby sauce can be used alongside grilled shrimp and fish dishes or stirred up with some sour cream and mayonnaise for a refreshing dip with crisp vegetables. I love eating it on its own with grilled smoky slices of baguette.

To bridge the winter and spring months, try making a salad using vegetables from both seasons. The variety of greens coming together all at once is uniquely pleasing and satisfying. The key is to use the freshest ingredients available. If you don't have a garden of your own or a farm nearby, try your local farmer's market or a specialty store.

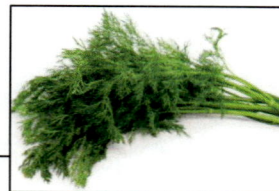

### Dill Pesto

This is a nifty way to use up all that dill that grows so well in our coastal environment. Lovely served with grilled fish, chicken or as a dipping sauce with bread.

| | | |
|---|---|---|
| 5 tablespoon walnuts or pine nuts | 1 teaspoon sea salt | 5 cloves garlic |
| 1 cup vegetable oil | 3 cup fresh dill, roughly chopped | zest of 1 large lemon |

Whizz up walnuts and garlic in a food processor until finely chopped. Add fresh dill, lemon zest, and salt and puree until it forms a nice paste. Gradually pour in the vegetable oil until it becomes as thick or thin as you want it. Store in the refrigerator.

# Bouquet Salad

### Serves 4 to 6

| | | |
|---|---|---|
| 2 garlic cloves, peeled & crushed | 2 tablespoon chopped dill | 60 ml champagne vinegar |
| sea salt | 90 ml olive oil | cracked black pepper |
| 8 radishes, slice ¼" | 1 sm red leaf lettuce heart, torn | ¼ cup Kalamata olives |
| ½ small red onion, thinly sliced | 1 sm cauliflower, divided into florets; cut into 1/8" thick slices | |

2 cucumbers, cut on an angle into 1/4" thick slices

¼ cup small parsley leaves, removed from stem

Assorted blossoms such as arugula, nasturtiums & broccoli.

In small bowl, whisk together dill, garlic, vinegar and oil, pinch of salt and pepper. Toss the salad ingredients (except the flowers) in a large mixing bowl. Drizzle the dressing over the salad – just enough to coat. Gently toss again; taste for seasoning. Serve garnished with assorted blossoms.

# Mom's Crispy Eggplant

by Karey Swartwout

One of my favorite food memories is my mother's Crispy Eggplant, pan-fried in seasoned homemade breadcrumbs, then smothered in a fresh tomato basil sauce under gooey mozzarella cheese. It is a recipe from her New Orleans' upbringing and one of many lip-smacking dishes she provided for me during my childhood in Houston. While running my catering company in London, I had the chance to explore countless exotic eggplant dishes. Smoked, marinated, grilled, pureed, braised, pickled, stuffed, roasted...so many cooking methods shared by cultures from around the world. There is a Persian recipe (Mirza Ghasemi) made from roasted eggplants, turmeric and lots of garlic that is so incredible, I have found myself consuming velvety, creamy spoonfuls straight from the fridge in the middle of the night. *Please don't tell my mother.*

Speaking of secrets, did you know that the eggplant is a fruit, or more precisely, a big berry? I recently discovered that the eggplant is a member of the nightshade family, a poisonous group of plants. Folks once believed it would cause insanity or even death.  It was not until the early 1900's, with the arrival of Italian and Asian immigrants, that the eggplant gained popularity here in the United States. Nowadays we benefit from a variety of eggplants, from the glossy violet "Black Beauty" to the "Bianca Rose" with its lavender and creamy white shading. Along the Texas coast, it can be difficult to grow fruits and vegetables in our sandy soil, but the eggplant thrives here.

If you can find an assortment of eggplants, this is a useful dish to showcase them, as the different shapes and sizes can be put on display. You will notice this recipe requires lots of salt, and I like to use sea salt to bring out the essence of the eggplant. An outdoor wood burning grill will bring out even more flavor, but when indoors, a very hot cast iron griddle pan on the stove works just fine.

When complete, this recipe results in a lovely contrast of flavors and textures: The smoky grilled eggplant lights up from the fiery heat of red chilies, then cools down with the minty crème fraîche (pronounced "crem fresh").  Do not let the fancy name intimidate, crème fraîche is like sour cream, just sweeter and creamier.  If you have trouble finding crème fraîche in your local store, I have included an easy recipe to make your own which only requires a day to set - well worth the wait. Note: My mother likes to salt her eggplants before cooking.  Many feels that's no longer necessary since we now harvest them sooner, eliminating the harsh taste.

# Grilled Eggplant with Red Chilies and Mint Crème Fraîche

By Karey Swartwout

1 medium globe eggplant, 2 long Asian eggplants, 1 large black eggplant

1 Tablespoon sea salt (or Maldon Sea Salt Flakes)

Olive oil

2 teaspoons finely minced fresh garlic

2 teaspoons finely sliced red chilies

Mint sprigs for garnish

Salt and pepper

**Eggplant:** Remove stems and slice ½ in thick, making sure they are all the same thickness. Preheat a grill, cast-iron griddle or broiler to a high heat. Brush both sides of the eggplant slices with the oil, sprinkle with sea salt, and cook 4-5 minutes per side. Keep brushing with olive oil and salting during this process. This can be done in batches. During the last minute of grilling, throw in a bit of the minced garlic and sliced red chilies, cooking long enough for the flavors can be released. Garlic should be golden; but not brown as it will taste bitter if cooked too long. Serves 4 to6.

**Crème Fraiche:**

2 cups heavy whipping cream

2 tablespoons buttermilk

2 tablespoons chopped fresh mint

1 large clove garlic, mashed to a paste

Salt and pepper to taste

Prepare this the day before it is needed. Mix heavy whipping cream with the buttermilk in a glass or plastic bowl. Cover with cling film and keep at room temperature until thickened to desired texture about 12-16 hours. You can then store it in the refrigerator for up to 2 weeks.

**To plate:**

Arrange the eggplant slices and spoon some of the garlic-red chile-olive oil-pan drippings over them. Place a few dollops of minty crème fraîche and crack some black pepper over the top. Garnish with mint sprigs and serve warm or at room temperature.

From the collection of Kam Wagert

# When life gives you lemons, say thank you.

By Karey Swartwout

When life gives you lemons, well…actually, it really depends on the lemon. I've learned the hard way that some lemons out there are just not right. Like the ones that look superlative on the outside, with their impressive size and bright, sparkly skin…the ones that seem to scream "Pick me! Pick me!" from the produce bin. Back home, you slice through the heavy outer peel (clue #1), and instead of succulent flesh on the inside, you find the core is dried up and hollow. Juiceless soul. Not even a squirt in the eye. Nada. Nuh-zing. Back in the produce section, you turn away from the lackluster lemons, prepare to forego your cravings for that zesty tang, when voila! You spy an open box of plump fruit off to the side. Hmm. These lemons look attractive, but in an unassuming way. You make a leap of faith and are rewarded with bitter-sweet juice beneath convivial thin skin. Your trust in citrus is restored.

The Valley Lemon is that kind of lemon. It won't let you down. It's the lemon that keeps on giving, with delightfully sweeter versions as the season unfolds. Don't just stop at lemonade. Imagine stocking up on lemon sorbet, candied lemon peels, lemon cookies, lemon infused olive oil, lemon meringue, preserved lemons, lemon cake…and…ohhh…lemon buttercream frosting!

Why are these so special anyway? Well, Valley Lemons are also called Meyer Lemons and are grown in the Rio Grande Valley at the southernmost tip of Texas. They are not actually true lemons, but are crossed with a type of orange. Mr. Frank Meyer discovered them in China in the early 1900s and brought them back to the US. However, it wasn't until Alice Waters from Chez Panisse in Berkeley, California began using them that they began to take hold in American kitchens. A few years later, a woman named Martha Stewart began showing them off in her now famous recipes and the Meyer Lemon Star was born. It's a likeable fruit, not too sour with aromatic hints of honeysuckle and herbs. Right now, these lemons are beginning their season, and still a wee green. If you prefer your lemons on the sour side, this is a great time to pick up a box.

I stopped by Jimmy Woods Produce last week for some onions and left with a huge bag full of Valley Lemons. Once you go there you will see how easy that is to do. Jimmy has been in business for over 30 years and has exquisite South Texas produce. Right now, you can find all sorts of Valley citrus as well as pumpkins, sweet 10-15 onions, and dried Indian corn, all displayed beautifully in his open-air market. There's also a refrigerated room with herbs and eggs plus locally made honey and preserves. Be sure to try the Mangopeno Jelly. Jimmy makes you feel right at home with his enthusiastic welcome and heartfelt customer service. When you go, please tell Jimmy to save some Valley Lemons for me. I've already used up my bag.

# Valley Lemon Tart with Almond Crust

Serves 12

| CRUST | FILLING |
|---|---|
| 1 cup butter, softened | 4 eggs |
| ½ cup white sugar | 1 ½ C white sugar |
| 2 cups all-purpose flour | ¼ C all-purpose flour |
| 2 tablespoons finely chopped almonds | 2 Valley Lemons, juiced |

Preheat oven to 350 degrees F. In a medium bowl, blend together softened butter, 1/2 cup sugar and 2 cups flour. Stir in the chopped almonds. Press crust mixture into the bottom of parchment paper lined 9x13 inch pan. Bake for 15 to 20 minutes until firm and golden.

In another bowl, whisk together the remaining 1 ½ cups sugar and 1/4 cup flour. Whisk in the eggs and lemon juice and pour over the baked crust. Smooth out mixture with the back of a spoon if necessary.

Bake for 20 minutes more until filling firms up a bit. Remove and cool to room temperature. Chill in the fridge to set further and slice into squares or triangles. Garnish with coulis and fresh berries or whipped cream.

This is a fast, easy recipe for those needing a quick citrus fix. Perfect for special occasions, too.

P.S. I'd like to dedicate this recipe to Grandpa Richard, who passed away last week. His witty rebuttals to life's bittersweet moments will be remembered forever. He loved this dessert.

WAGON LOAD OF
JEW OR JUNE FISH
ROCKPORT, TEX.
PHOTO BY DYE.

From the Collection of Gordon Stanley

# Fishing

A flourishing fishing industry was established in the Aransas County area as early as the 1890s. Fishermen used scows to gather their catch. Three well-established fish houses owned most of the boats, usually sailing scows, which pulled nets and seined for fish. It was not uncommon for a fleet of three or four fishing scows to bring in a catch of 2,000-3,000 pounds of fish.

Early fish houses purchased the catch of the individual fishermen. At the turn of the century, D. R. Scrivner established two locations for Miller Bros, one in Rockport and one in Fulton.

In 1905, Roy Jackson bought out Scrivner's Rockport business and formed the Jackson Brothers' Company. After the 1919 storm, S. F. Jackson changed the name to Jackson Seafood Company.

From the Collection of Jim Moloney

Rockport, Tex.
Front of Cobolini Fish House

From the Collection of Jim Moloney

The Union Fish Company, co-owned by Louis Cobolini and Mr. Gentry, was located behind a saloon on Water Street. However, the company was sold in 1907 to Ernest Camehl and the location was moved to railroad property – just north of the tracks and across from Jackson Fish Company. Until the hurricane of 1919, Union Fish Company flourished. After the hurricane, Camehl found a small typewriter in the debris, but the company's huge safe was never found.

With trusted friends and fishing crews, which included W. F. Close, Sr., John Weber and Wesley Atwood, the Union Fish Company was soon reestablished and prospered.

Local fisherman remembered having nets about 1,000 feet long with a bait bag in the center. The men would grab the net, walk in a circle and then the fish would be pushed into the center. The bag would be hauled to a boat and delivered to the fish companies. The fishermen would be paid 5 cents a pound for trout and 2-3 cents a pound for redfish and drum.

The Rockport Fish and Oyster Company was owned and operated by C. W. and C. R. Gibson. The Gibsons also owned and operated the Lone Star Fish and Oyster Company in Corpus Christi. Gladys Bruhl Gibson managed the businesses after her husband's death. She was the daughter of Albert Bruhl and Hattie Fulton Bruhl.

Travis Johnson went to work for the Gibsons in 1922. Later he entered a partnership with Charles Picton and founded Johnson Fish Company in 1935. He then bought the property from the Gibsons but continued to use his company's name. The Union Fish Company quit selling fish in 1932 and became a ship chandlery.

The average selling price for the fish was about 6 cents per pound, but at times it went as high as fifteen cents per pound.

Mrs. Myra Allen, Camehl's daughter, remembered many nights when 40 to 50 barrels of fish were packed and shipped from Rockport on the train. The first

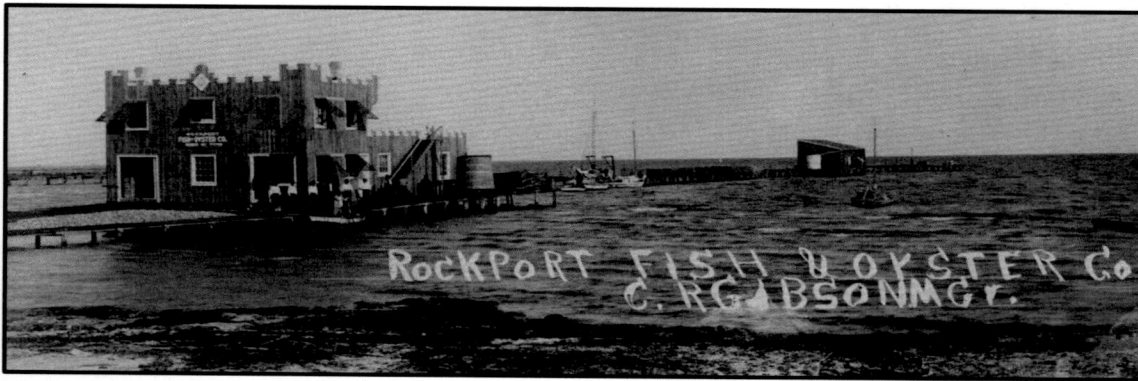

From the collection of Jim Moloney

ice shipped to Texas came by schooner from the lakes of Maine and New York. In a *Caller-Times* article (1958), Andrew Sorenson stated that the ice was cut into slabs four feet square and packed in sawdust.

From the collection of Jim Moloney

### Baked Redfish
By Dorothy Morrison Leslie

1 large redfish (2 ½ lbs.) (Leave scales on)     Lemon Juice     Garlic Salt
Melted butter or oleo     Worcestershire Sauce

Remove the head and large fin from the fish. Your seafood dealer can dress your fish using these directions. Mix together all ingredients and pour the mixture down the fin cavity. Put this side up. Bake in a moderate oven until fish is tender which is usually about a half hour depending on the size of the fish. When ready to serve, take off the scales and skin. They should peel off like a banana. Fish will be moist and delicious.

19 FISH, OVER 100 LBS
CAUGHT HANDS ONLY
ROCKPORT, TEXAS,

PHOTO &
COPYRIGHT 1907
BY W. D. L. DYE.

From the collection of Gordon Stanley

In the 1930s, the Casterline brothers, as Casterline Fish Co., and the Rouquette & Wendell Fish Company began their operations in Fulton. By the 1950s, the Fulton harbor front also included the Dietrich Brothers Seafood, Fulton Fish Co., Fulton Fish and Oyster Co., and Johnson Fish Co. From those early days until today, the fishing has *lured* people to visit and live on the Texas coast.

A TWO-TONED SYMPHONY: Rockport's "Fishbowl"

Outlet to the bays which surround Rockport is that town's "Fishbowl" harbor.

### Red Snapper Tampiquena

| | |
|---|---|
| 1 ½ fresh red snapper fillets | Onions |
| Butter | Green Peppers |
| Fresh tomatoes | Minced jalapenos |

Broil fillets in butter for about five minutes. Turn, then bake in pre-heated 400° oven for 3-5 minutes. Sauté onions, peppers, tomatoes and jalapenos till crisp and tender. Place vegetables on top of fillets.

# Red Snapper Run

By Lucretia Wright

Nathan "Peanut" Wright

While out shrimping, one Wright brother happened upon the red snapper run and dropped his lines of hooks. Bringing in an abundant amount of snapper, he radioed his position to his brothers. As the other boats arrived, deckhands dropped hooks on cane poles into the water and pulled out snapper as fast as they could. The fish were laid on ice and hauled to one of the local fish houses. That day was successful for all the Wright Brothers!

This historic Red Snapper Run was documented in the local papers. A series of 33mm films taken between 1947 and 1951 were compiled to depict the working lives of the Wright Brothers of Rockport, Texas as well as this red snapper run. Well-known shrimpers, these gentlemen made an impact on the local shrimping and fishing industry. They docked their boats in Rockport Harbor.

Also seen is "a clean pick catch". This occurs when the shrimp net is emptied onto the deck of the shrimp boat and very little culling is needed. When the catch is mostly shrimp, with no "trash", it was a deckhand's dream. When the net was opened behind the boat, fish were funneled into the net, so a school of sharks can be seen. Even in the old film, the shrimp are white, clean, abundant and beautiful. This industry continues to impact the economy of Aransas County today.

In the video a glimpse of the first Aransas County Courthouse can be seen. The Wright family has donated this video to The History Center for Aransas County. For more information, please contact The History Center.

Tom Betz (l) and Leslie "Bubba" Casterline (r) watch "Red Snapper Run".

# Raw, Superfrozen, Ike-Jime'd Fish

By Karey Swartwout

A friend of mine has one of those nice offshore fishing boats, you know the shiny ones that sail off into the big blue water, catching gorgeous things like red snapper, bonito, tilefish, and mackerel?

After a good catch, he tells me about the deliciousness of our gulf fish, especially when just caught and sliced into juicy chunks, finished with just a squeeze of lime and splash of soy sauce.

I patiently wait for my nice friend to finish his story, while my salivating taste buds are about to explode with envy. Many folks who enjoy fishing in deep water know that eating a just-reeled-onto-the-boat-fish is an eye-opening culinary experience.

How do I get some of that fish? How does one without a shiny offshore boat experience that? I researched to find a local supplier of good quality raw fish, and finally came across Jim Naismith, who until recently operated a small business supplying sashimi grade from our local waters. I wasn't familiar with sashimi grade fish from our local waters, and begged Jim to meet me at the restaurant. Jim kindly walked me through the process that originated in Japan called "Ike Jime", which results in superior, great-tasting fish that lasts for long periods of time.

Most people that I know will catch the fish, reel it in and let it slowly die in a slurry of ice. But with the Ike Jime process that Naismith uses, the fish die instantly, and their flesh contains low levels of lactic acid, that pesky culprit behind the fishy smell in decaying seafood.

So, what is this Ike Jime method? Basically, once the fish is caught and reeled in onto the boat, a long spike is quickly inserted directly into the brain. I have also seen it done where the tail is cut and the spike is inserted up the spinal column, while the fish bleeds out. The fish relaxes and is dead immediately.

Big Jew Fish caught Rockport T.

At the restaurant I have experienced the results first hand. The extended shelf life on Ike-Jime'd fish is remarkable. Even after thawing out the fish caught ten days ago, the fish has virtually no odor. The next critical step is storing the Ike Jime'd fish.

Naismith taught me about super-freezing, which effectively "stops time" for the fish and when it's thawed properly, the quality of the fish is the same as if it was caught just a few hours before. The FDA requires that raw fish sold in restaurants, like sushi, must be frozen to cold temperatures. Super-freezing exceeds those requirements. The mass public can safely consume the fish. Aside from safety benefits, super- freezing allows for flexibility, which means we can enjoy high quality fish anytime. Even without a boat!

---

**Broiled Fish**

By Susie Black

1 c. mayonnaise      ½ c. melted butter

1 c. Dijon mustard      4 oz. lime juice

Pepperidge Farm bread crumbs

Fresh fish filets

Mix mayonnaise, mustard, butter and lime juice. Spread thickly on fish filets. Roll in bread crumbs. Broil until fish is flaky.

---

# SNAPPER CRUDO

Karey Swartwout

*Makes about 8 servings*

One of my favorite ways of eating raw fish is Crudo, a dish that is popular in Italy. You will need the finest ingredients to make this dish, so make sure to use a high-quality extra virgin olive oil along with your sashimi-grade fish. If you don't have snapper, sashimi-grade tuna is fine.

| | |
|---|---|
| 2 ounces red snapper fillet, sashimi grade | 1 plum tomato |
| Juice of one lime squeezed | 1/2 teaspoon finely chopped shallot |
| 1 red chili, very thinly sliced | Extra virgin olive oil and sea salt |

Make sure your fillet is super cold for a nice, clean cut. Thinly slice the fillet into 1/4-inch slices, using a super sharp knife cutting against the grain. Wrap the slices in clingfilm and keep in the refrigerator.

*To make tomato water:* Cut the tomato in half and scoop out the seeds. Whizz the tomato in a food processor or blender then strain through a fine sieve. Mix the remaining tomato water with the lime juice, shallot and red chili.

Spoon the tomato citrus marinade over the fish and gently toss. For presentation, you can either arrange the pieces in a loose fan shape on chilled plates, or in small bowls. Garnish with slices of red chili, sea salt and a drizzle of olive oil. Serve immediately.

# Crabbin'

The best places to find blue crabs are near the bay's sandy bottoms lined with sea grass. Avid crabbers recommend adding the head of a sheepshead or the cheapest raw chicken for bait to the inside of a crab trap. For more sugar, soak the chicken in Big Red overnight.

John Freeman remembers, "In the early hours of the summer mornings, Little Bay was so calm that the water looked like a large sheet of glass. Its shallow protected water made it an ideal place for the plentiful blue crabs to grow. It was common for us to be there by six or seven in the morning with our crabbing gear: a washtub and a gig for each of us. We happily greeted other groups for we were glad to have company and there was plenty of room and crabs for everyone. It usually took about two hours to get our tubs filled with several dozen crabs to take home. Occasionally, we would stop at one of the houses on our way home and sell to the Picton sisters for 35 cents a dozen" (p. 52).

Courtesy of Kay Barnebey©

COPYRIGHT 1907 N.Y.O.V. DYE.

"81 CRABS IN 2 hrs.     ROCKPORT, TEXAS.

*You could have done better than this, when you and father were boys at close range*

From the Gordon Stanley Collection

## Mrs. Charles T. Picton's Deviled Crab Recipe

| | |
|---|---|
| 1 lb. white crabmeat | ¼ c. Worcestershire sauce |
| 1 lb. claw crabmeat | 1-2 T. cream or canned milk |
| 1 medium onion, grated | 3 thin slices of toast |
| ½ c. finely chopped celery | salt and pepper to taste |
| ½ c. green pepper, minced | dash or two of tabasco |
| ½ c. melted margarine | |

Pour small amount of boiling water over toast and chop up with fork. Mix all ingredients together lightly so that crabmeat remains flakey. Put mixture into crab shells or ramekins. Cover the top with toasted bread crumbs. Dot with margarine. Bake in 375-degree oven for 20 minutes or until bread crumbs brown.

Submitted by Mary Jeffries, whose husband's grandmother was

Mrs. Charles T. Picton

Photo by Doc McGregor, Corpus Christi Public Libraries

# Oystering

"The Pearl" Oyster Boat

Courtesy of The Texas Maritime Museum

# An Oyster Token of Change

By Karey Swartwout

Driving up to Casterline's Seafood, you will find the rolling shutter doors wide open, welcoming any curious visitor. Piled several feet high are layers upon layers of recycled burlap coffee and chocolate bags, cleaned and ready to be stuffed with local oysters. A forklift stands at the ready, waiting for the arrival of the oyster boats, and, as usual, I catch Bubba Casterline at the helm. He sees me approach, turns off the engine and says with an earnest smile, "Hey girl, how's it going today?" It's good to see him.

Bubba's family history is well-recorded and thought-provoking. A third-generation fisherman, his great-great-grandfather, Jonas Casterline, is credited with setting up roots on the Texas coast. Born in Fayette, Seneca County, New York, on a Tuesday in the summer of 1810, Jonas grew up a long way from South Texas. In 1837, at 27 years old, he enlisted in the Army and fought under Zachary Taylor in Oklahoma, Florida and Texas. Jonas was with Taylor during the annexation of the state of Texas and made his way down with his wife, Rebecca, to Rockport-Fulton, even living on St. Joseph's Island as many settlers did during the late 1800s.

Jonas' son, Frank, the youngest of nine children, was 8 when his father died in 1869. Frank went on to have a son, Frank, Junior, who was Bubba's grandfather. Bubba's father, Leslie Eugene, or L. E. as he was known, was the first mayor of the town of Fulton and partnered with his brother Cecil in the seafood business, which they started in the 1940s. He was also known as a champion oyster shucker.

By the 1950s, the Fulton harbor front was nearing its peak with numerous fish markets and boat-yards for building commercial vessels. On any given day, one could find rows of tables with 50 or more men and

## Fulton's No. 1 shucker
B1

# LOCAL

La – Editor/Designer: Gary Fulghum, 886-3600          Copyright © 1996 Caller-Times Publishing Company          Wednesday, March 20, 1996

# Oysterfest champion keeps on shuckin'
## 77-year-old Casterline has known his way around an oyster since he was 7

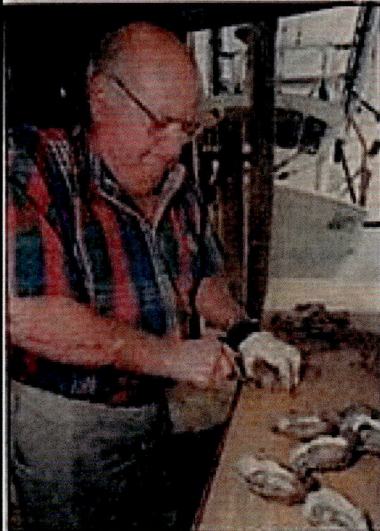

L.E. Casterline once again was the Oysterfest oyster-shucking champion. He has won the event 14 of the last 16 times he has competed.

FULTON – L.E. Casterline learned to shuck oysters when he was 7 years old.

"I cut myself a few times," he recalls. "You let that knife slip and you're in trouble."

Seventy years and thousands of oyster shuckings later, Casterline doesn't cut himself much anymore.

In fact, at 77 years old, Casterline has been Fulton's Oysterfest shucking champion for 14 of the 16 years he has competed. His last win came March 3.

"It's just been a lot of fun for me – competing with these young fellows and beating them," he said.

Casterline has lived in Fulton all his life. He served as Fulton's first mayor after the town incorporated in 1978.

Casterline's family has operated Casterline Seafood Market since the early 1930s.

Casterline worked at the market for 45 years, retiring about five years ago. He still visits the waterfront business often.

"You never get it out of your blood. I just sit around and talk to the boys. I never lift a finger anymore (to work)," he said, laughing.

Casterline gave an oyster-shucking demonstration one day recently for a

### D a n
## PARKER
#### South Texas Tales

visitor at the market.

First, he displayed his three oyster shuckers – stout metal blades with wooden handles.

"This is my favorite," he said, pointing to a shucker with a blade worn down by about an inch from 25 years of shucking and sharpening. "It's getting so it's not long enough to do the job."

The secret to winning oyster-shucking competitions, Casterline said, is not just speed. It's also being delicate enough with a shucker not to tear up the mussel while

forcing open the shell and separating the mussel from the shell.

Destroying the mussel costs a competitor points in an oyster-shucking contest.

Before shucking an oyster, Casterline puts a glove on his left hand. He holds the oyster in that hand.

With his right hand, he jams the point of the shucker into the oyster's hinge, forcing the two shells apart.

He slides the blade along the inside of the oyster, separating one side of the juicy mussel from the glistening white shell.

Then, almost too quickly and gracefully for onlookers to notice, Casterline flips the mussel-bearing shell on top of the other shell and he slices the underside of the mussel from the top shell.

For this master shucker, the whole process takes only a few seconds.

In addition to competing in the Fulton contest, Casterline has competed six times in a national shucking contest in Maryland. One year, he took second place.

Back problems almost kept Casterline out of this year's Fulton competition.

But he plans to keep on shucking "if everything's going all right, Lord willing."

women (mostly women) heading shrimp from the day's catch. When boats arrived, a truck would drive the streets of Fulton, blowing a whistle or honking the horn to signal workers that the boats were in and shrimp needed to be headed and oysters needed to be shucked.

Tokens paid to workers
Courtesy of Leslie "Bubba" Casterline

Cecil, Frank and L. E. Casterline had a warehouse where workers packed shrimp and oysters in barrels. Workers' wages were paid in tokens that could be cashed or spent in town. Inside his office where the warehouse once stood, Bubba pulls out a drawer on an old desk loaded with fading family photos and cherished mementos. He holds out his hand and shows me a half dozen weathered coins, which upon closer inspection appear to be tokens.

"These were used by my family to pay oyster shuckers back then," he says softly, the edges of his mouth lifting into a reminiscing grin. "It would have been good in our office for a few cents today. The boys could use them as money in Aransas County and were accepted by local businesses." Then he adds with a wink, "Also used quite a bit in games of chance."

We go on to chat about the oyster business, how this season is predicted to do versus the drought-heavy couple of past years. Bubba pulls up the National Estuarine Research Reserve System's local website, showing me the current salinity level readings for our waters.

"It's interesting, you know? A lot of people don't know about all the hassle, but also the benefit that goes into harvesting wild caught oysters. Our local customers complain that the farm-raised oysters are too bland or just not right." I nod in agreement and have noticed a difference when tasting products from oyster aquaculture. "Shipping these local oysters can be a real headache," he goes on to explain. "Some buyers refuse our oysters if they are too irregularly shaped or if their thin lips are cracked. They want them tidy and round."

He pauses for a moment, and glances at the tokens still in his palm. In the brief silence, it occurs to me that while our oysters may not be attractive on the surface, they are essential relics filled with delicious character. And surely there is still value in that.

### Drunken Oysters
#### By Steve Russell

```
1 doz. Oysters            Touch of flour
Smidge of catsup          Garlic powder
Tad of salt and pepper    Hardy Burgundy
Teriyaki sauce
4 Tablespoons Olive Oil
Sour dough French Bread
```

Wash and dry the oysters, season with salt, pepper and garlic powder, then dust with flour. Stir fry them in a wok with olive oil over fairly high heat until crunchy brown. Mix a dash of catsup, teriyaki sauce and about three fingers of burgundy in a cup. Stir well and pour in the wok to deglaze the oysters. Continue stirring until the mixture thickens.

Pour this mess in a bowl; break bread and start eating. Feeds one at a time. Next person gets the wok to do the same. Caution should be used here, as this could do to what blackened red fish did to our red fish. Oysters in AA>

### An Oyster Roast

*This recipe has been the same for hundreds of years, probably developed by the Karankawas or other coastal Native Americans. Oysters are at their best from September to March.*

Build an outdoor fire, often of live oak, and when hot, cover with oysters in their shell. Periodically, turn them over with a shovel or tongs until the shells begin to open. Use a stick or oyster knife to open the shells. Serve with crackers, cocktail sauce, lemons and hot sauce…and maybe beer.

# Shrimping

Countless numbers of individuals and families in Aransas County have been engaged in fishing and shrimping. Family seafood businesses often began by building a boat in the backyard. Individuals sold their catch to fish houses.

Around 1930, the shrimping industry was established when Jim Tuttle accidently discovered the abundance of shrimp in Aransas Bay. By 1935, Travis Johnson and Charles Picton founded the Johnson Fish Company; shrimp was its main product.

The shrimping industry reached significant proportions by the 1940s, possibly due to an emphasis on seafood being an important part of the American diet during World War II. During

Jumbo size, these shrimp are sorted and sent on their way to market.

From the Houston Chronicle, 1956

Courtesy of Leah Nguyen Oliva

There are two kinds of shrimping - Gulf Shrimping and Bay Shrimping. Gulf shrimpers use 50 to 80-foot long wooden or steel-hulled trawlers with nets that drag along the sea bottom. Gulf shrimpers usually fish for up to three weeks before returning to port.

Bay shrimpers are a historic part of many Texas coastal communities. Along the Texas coast, shrimping, combined with the commercial netting of other species of fish including trout, redfish, flounder, and drum, can be traced back to the middle of the nineteenth century. These smaller shrimp boats work daily from early morning hours until noon when they return to port.

the 1970s, shrimping funneled approximately $2,000,000 per year into the local economy.

A wooden "door" keeps the mouths of the nets open as chains at the bottoms of the nets stir up the shrimp and drive them in.

In 1975, the family of Nguyen Can Ban became the first of Vietnamese immigrant families to move to this area to work in the shrimping industry. Within a few years, several had built their own boats. Others sought higher education or became entrepreneurs.

In 1989, 62,453,900 pounds of shrimp were collected in Texas waters for a value of $119,761,700. This accounted for 84 percent of the value of all commercial marine products that year.

The following is a copy of a Rockport Pilot article from June 5, 1991 written by Charles Steward

SHIP YARD AND FISH FLEET AT ROCKPORT, TEXAS.

PHOTO BY DYE.

DeGolyer Library, Southern Methodist University, Texas: Photographs, Manuscripts and Imprints

entitled, *Jackson Gulf boats sold, described as 'end of an era'.*

Roy Jackson, a businessman from the Sinton and Mathis area, purchased the initial location of Jackson Seafood Co. in 1904. His brother, Stephen Ford Jackson, bought his brother's interest in Jackson Fish Company and changed the name to Jackson Seafood Company. Jackson added shrimp to his harvest. The local shrimping industry developed rapidly after 1930.

In 1945, Jim and Norvell joined their

TURNING BASIN AND CHANNEL. PLEASURE AND FISH FLEET. LOOKING EAST
ROCKPORT, TEXAS

DeGolyer Library, Southern Methodist University, Texas:
Photographs, Manuscripts and Imprints

father in the business after serving in the military. Norvell Jackson recalls, "Sailboats were used for fishing back then. The cabin would be aft and there would be a hold for the fish. The fish would be caught with drag seines. The seines were dragged by hand." The commercial catch was predominately redfish, trout and drum. "There was hardly any sport fishing here in those days," he says.

He adds, "Nobody knew what shrimp were in those early days. Shrimping started after 1930. It took about five years to educate the public that brown shrimp were good to eat. People used to think they were spoiled white shrimp.

I remember as a kid in high school, the shrimp would all come

Jackson Seafood Company and Boats
Courtesy of the Jackson Family

in with the heads on and we would come in after school and head them. My dad would catch lots of white shrimp in the spring then. There are a lot of old timers here, whose first job was heading shrimp for my dad."

During the 1920s, much of the fleet was converted to gasoline engine-powered craft. "We would buy old Buick engines from a scrap heap for $35," says the older Jackson. "With some of those engines, we didn't know if we would make it out, let alone make it back in. Some of the old scowls even had engines put in them.

In 1930, Stephen Ford Jackson bought the railroad pier at Rockport Harbor. In 1935, the Jackson Channel & Dock Co. was formed. "The company had a charter from the state to maintain the channels, docks and bulkheads in this area,"

says John Jackson. His father adds, "There were fewer than a dozen charters like that issued in the state."

According to Norvell Jackson, Jackson Seafood Co. boats converted to diesel engines after World War II. "Back then, the boats would leave here at 2 a.m., go through Port Aransas and fish the Gulf and come back the same night, and then turn around and do it the next day."

If there was a year of adversity for the Jackson family, it was 1970. Stephen Ford Jackson and Jim Jackson died within 16 days of each other. Hurricane Celia also ripped through the Coastal Bend.

"Our main building was a Quonset hut and we had covered boat stalls", says John Jackson, who joined the company in 1974. "We lost both of those with Celia. We had a fleet of wooden boats then and we were constantly changing the ropes and pumping out water. Then it got real hairy and we went to the sheriff's department." While structures were lost, the boats were intact after Celia.

In 1980 as Hurricane Allen approached, several Jackson boats were anchored in Aransas Bay. The Sarah J broke loose during the rising tide and was found in four feet of water near Cove Harbor. It took a twin-engine tug to pull the Sarah J free.

The appearance of Rockport Harbor was changed forever in May 1991 with the sale of eight gulf shrimp boats from Jackson

Rockport Yacht and Supply Co.: Local builder of boats
From the DeGolyer Library, Southern Methodist University, Texas:
Photographs, Manuscripts and Imprints

Seafood Co. "You could call it the end of an era," said owner operator, John Jackson. "We are happy we sold them, but it is a sad commentary on the shrimp industry," he added. "For a fleet owner, it hasn't been profitable for the past several years. We had two decent years in all of the 1980s. We can't afford to keep the boats up. Replacing the boats would now cost two to three times what they previously cost."

Six of the boats went to a Mexican company out of Ciudad Del Carmen and the other two went to a buyer in Palacios. Jackson was on the Rockport Harbor Jetties on May 18, 1991 to watch the boats to pass through for the last time as they sailed for their new homes. "I like to tell people I shed one tear as the boats went by, but that tear only went halfway down my cheek," he says. "It was minor

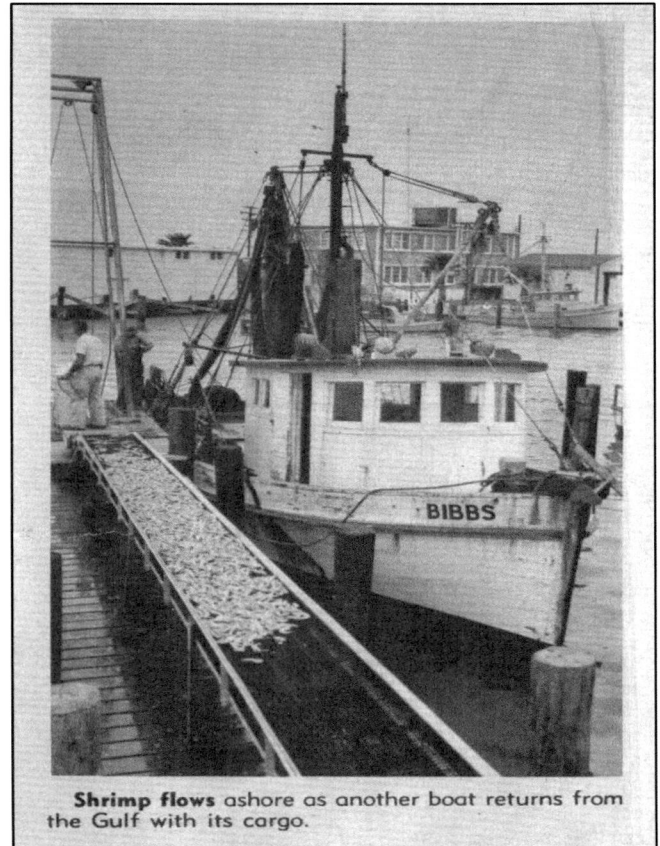

**Shrimp flows** ashore as another boat returns from the Gulf with its cargo.

From the Houston Chronicle, 1956

miracle I was able to sell the fleet of boats in this day and age".

"We had 25 to 50 employees at any given time, depending on the season," he says. "The majority of our workers were Hispanic. They are the ones I worry the most about."

He continued, "The shrimp plant will still operate, but we are looking for someone to lease or rent the property. We will continue with the shrimp, fuel and ice docks, but not as boat owners. We have a vacant marine supply store over there that would be a prime location for someone interested in the marine supply business."

A fifth-generation Rockport native, Jackson wrote "Taking the Tide" in 2011, working with

From the work of Rip Harrison

### Shrimp Gumbo

Cut three-inch square of fat bacon into small pieces. Fry it with a good-sized onion that has been sliced. When this is done, add a can of tomatoes and a small quantity of okra. If fresh okra cannot be obtained, okra and tomatoes canned together will do. When this has cooked awhile, add rice which has been previously cooked (1 cup) and two pounds of shrimp. Season to suit taste. This is enough to serve ten or twelve people.

Mrs. S. F. Jackson

Sue Hastings, author of "Aransas: The Life of a Texas Coastal County," the definitive history of the area. Jackson's book is a personal narrative of the trials and tribulations of his family's seafood business and their deep ties to the rich history of Rockport. The book contains many evocative images of his family's seafood business from the late 1800s through the early 1990s.

---

**World Famous Shrimp**

2 lbs. shrimp, cleaned, washed and dried

2 lemons                          2 T. parsley flakes

2 Sticks margarine or butter  ½ tsp. chili powder

5 cloves chopped garlic

Paprika, salt & pepper to taste

2 dashes of Worcestershire sauce

Arrange shrimp in a large baking dish. Squeeze lemon juice over them; place slices of lemon on top of shrimp. Sauce: Melt butter or margarine, add garlic, parsley flakes, Worcestershire sauce and chili powder. Bake 15 to 20 minutes or until shrimp turn pink. Sprinkle paprika, add salt and pepper to taste. Serve shrimp and sauce in a large bowl with a loaf of French bread for dunking.

Lucille Hartley

# Purchasing Shrimp

Courtesy of Kay Barnebey©

Shrimp is sold according to size and is based on the number of shrimp per pound or "count". The terms, "Jumbo", "Large", "Medium" or "Small" are not often uniform among those who sell shrimp. They are also sold as "Heads-on", or "tails", if you want them without heads.

A lower count indicates larger shrimp; therefore, there are fewer shrimp to the pound. They are available from 15 (or fewer shrimp per pound) to as many as 60 (a large number of shrimps per pound.)

When purchasing shrimp, select those with a mild, clean smell and firm texture. Shrimp, which have an offensive odor or black or brown spots on the tails or signs of freezer burn, are of poor quality.

After purchase, have the seller pack the shrimp in ice. Before preparation or freezing, drain off the water and keep them in air-tight containers.

To determine the number of pounds to buy: multiply the type of shrimp by the following multipliers:
- Peeled (cooked) – Multiply by 1.0
- Peeled (raw) – Multiply by 1.6
- Tails – multiply by 2.3
- Heads-on – Multiply by 3.1

Chefs recommend that regardless of how shrimp are prepared, cook them for only 2-3 minutes so that they are tender and juicy.

## BOBBY'S FAMOUS SHRIMP DIP

2 lb. cooked shrimp
1 (8 oz.) pkg. cream cheese
1 bunch of green onions
2-3 jalapenos
Hellmann's mayonnaise

2 Tbsp. lemon juice
Salt
Pepper
Red pepper

Boil shrimp and grind in food processor, along with green onions and jalapenos. Mix cream cheese and lemon juice together and mix shrimp; add mayonnaise to moisten the shrimp mixture. Stir in salt, pepper, and red pepper.

I serve this with Fritos!

*Debbie Jackson*

**Recipe** Neva's Shrimp Salad **Serves**

Shrimp 2 lbs          Salt, Pepper, Red pepper
Celery 2-3 stalks optional  Sliced Avacados
Green Onions 3-4      Sliced Tomatoes
Boiled Eggs 2-3       Mayonaise - enough
Lemon Juice          to moisten to your taste

Peel, devein, cook shrimp, Chop celery, green onions and hard boiled eggs and add cooled shrimp. Squeeze lemon juice, add salt, pepper and red pepper and mix in the mayonaise. Taste & add more seasonings if needed. Lots of pepper.

## Seafood Salad

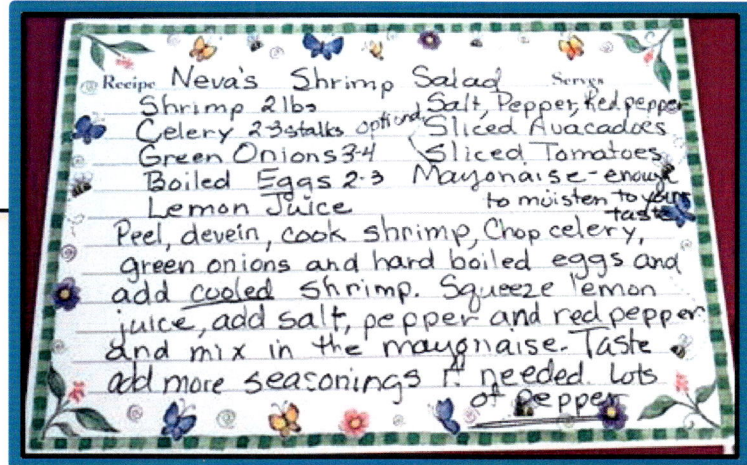

| | | |
|---|---|---|
| ¾ cup minimum cooked shrimp or crabmeat or both, diced | | ¼ c oil |
| ½ cup sliced pimento-stuffed olives | 1 medium tomato, chopped | 3 cups shredded lettuce |
| A pinch dry mustard | 1 tsp. salt | Pepper to taste |
| ¼ cup sour cream | ½ tsp. grated onion | 1 ½ Tbsp. lemon juice |

Combine oil, lemon juice, salt and pepper with onion, mustard and sour cream. Beat well. Place seafood, olives, tomato, lettuce in salad bowl. Toss with dressing. Serves 4 as an appetizer.

Old Woman of the Sea

From the work of Hal McCaskill

# Hunting

Aransas County is the ancestral wintering grounds of countless millions of waterflow. Deer and wild turkey roam in numbers greater than when the Indians ruled this land. Texas deer herds alone are estimated at nearly three million animals.

During the winter, mallards, redheads, wild geese, redheads, bluebills, pintails and other game migrate to Aransas County as do hunters from all over the country. The large bays welcome waterfowl by the thousands. Huge ranches and land holdings provide the oak motts and coastal prairies, where white-tail deer and javelina roam and quail intermingle with mourning doves. In this fertile environment, hunters supplied the local table.

GEESE AND DUCKS KILLED BY THOS. E. MATHIS AND ARTHUR MATHIS OF ROCKPORT, TEXAS. SAM C. BELL AND J.M. VANCE OF SAN ANTONIO, TEX.

PHOTO TAKEN THANKSGIVING DAY 1911 BY W. D. L. DYE.

From the Collection of Gordon Stanley

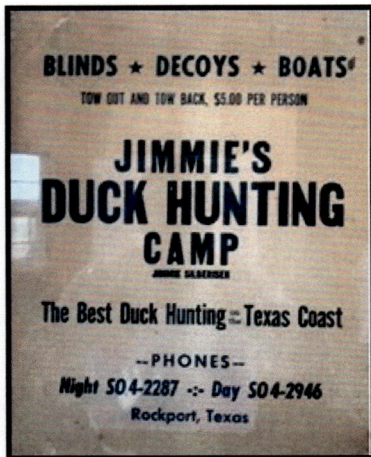

BLINDS ★ DECOYS ★ BOATS
TOW OUT AND TOW BACK, $5.00 PER PERSON

JIMMIE'S
DUCK HUNTING
CAMP
JIMMIE SILBERISEN

The Best Duck Hunting ~ Texas Coast

—PHONES—
Night SO 4-2287 -:- Day SO 4-2946
Rockport, Texas

Several hunting clubs were
established in our area.

From the Collection of Gordon Stanley

Jimmy
Silberisen Photos
courtesy of Donna
White Schott

148

# Mills Wharf

From the postcard collection of Jim Moloney

Mills Wharf has long been a Coastal Bend hunting and fishing hot spot. In 1932, Capt. Howard Mills chose the location of Mills Wharf. Because a deep-water basin was left when the fill for the causeway approaches was dredged, he selected the site and built a fishing and hunting camp there.

The location offered a pier with living quarters for the family with about 20 boats for rent. Twenty-five years later, the camp had several rental cottages, a café, hunting and fishing supplies, five charter boats and all kinds of wooden, aluminum and fiberglass skiffs.

Mills once said, "I remember when we used to laugh at people with rods and reels. They were always having trouble with them and they were just too slow. Before the day was over, they'd usually put the rods and reels in the bottom of the boat and pick up a cane pole. We hardly ever rent a pole and line these days."

Howard Mills, an Aransas County Commissioner for more than 25 years, said that geese and duck hunting was "getting worse," but fishing was holding its own. If anyone ever had any doubts about the place being a prime hunting and fishing spot, just go inside the café and take a gander at the

photos of the ones that didn't get away. Some of the big "hauls" of game fish and birds are almost hard to believe.

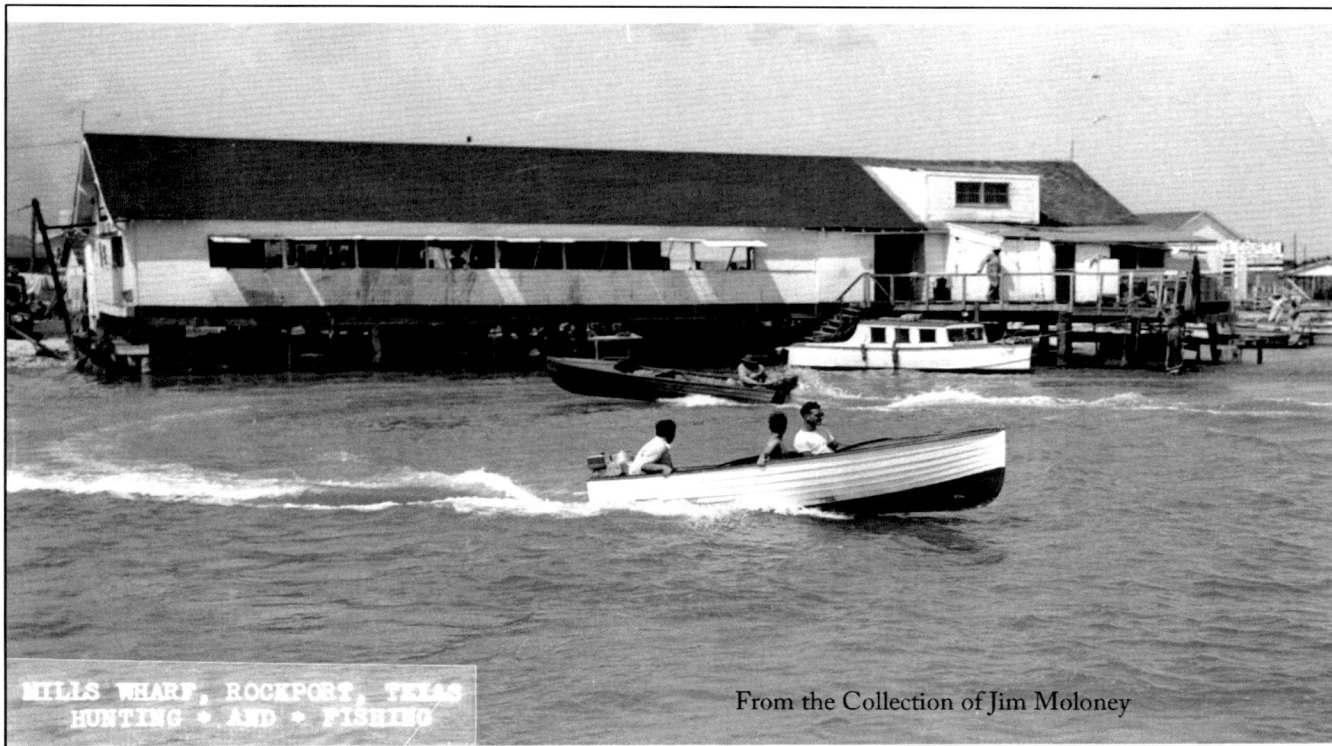

MILLS WHARF, ROCKPORT, TEXAS
HUNTING * AND * FISHING

From the Collection of Jim Moloney

## Chicken Fried Duck Breast

Breasts of 2 ducks          Flour

½ C. milk                   Salt & Pepper

1 egg                       Oil

To reduce the wild taste, soak the duck breasts in extra milk at least one hour before cooking. Pound duck breasts thin. Mix milk and egg together. Coat breasts with seasoned flour. Dip into egg and milk. Pan fry in hot oil. Good with cream gravy made from the drippings.

From the photo collection of the Mills Family

# Grocery Stores

**SPECIAL**

MARCH OF **FOOD** VALUES

FRIDAY and SATURDAY, JUNE 27th and 28th

| | | |
|---|---|---|
| | **BACON** Sliced | 16c |
| **SUGAR** 10 Lbs. 51c | FRESH YARD **EGGS** Dozen | 28c |
| | 4 PACKAGES **My-T-Fine** | 25c |
| GREEN BEANS No. 2 Can | | 07c |
| **Camay Soap** Bar | | 05c |
| **Rainbow Bleach** Quart | | 10c |
| **Marshmallows** Pound Boxes | | 13c |
| | | 20c |
| **Steak** Good Beef Pound | | |

**KELLY'S CASH**

Rockport                Aransas
Dial 3321

---

he Quality of our Groceries

Will be Remembered long after

## THE PRICE HAS BEEN FORGOTTEN

Over 20 years experience in the
Grocery buisness enables us to
offer you the choicest selections
of Pure Food Products at the low-
est possible prices consistent with
good service

# A. L. Bracht's
### The Pure Food Grcoer

---

## QUALITY GROCERIES

### SHIVERS' GROCERY
### A FOODCRAFT STORE
We Have a Full Line of School Supplies

---

**PIGGLY WIGGLY**

GROCERY AND MARKET
CHAS. A. ROE, Prop.

DIAL 233                ROCKPORT, TEXAS

**January 1957**

December

| S | M | T | W | T | F | S |
|---|---|---|---|---|---|---|
| | | | | | | 1 |
| 2 | 3 | 4 | 5 | 6 | 7 | 8 |
| 9 | 10 | 11 | 12 | 13 | 14 | 15 |
| 16 | 17 | 18 | 19 | 20 | 21 | 22 |
| 23 | 24 | 25 | 26 | 27 | 28 | 29 |
| 30 | 31 | | | | | |

January

| S | M | T | W | T | F | S |
|---|---|---|---|---|---|---|
| | | 1 | 2 | 3 | 4 | 5 |
| 6 | 7 | 8 | 9 | 10 | 11 | 12 |
| 13 | 14 | 15 | 16 | 17 | 18 | 19 |
| 20 | 21 | 22 | 23 | 24 | 25 | 26 |
| 27 | 28 | 29 | 30 | 31 | | |

February

---

Here's
Your
Food
Specials

**FRIDAY & SATURDAY, JUNE 20 & 21**

| | |
|---|---|
| SUGAR, Imperial Cane, 10 pounds | 53c |
| CRUSTENE, 3-pound carton | 39c |
| CRUSTENE, 3 Pound Carton | 39c |
| SNOWDRIFT, 3 Pound Pail | 39c |
| SOAP, Giant Bars P. & G. or C. W., 3 for | 48c |
| FLAKY BAKE FLOUR, 12 lbs. | 10c |
| 24 pounds          79c; 48 pounds | 42c |
| | $1.47 |
| PINEAPPLE, Sliced or Crushed, 3 No. 1 cns | 25c |
| MILK, Red & White, 2 lge.    15c; 4 small | 15c |
| BACON, Sliced, no rind, Flavor Full, lb | 25c |
| TOILET SOAP, Lux or Camay, 2 bars for | 11c |
| LIMES, Mexico, lge. size, dozen | |
| COFFEE, Chase & Sanborn's Vac-Pack Cans, Drip or Percolator Grind, pound | 27c |
| LEMONS, Large California, dozen | 19c |
| YAMS, Kiln Dried, 3 pounds | 10c |

THE **RED & WHITE** STORES
The Sign Of A Dependable Store

# Grocery Stores

As the frontier was being explored, trading posts sold food as well as clothing, household items, fabric, tools, furniture and other merchandise. These businesses evolved into general stores, which dealt in "dry" goods, such as flour, dried beans, baking soda and canned foods. Families purchased or traded perishable foods such as meat from the butcher, milk from a local dairy, eggs and vegetables from a family, who grew more produce than could be used.

Grocery stores brought together the producer, or farmer, milkman, and the consumer.

Small, neighborhood, family-owned "Mom & Pop" grocery stores were established throughout the county such as Casterline's, Ormands', Shivers', and Kelly's IGA among others. Upon entering the store, customers were often greeted by name and asked which food items they wanted to purchase, or they might hand over a grocery list. The clerks would then fill the list and charge the customer for the goods. Such were the general stores of The Bracht Brothers, A. L. Bracht, and Simon Sorenson, which were established in the late 1890s, and Roe's Food Store and Red and White Grocery Stores, popular during 1940s-1970s. This book highlights a few of the grocery stores located in the area over a period.

## The Bracht Brothers

In 1877, Leopold Bracht and Roland Bracht established a mercantile business, Bracht Brothers, in a two-story building at the corner of Austin and Peter. This building also included a post office

Courtesy of Janet Taylor

managed by Victor Bracht, their father. The second floor was used for dances and meetings. Later L. M. Bracht and Roland Bracht opened a furniture store behind the mercantile.

Bracht's Red and White Grocery Store was destroyed during the 1942 Hurricane. The store was then owned by Fred Bracht, the son of L. M. Bracht. After the hurricane, A. O. Freeman renovated the building, modifying it to a one-story, white stucco building, Mr. Bracht continued serving the public through his mercantile business. The building is still standing on Austin Street between North and Peter Streets.

## A.L. Bracht Grocery

Adolph L. Bracht, the youngest Bracht brother, worked for his brothers for a few years in their mercantile store. He established his own wholesale and retail grocery business in 1899. Adolph sold farmers the cans and crates for packing tomatoes and other can goods. Later he purchased and labeled canned goods with his own label, "Packed by A. L. Bracht". Further, he stored and arranged for shipments of canned goods to the wholesale market.

The hurricane of September 1919 severely damaged Adolph's Rockport grocery store. The store had the only dry flour and sugar in town after the storm. Federal authorities took charge and parceled the goods to those in need. Between 1919 and the early 1930s, the A. L. Bracht store in Rockport was closed. The family moved to the Valley in south Texas where he held several jobs managing vegetable grower associations. In 1929, he managed the San Benito Vegetable Growers'

Association and the Rio Hondo Association. Through these growers' associations, Bracht shipped vegetables grown by local Valley farmers to other cities.

According to Charles, his son, Adolph was in poor financial condition during the Depression. He moved his family back to Rockport and reopened his grocery store on the corner of Wharf and Austin Streets with his son, Arthur. A plaque can be found on the side of Treasure Islander, the site of A. L. Bracht's store.

From the Collection of Janet Taylor

In 1935, Arthur began a store in Fulton, Fulton Cash Grocery.  In 1942, Adolph's store in Rockport again flooded and the property was sold to Arthur, who continued the businesses.

Later A. L. Bracht built a small concrete block store at the corner of Austin and Liberty (Highway 35) directly across from Thompson's Spa.  Late one night, the building was destroyed due to two butane explosions. The first did the greatest damage and the second immediately followed. The

store was demolished along with many living room windows on nearby streets. The blast scattered the contents of the store over a wide area.

As curious students on their way to school viewed the devastation, they picked up boxes of chewing gum and distributed them to all their friends at school. After lunch that day, many students had severe cases of diarrhea. Teachers solved the mysterious disease when they learned that the gum that had been shared was Feniment Gum, which at the time was a commonly used laxative. A. L. Bracht retired in 1947.

### Sorenson's Ship Chandlery

Simon Sorenson came to Rockport on the schooner, *Alfred and Sammy*. He was mate to Capt. Charlie Hughes. When Hughes fell overboard, Simon quit sailing the sea and began a new life in Rockport. He purchased a wooden two-story building called Brunners in 1886 on Austin Street.

Using this storefront, Sorenson operated a ship's chandlery and grocery. This type of business gave a high level of service demanded by ships. These special orders had to be filled and delivered to the ship in a short amount of time. The chandlery specialized in supplies and equipment for ships as well as supplies of water

Courtesy of Lisa Baer Frederick

and fresh produce to stave off scurvy. Later he added feed and grain to his offerings.

Paul Sorenson remembered rowing a small boat out to the ships to receive an order, rowing back to shore, filling the list of supplies, rowing back to the ship with the ordered goods, receiving the money, and then returning to the store. This often occurred during the night.

In 1890, Sorenson's Store burned when the *The Finish*, a local tavern, caught fire. Many nearby buildings were also destroyed. After that fire, Sorenson rebuilt his business as a two-story brick building. In 1895, the store was again damaged due to another devastating fire. After this fire, Sorenson rebuilt the store as a one-story brick building called Sorenson & Hooper. The floor was dirt, walls were dark brick and held together with shellcrete mortar. The sturdy ceiling beams recalled the shipbuilding background of the store's designer. Sorenson's first renovation was laying planks over the dirt floor.

In 1913, the business became Simon B. Sorenson, Sr. and Sons and in 1935, the name changed to John C. Sorenson & Sons.

Three generations of Sorenson displayed weather warnings in the store windows and hoisted signal flags on a tower behind the store. Later the mast was moved to a location between his store and the beach. As soon as the railroad agent received weather reports from Western Union, he would deliver them to Simon, who then placed them in the window of his store. Manning the weather flags was greatly appreciated by fishermen and their families. Sorenson also allowed many to buy on credit during the non-fishing season.

Because Hurricane Celia badly damaged the store in 1970, the business closed. In 1978, the Rockport Art Association occupied the building. Estelle Stair purchased it in 1984 and used it as an art gallery and Stair's niece, Lisa Baer Frederick, has continued that practice.

### Hooper's Grocery

Hooper's Grocery was located on Austin Street. Mr. Hooper had a large screened wire cage in the center of the store containing salt pork, bacon and other dried meats. Families usually feasted on some type of beans. The family mom usually shopped there to get salt pork to season beans. Mr. Hooper, on occasion, would hand out candy to the younger children.

## Roe's Piggly Wiggly

Charles Roe, Sr. arrived in Robstown with his dad as a very young man. While his father was building a home in Robstown, Charles would fish in Rockport. Charles married Ruby Green Roe and they had four children. During the Depression, Charles Sr. worked for The Swift Company. When it closed, he was given a choice to go to Arkansas or be without a job. He quit Swift,

From the collection of the Roe family

163

became an itinerant butcher, and moved to Rockport.

Charles Roe, Sr. would purchase one or two cattle from individual families. At one time, he bought over 300 cattle, including extra calves from different ranches and family farms. Many cattle were butchered under a tree with help from Joe Valdez and Mr. Sparks. After they were butchered, the meat was delivered to the grocery store and then sold to customers. A slaughter house was later built on Market Street.

Ruby Green Roe died in 1942. After a while, Charles, Sr. married Elizabeth "Libby" Sterling, whose family owned the Sterling Building at St. Mary's and Austin Streets. This became the location of Roe's Food Store. First, Roe's was a meat market and produce were later added.

Charles, Sr. grew the produce on 50 acres near Sparks Colony. Additional produce was purchased from local truck farmers such as Abraham Sanchez.

Charles Roe, Jr. graduated from Aransas County High School and attended Schreiner College in Kerrville on a football scholarship.

When war broke out, he enlisted in the Army Air Corp and was sent to Texas Tech in Lubbock, Texas for pilot training. He toured the west and southwestern United States. After World War II, he graduated from Texas Tech with a degree in Economics and returned to Rockport in 1945 and taught bookkeeping and typing at Aransas County High School. He also coached football, basketball and track. In 1947, he married Dixie Townsend, who later taught kindergarten and first and second grade at Fulton Elementary.

made sausage, and raised and butchered turkeys near the holidays.

While at Texas Tech, Charles, Jr. researched self-serve meat markets. He convinced his father that this practice was less labor intensive as well as being the next trend in serving customers. Roe's Food Store was the first store in the area to offer this service. Roe's Food Store processed deer, castrated roosters and sold them as capons,

Charles Roe, Jr. second from the right.

From the collection of the Roe family

Customer Service was a priority at Roe's Food Store. They offered customers a delivery service. Groceries were always carried to the customer's cars; customers could tip the bag boys; meat was cut to the customer's specifications; and when asked where merchandise was located, workers found the item for them. Often in the middle of the night, they delivered groceries to boats servicing off-shore wells.

The 1950s brought the creation of the "Good Food Line" train, which featured Elsie, the cow,

Charles, Jr., Libby and Charles Roe, Sr.
From the Collection of the Roe Family

and her family, her husband, Elmer, and her two children, Beulah and Baby Beauregard, promoting Borden's milk, ice cream, and cheese. This photo shows that train with The Roes- Charles, Jr., Libby, Charles, Sr. In 1958, Borden's commissioned Ringling Brothers to build a special car for the live Elsie to ride on that was used in thousands of parades until the early 1990s. After that, Elsie had faded into history. She spent her last days on a farm in Texas.

Charles III remembers being very young and in charge of selling Christmas trees outside the store when it was very cold. He wasn't paid; that's what kids did to help the family. Charles III worked mostly as stock boy/sack boy. He briefly worked in the meat market and recalls receiving whole chickens packed in ice inside flimsy boxes. His daily take home pay was $5.00.

Theresa Roe Smith, his sister, remembers building forts using the big boxes in the back of the store. Theresa also worked in the meat department. She also remembers going to the air-conditioned store for a while, since their home wasn't.

When Roe's bought Bracht's Food Store in Fulton, Charles III worked there. When he was elementary age, he would put Roe's fliers in mailboxes and at homes in Fulton advertising Roe's Food Store. Inadvertently, he left a flier on the home of Mr. Ernest Jones, owner of the Fulton Red and White Grocery at the corner of Broadway and Fulton Beach Road. The Fulton store was sold in 1963 when Charles Roe, Sr. passed.

As time passed, few, if any, truck farmers were operating in Aransas County. The main store in Rockport bought produce from Groce-Wearden in Corpus Christi. During the first part of the summer, watermelons and cantaloupes would be purchased from Mexico and the Valley, then Skidmore and then, as the summer ended, from Brenham.

When the store closed, Charles, Jr. worked as a Business Manager for ACISD. The store was renovated into the Austin Street Mall.

## Weber's Grocery

In Fulton, cattle, hogs and donkeys roamed at will since Fulton had no stock laws. Weber's Grocery was previously owned by the Caruthers family. It was located on Cactus and Fulton Beach Road. They sold supplies in a wire shed on the side of the little house and in the main store they had everything including kerosene – even cheese-which sat out in the open. Mr. Weber weighed out beans and sugar from the

**RED & WHITE GROCERY**

RED & WHITE BRAND FOODS

QUALITY GROCERIES
FRESH MEATS
FRUITS - VEGETABLES
Air Conditioned

SO 4-6209
FULTON, TEXAS

sacks for his customers. He bought meat from Roe's Grocery.

Courtesy of Leslie "Bubba" Casterline

### West's Grocery Store

Grady West left the Red and White Store that was in the Bracht Building and built a "new" building located on Magnolia and Concho Streets facing the harbor.

When West's Grocery Store opened, a set of water skis were given away. Dixie, CharlesRoe, Jr.'s wife, won the prize.

After a few successful years, HEB bought the property between Magnolia and Austin Street and Liberty Street (Business Highway 35). The HEB Company planned to build at that location. Eventually, West sold to HEB.

Some remember that every Thursday night, the high school kids would pull into the parking lot in their cars, cut the engines and visit with

BETTER GROCERIES

WEST'S
SUPER MARKET

G. A. WEST, Owner

Phone SO 4-6209

Rockport, Texas

169

whomever was there- until the police came by and sent everyone home.

## HEB

HEB purchased West's building in the 1970s before it built a new store. Later it also purchased the street that ran parallel to Concho Street. Many students found their first job there outside the family business. They were cashiers, worked in produce, stocked shelves at night and even worked in the meat market. Sometimes on Fridays, rotisserie chickens were shared along with fresh guacamole.

### David's Grocery

David's Grocery was opened in Fulton at the north end of Harbor Oaks Shopping Center (now the AC Courthouse). This store was a warehouse store, which was the current trend in supermarkets.

In 1954, the main grocery stores were West's Red and

Your One-Stop Shopping Store

White, Kelly's IGA, and Roe's Piggly Wiggly. In 1964 when HEB purchased West's, the smaller grocery stores couldn't complete.

At one time grocery stores found in the area also included Butch's Grocery and Market, Casterline's Food Store, Earl's Drive In, Earl Harle Drive-In Grocery, John W. Haynes Grocery, Ormands', and Trep's in Fulton among others.

Pictured Joe Rodriguez (l) and Debra Picarazzi Gifford (r). Photo courtesy of Debra Picarazzi

*Facebook Comments about Roe's:*

"We used to sit in the car and wait while our mother shopped for groceries at Roes. My little brother, Randy, age 5, would whistle and say 'Hubba, Hubba, Baby' at any woman who passed by. During one trip, he slipped out and went into the store. We didn't discover him missing until we unloaded groceries. My mom went back to get him, and staff had given him candy and ice cream. He was upset that he had to leave!"

"A nice little store with a great atmosphere. Drugs and hardware were right in front as you came in. The produce was located on the east wall - the frozen food and meat section was on the north. They sold Christmas trees during the Holiday Season, and they distributed S & H Green Stamps."

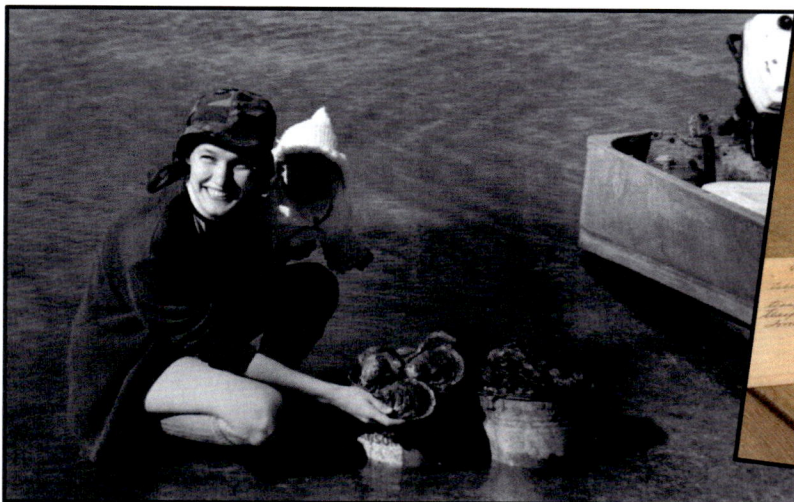

Donna & Jennifer Husak gathering oysters for a tasty home cooked meal. Courtesy of Ty Husak

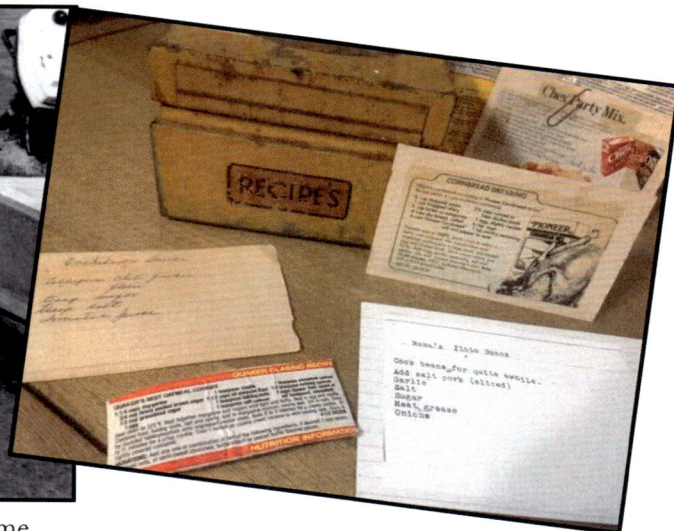

Courtesy of Laura and James Fox

# Home Cooking

Home cooks in Aransas County have been serving up great meals for family and visitors for decades. As much as they loved their beloved diners, drive-ins and cafes, they enjoyed being in their kitchens, serving up dishes passed down through the generations.

Early settlers had a hard-scrabble life, whether on the barrier islands or the mainland. Naturally, what they could hunt, fish or gather often appeared on the table. Game, shellfish and other wildlife were so much a part of early foodstuffs that numerous residents will say they don't care for deer or oysters. Early on, whatever protein was on the table was fried in lard or bacon grease, covered in cornmeal, crushed saltines, or flour, whether it was a goose, quail, dove, turtle or alligator. Children were usually taught to hunt, fish, go crabbing and

**FIRST PRESBYTERIAN CHURCH OF ROCKPORT, TEXAS PRESBYTERY IN SESSION, APRIL, 1907**

From the collection of Jim Moloney

gather oysters. Often, the experiences of gathering crabs in Little Bay or along Water Street or catching the first redfish at Mill's Wharf, where "Fish Bite Everyday", or on St. Joe Island have become the definitive experience of what Aransas County is about.

Many locals grew a variety of vegetables in their yard but would shop for hard to find items at one of the local groceries such as Roe's Piggly Wiggly, Ormands' Grocery, West's, Casterline's or Weber's in Fulton.

Locals also remember going around town to buy specialty items like tamales or cheese from a cook, who would make extra for purchase, or from a stand maintained by a

Fred A. Bracht, Sr. and Inez Bracht 50<sup>th</sup> Anniversary Celebration

From the collection of the Bracht Family

truck farmer. And, they often canned their harvest including a variety of jellies and preserves.

Sunday dinners after church would often include the extended family with fried chicken or roast beef with scalloped potatoes or macaroni and cheese, homemade rolls and pickles. This was followed by several kinds of pie. They would also try and duplicate some of the local café delicacies they loved like the Duck Inn's sourdough bread or Tony Dominguez's Enchiladas from the Key Allegro Marina or the Campus Inn's onion rings.

Having desserts seemed to be a big part of our food heritage. Many local cookbooks have larger sections for sweets than for savory. Home cooks in Aransas County here have always been known for baking cookies, candies, and special preserves during the holidays and sharing them with friends in special jars and tins.

Cooking for showers, church socials, anniversaries, Bridge or Garden Club get-togethers and fund-raisers was also a large part of our community life. Favorite Punch, also known as the Presbyterian Punch, served with shrimp salad canapés, fancy Jell-O fruit molds and aspics, chicken and tuna casseroles, appear in many a family or organization's photographs.

Holidays like the Fourth of July, Thanksgiving and Christmas, as well as birthdays, graduation and anniversaries, evoke many special food memories for those who grew up in the area.

Traditional menus with special family dishes were treasured and repeated year after year, generation after generation, and often were included in family reunions with those who had moved away.

Whether participating in a formal, sit-down dinner, informal backyard or a beachside picnic, these special meals evoke the deepest feelings for many

### History Center Refreshments

Lucretia Wright was the "personal chef" for the History Center from 2016-2018. She researched recipes that emulated the theme. During the *Aransas County Strong* Exhibit, focusing on Grades 1-5 Gifted and Talented Student's creations from

Hurricane Harvey debris, she served *Hurricane Smoothies and Debris Stacks.* For the quilting exhibit, she researched patterns for the squares. Using puff pastry, she crafted pinwheel sausage snacks.

For exhibit openings, bridal or baby showers, senior proms, or wedding celebrations the following punch was often served:

---

**Favorite Punch**

2-12 oz. bottles lemon concentrate

1-46 oz. can of pineapple juice     1-46 oz. can of orange juice

10 cups Water     8 cups sugar

6 teaspoons vanilla     Food coloring (optional)

2 bottles almond extract

Combine 10 cups of water and sugar. Boil together until a syrup is made. Cool. Mix all other ingredients. Add cooled syrup. Then add 10-12 quarts of water. If extra guests arrive at the party, more water can be added. 1 recipe equals 4 gallons of punch.

---

For the exhibit, *Foodways: Culinary Traditions of Aransas County*, Lucretia made Puffy Chicken Tacos and her dad's crab cakes.

### Puffy Chicken Tacos

1 Package Wonton wrappers

Chicken

Taco seasoning

Chicken stock

Oil for frying

Place chicken in a crockpot with an inch or so of chicken stock (broth). Add taco seasoning. Cook on high for 6 hours or low for 8 hours. Debone chicken.

Place wonton wrappers in a damp towel after opening. They dry out very quickly Using one wonton wrapper, spoon approximately 1-2 teaspoons of the chicken mixture in the center of wrapper. While wrapper is still open, dampen all sides with water with your finger or pastry brush. Form a triangle by placing one corner of the wonton wrapper on its diagonal corner. Triangles should be formed. Seal with a finger press. The water will make the dough sticky enough to seal. Drop triangles (tacos) in hot oil and fry until golden and crispy.

*Sauces for dipping:* Salsa, sour cream or avocado sauce.

*Avocado Sauce:* Mashed avocado, add sour cream and chicken stock, squeeze of fresh lime, cilantro, salt and pepper to taste.

Lucretia Wright

# Lucretia's Helpful Hints

*By Lucretia Wright*

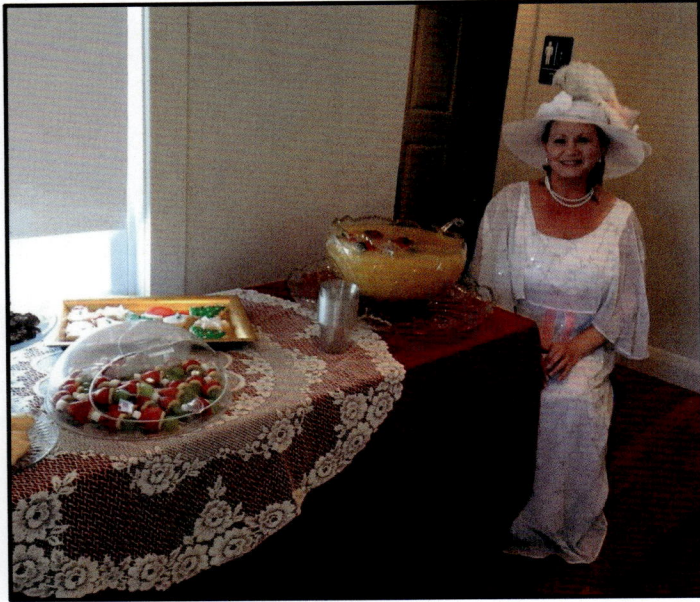

Consistency is the key in calculating the ingredients needed for an event. Generally, the general rule is two to four appetizers per person.

AN ACCURATE HEAD COUNT: This will make shopping and menu preparation easier!

CREATE A CLEAN ENVIRONMENT: Try these tips: utensil free foods, use toothpicks, individualized servings and think outside the box for serving. For example, instead of serving French Toast on a plate with a fork all covered in syrup, try French Toast Sticks served in a hard-plastic cup with a puddle of syrup at the bottom of the cup.  Everyone loves dipping and there is absolutely no waste!

## PAY ATTENTION TO DETAIL WHEN IT COMES TO YOUR SERVICE TABLE:

Place utensils, cups and plates in the order they will be used. Place cups near or before the drink dispenser.  Place flatware and plates before the food, etc.

## LANDSCAPE YOUR SERVICE TABLE.

Use small boxes or pans underneath the tablecloth to serve food from varying heights. This brings interest and saves room on your table!  Having something green and alive on the table is also important.  A vase of flowers or a large sprig of rosemary laid among the trays or palm leaves used as a tablecloth are simple touches I've used.

ALWAYS REMEMBER: Serving utensils like large spoons and tongs, ice, scissors, duct tape, napkins, bug spray, pad and pen, menu board, music (if required), and trash cans strategically placed. board, and trash cans strategically placed.

**Factors to be considered when cooking for groups, no matter the size.**

1) Know the general age, gender and preferences for the group attending.
2) When preparing the menu, consider guests who might have diabetes, dentures and peanut allergies. Every special diet can't be addressed. But

those considerations should affect your menu planning. Rather than peanuts or peanut butter, use almonds substituting 1 for 1.

3) Use the theme of the event to plan the menu. If I'm preparing refreshments for the 109th Annual Picnic where kids are sack racing and playing stickball, I am going to find a recipe that coincides with the historical events of that time such as homemade ice cream and applesauce cookies. When planning the menu for the Quilting Exhibit, I found a recipe for wrapped sausage balls. When wrapped in croissant dough, they looked like the pinwheels that the quilters used as patterns for their quilts!

The quilters went crazy over those very simple sausage puffs! I'm convinced that it was their shape, more than the taste. The quilters were comforted by a common pattern they see often...the pinwheel!

4) Another consideration is your geographical location. I resource local ingredients as much as possible. People appreciate local fare and networking. Because we are situated right on the bays adjacent to the Gulf of Mexico, you'd be hard pressed to find one of my service tables without at least one seafood dish except for breakfast, although Crab cake Benedict is DELICIOUS!

5) Finally, no matter what the size of your crowd, it's always better to have more than you need rather than run out. Prepare plenty; they can always take some home. See the chart of Lucretia's Helpful Hints for help with amounts to prepare appetizers.

---

**Frying Shrimp**

Wait to season raw shrimp. Instead season them with flour and sea salt as the cooked shrimp are fresh from the hot oil.

---

**Best Tasting Shrimp Cocktail**

Clean shrimp thoroughly.

Lay shrimp on a cookie sheet in a single layer. Season shrimp with sea salt and lemon pepper.

Broil for 3 minutes on one side. Remove shrimp from oven; flip each shrimp and then season this side of the shrimp. Broil for 2 minutes.

DO NOT OVERCOOK THE SHRIMP!

By preparing the shrimp in the oven rather than being boiled, the flavor is preserved. Serve with cocktail sauce.

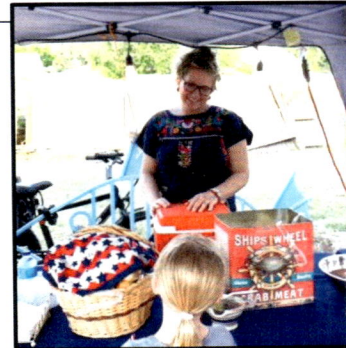

| Appetizer | Pieces per person | Helpful Hints |
|---|---|---|
| Meatballs/Mini sausages | 3 per person | Use a small ice cream scoop for consistently-sized meatballs. One pound of ground meat will serve 12-15 guests. |
| Shrimp | 3 per person | If 30 people are expected, using 16/20 sized shrimp, plan for approximately 20 shrimp per pound. Calculate 3 shrimp per person times 30 people equals 90 shrimp. If there are 20 shrimp in a pound, about four pounds of shrimp is needed. Some guests will not eat shrimp. Using the packaging, the number of shrimp will be indicated. |
| Fruit, Veggie and Cheese trays | 2-3 items per person | On a cheese or vegetable tray, usually a guest will take a total of 2-3 pieces per tray. |
| Bruschetta/Mini Sandwiches; on crackers | 2-3 per person | Using sliced deli meat, up to 25 people can be served with one pound of shaved deli meat – depending on the sandwich's thickness. |
| Desserts | 1 per person If small, 2 per person | With cupcakes, cakes, pies or cookies, most will eat only one due to the sugar content. |

# Food Memories from Aransas County

## Jackson Family Cookies

### By N. F. Jackson

"For years, starting when I was stationed overseas during my active duty Navy time, I would package and send Christmas gifts to my family, usually around Thanksgiving to ensure that they would arrive in time. My mother did likewise. Knowing of my sweet tooth, especially cookies, she would send me my favorite cookies, much like she and my grandmother routinely sent to my father during World War II. Sometime during that era, she sent me cookies in an oval, metal cookie tin.

I would religiously send it back with the *wink-wink, nudge-nudge* inference that it should be filled again and sent my way at the soonest opportunity.

About the time I moved to Washington in 1982, my mother was less able to do the time-consuming work of days of cooking Christmas goodies. Knowing that my father's sweet tooth was as dominant as mine, I began the practice of baking his favorite cookies and using the same tin to ship them to Rockport. I would pick up the tin each time I was in Rockport and send it back again usually for Christmas and my father's birthday in June."

## OATMEAL COOKIES

| | |
|---|---|
| 3/4 cup. Crisco | ½ tsp. salt |
| 1 cup sugar | ½ tsp. soda |
| 2 eggs | 1½ tsp. cinnamon |
| 2/3 cup raisins | 1 tsp. cloves |
| 2 cup raw oatmeal | 1 dash nutmeg |
| 2 cups flour | 1 cup pecan pieces |

Mix. Drop onto greased cooky sheet. Bake at 400° till delicately brown.

---

### Cobbler Topping

| | |
|---|---|
| 1 cup sugar | 1 tsp. baking powder |
| 1 cup flour | 1 egg |
| ½ tsp. salt | 2/3 c. melted butter |

Mix dry ingredients and add egg. Mix until it's the consistency of coarse corn meal. Pour over seasoned fruit. Add melted butter to the top. Bake at 350 degrees about 4 minutes or until golden brown. Optional: Add cinnamon to dry mixture.

Lou Dick

# Traditional Family Reunion Held At Picton Home Sunday

Members of the Picton family from Houston and Port Arthur joined with those living here to celebrate the traditional family reunion on July 5 in the home of Miss Velma Picton and Miss Vivian Picton.

A chicken barbecue was served at a picnic table on the lawn Sunday to the thirty one members present. Two young men in service, Lieut. Dick Picton now stationed in Florida and Ensign DeWilton Jeffries now stationed in Virginia were the only absentees from the family gathering.

The custom of the yearly meeting began many years ago during the lifetime of the parents, the late Mr. and Mrs. D. M. Picton, and has been continued with few exceptions ever since The date is traditional, being the birthday of their father.

Those present were Mr. and Mrs. John Picton of Port Arthur, who returned Tuesday to their home, while others are staying over this week. They are Mr. and Mrs. David Picton of Houston with their family, Mr. and Mrs. Jess Hines, Mr and Mrs. Harvey Shuttles, Miss Grace Vivian. Alice, Ellen and Julia; Mr. and Mrs. Charles Picton and their family, Mrs. DeWilton Jeffries, Miss Mary Beth Picton and Harold Picton, all of Rockport, and Mr. and Mrs. Gerald Picton and their daughter Geraldine of Port Arthur; Mr. and Mrs. Will Picton with their daughter Sarah Frances and son Bill Jr., of Port Arthur; Mr. and Mrs. Ed Picton and daughters Evelyn and Marianne and son, Edward, Jr., of Port Arthur; the Misses Velma and Vivian Picton and Miss Grace Smith.

---

Rum Pudding

By Mary Nance Picton

2 eggs (separate yolks and whites)
½ cup sugar
½ pint whip cream
4 Tablespoons rum
1 ½ dozen lady fingers

Beat yolks well. Add sugar. Mix well. Gradually add rum and set aside.

Beat egg whites stiffly with pinch salt. Add whites to yolk mixture. Whip the cream. Fold in whip cream.

Line a serving bowl with lady fingers. Add mixture. Refrigerate. Garnish with strawberries and whipped cream.

# James Richard Fox's Childhood Memories

James Richard Fox, longtime Aransas County fishing and hunting guide and ardent conservationist, is a lifelong resident, born and raised in Rockport on East Cedar Street. His grandfather, Bernard Fox, was Aransas County Judge for 16 years. Bernard was an Irish immigrant who was the first commercial nurseryman in the San Joaquin Valley in California. He later worked on the Hearst Ranch in Mexico. When Bernard first came to the

Courtesy of Steve Russell

county, he opened a truck farm with Mr. Ferris. His wife, a native of Mexico, cooked many Mexican dishes including homemade flour tortillas.

James grew up in Old Rockport and remembers roaming around the neighborhood freely as a child. His grandmother had a peach orchard with twelve trees across from the current Law Enforcement Center where the Community Gardens were. She, like many in town, had a big garden where she grew garlic, potatoes and tomatoes and then canned the yield. She would make delicious, light and fluffy yeast rolls for Sunday dinner after church. His family also raised chickens and rabbits, which was helpful especially during the War when food was rationed.

Both his Mom and Grandmother cooked three meals a day, often frying seafood in cornmeal including game like duck or geese, fish, shrimp and an occasional turtle that would end up as part of the by-catch in shrimp nets. The

James Fox (l); Bobby Close, cousin (r)

family had an ice box, going once or twice a week to get ice from the ice house located behind Ready Mix Concrete Plant near the Catholic School.

James remembered that locals would often carry a bottle of Tabasco Hot Sauce and packaged saltines in their pocket and walk down to the beach to harvest raw oysters for a quick snack. Widow Mrs. Smith would often catch blue crabs in Little Bay and carry them in big wash tubs.

At that time, there were several grocery stores including Bracht's Mercantile, where James' Dad worked. There was also Roe's, which also had a slaughter and butcher shop and the Shivers' Store on Live Oak Street across from the Rockport School, like a convenience store where cheese was cut off a big block. And, of course, only a few stores used air-conditioning.

The Smith Family down the street had a milk cow and there were several dairies, including the Wheeler Dairy. Mr. Howell had a large truck farm off Rattlesnake Road with fields of watermelons and vegetables.

A holiday tradition from Christmas through New Year's for several friends and family was enjoying a glass of whiskey along with a sack of oysters.

When James was growing up, there were no deer on the Live Oak Peninsula. His dad and other men would lease land in Webb County for $100 a gun. They would camp out and upon their return, they would drive around town with a buck on their car fender. Deer steaks were usually fried.

James was an active boy, who sometimes could be mischievous. He and others would visit the nearby DeWitt strawberry patch at night. He also recalls a switch or two from his grandmother's peach trees being used to try to correct his behavior.

Connie Hagar and Patches
Courtesy of the Friends of Connie Hagar

One morning when he was about six, he was in his front yard with his trusty Red Ryder BB Gun and a sack full of migrating birds he had shot earlier. Connie Hagar, the famous First Lady of Texas Birding, stopped her car, walked over to him, and gave James what he remembers as a stern, long lecture about what he had done with an admonition that if she ever caught him doing that again, he would get a good whipping from the diminutive Hagar.

On another occasion, James decided that he would cook up a feast from the large goldfish in Mrs. Freeman's pond. Though he tried to hide the goldfish he had netted underneath his t-shirt, their tails were flipping in sight.

James worked as a duck hunting guide for the St. Charles Bay Hunting Club and on charter boats in Rockport Harbor. Growing up, Little Bay would be covered black with thousands of migrating ducks, pintails, teals, redheads and others. Duck was usually baked medium rare. At St. Charles, Mrs. Heldenfels would cook for the visiting sportsmen from San Antonio and Houston, who wanted fried seafood when they came to the coast.

Going out to eat was a rare treat for his and others' families. He remembers going to Thompson's Spa in the 1940s and early 50s, as well as Kline's, Los Amigos, La Cocina, and later Duck Inn. There were few bars in town until the Duck Inn, though set-ups were provided for BYOB, and many served beer. The Duck Inn was a favorite eating place with their broiled and stuffed flounder, soft shell crab, shrimp salad, and Burt's Habanero Hot Sauce.

James would contribute his talents to the growth of the local art colony when he worked for Carl Krueger at Key Allegro, often taking out prominent artists like Jack Cowan and Herb Booth.

He was also a leader in several conservation movements including the *Save Our Seas*, one of the forerunners to the Gulf Coast Conservation Association (GCCA) and later the Coast Conservation Association (CCA). Formation of these organizations was imperative to preserve areas like Cedar Bayou and limit the overharvesting of bays.

At a Memorial Service for Al Barnes, another local artist, Meredith Long, the owner of an art gallery in Houston as well as one on Key Allegro, was talking to James. Discussing their time together with friends when an abundance of game and fish had limited impact on the local environment, Meredith commented to James, "We had the best of it, didn't we?" James agreed.

Jo Ann Morgan shared some memories of the Fox family: "Growing up, my family lived next door to my aunt and uncle, Lois and Dick Fox, and their family. My mom and Lois were sisters AND they were both very good cooks. Four things Lois cooked really stand out in my mind. I probably ate there a lot – or I ate a lot there. She made wonderful scrambled eggs. I don't have any idea what she did to make them so good, but they were. James wouldn't eat them without ketchup all over them. Do you still do that James?"

Jo Ann Morgan remembers, "Another thing your mom made that was so good was lemon bars. Funny thing about lemons and

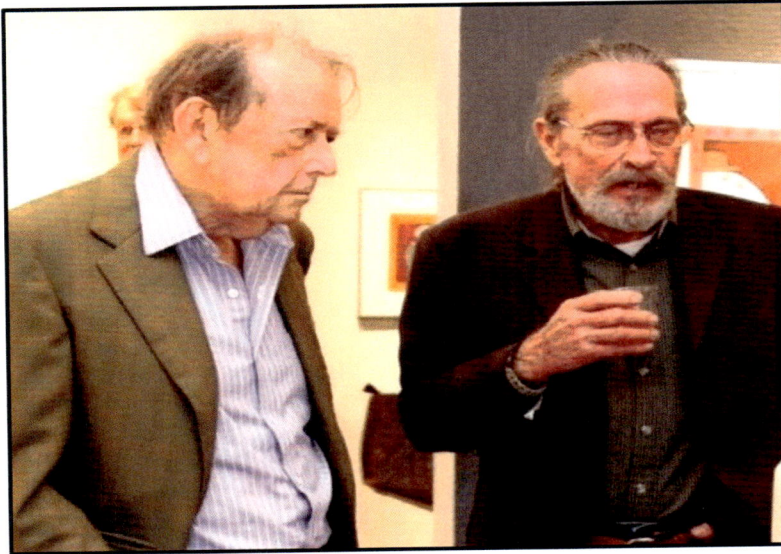

Meredith Long (left) and James Richard Fox

the Close family, they all loved lemons. My Grandmother Close made a very good lemon pie and my mother would always make a white cake and split the layers and cook a lemon filling to put between them. Lois would visit me at work occasionally and we would have coffee and lemon bars.

Another of her dishes that she would make on special occasions was a broccoli/rice/shrimp casserole. It was usually when my sister, Colleen, came for a visit from Colorado. My mother, Janet Smith, my sister-in-law, and myself were always invited to that delicious meal.

**Pinto Bean Casserole**

Left-over pinto beans, mashed

Chopped onion

Chopped green bell pepper

Cheese

Layer beans, onions, green peppers in a casserole dish. Top with cheese. Cook at 350° above 20 minutes.

Courtesy of James Richard Fox

I guess my favorite of all she cooked was a pinto bean casserole. She would take left-over pinto beans and mash and layer them in casserole dish with chopped onion, chopped green bell pepper and grate cheese. James has that recipe down to a "T". It was delicious tonight, James. Thanks, a bunch".

# Daughter of a Man of the Sea

## By Lucretia Wright

Lucretia and Nathan "Peanut" Wright

As a child, I would pray for windy or stormy mornings. My father, Captain "Peanut" Wright, was a shrimper. If the weather was bad, that meant Daddy was not a captain that day. Wind and rain meant he could stay home and be "Dad" that day, or at least, until the weather passed. Oh, how I prayed for wind and rain. If he stayed home, that meant that my mother usually got a break in the kitchen - at least for one meal. My father enjoyed cooking but had little time to do it. Shrimping is hard physical labor and required working long hours. So, most of the time, Daddy worked from before the sun was up until after it was dark.

If the weather kept him home, he would usually make breakfast. He was up by 4:00 a.m., making coffee, whipping up some wonderful pancakes from scratch, while not measuring a thing! He seemed magical, whipping up breakfasts from absolutely nothing at all. Some of my favorite childhood memories are in my childhood kitchen with my mom or my dad, brothers and sisters everywhere (I'm 1 of 12), food and utensils flying.

Fast forward to today, it's so early; it's still dark and the reality is that I'm assigned to make mini crab cakes for our big opening for our Foodways Exhibit at the History Center. Blurry eyed from my week of work, I review Daddy's crab cake recipe in my mind. Well, there's no written recipe, but I've made these with Daddy so many times, I can make them in my sleep. I wash and clean the vegetables, set out the cutting board, dig out the mixing bowl, look for my large, old, wooden spoon that is the perfect tool for the job. My feet are already burning; my hips tired; and no one in my house is even awake yet. Where's my coffee? All right, I think I've got everything I need. Let's get this show on the road!

No matter where you buy your crab meat, it's a must that you check the container of meat for shells from the crab's shell. It's like finding eggshell in your scrambled eggs; Yuck! I readied my large mixing bowl, opened the container of crab and into the bowl it went. I leaned over the bowl and the smell of the crab met the end of my nose.

Immediately, I was transported, standing next to my Daddy, cleaning crabmeat in the kitchen of my childhood. Memories flooded me as I reached down to put my hands in the crabmeat. Meticulously, I hunted through the crabmeat for tiny pieces of shell, while memories after memories of so many hours in the kitchen with my dad flooded over me. It was like he was there. Eight containers of crabmeat later, I'm washing my hands, tears streaming. Not because I was sad, but because I was so extremely grateful. He had taught me not only be comfortable in

From the work of Hal McCaskill

a kitchen, but he taught me what a kitchen is really for. *Love is made in a kitchen*! Sure, food and fuel, sustenance; we all need those things, but Daddy taught me beyond that. I'm so very grateful.

So, Daddy and I made crab cakes today even though he's been gone for 7 years, but he was with me today. We hung out in the kitchen like we used to. It was a joy and pleasure to cook with him again. The crab cakes turned out perfect; of course, made with joy and love. They were a hit at the opening. Daddy would have been tickled pink to hear people ask, "What restaurant do you own?" "There's no restaurant, just my old kitchen." Food is so much more important than just being used as fuel, isn't it?

Growing up on the back of my daddy's shrimp boat on the Texas coast presented me with blessings that I will carry the rest of my life. The simplicity of the style of cooking in this area, highlighting the fare from our local waters, is just priceless to me. Lunch on his boat usually consisted of an old Folgers can sitting atop a Coleman camping stove with boiling bay water in it. Yes, bay water. It's the best, salted water there is! The deckhands and I just dropped whatever we wanted out of the catch into the salty, boiling water and lunch was served. You can't get fresher seafood than that!

# Daddy's Famous Crab Cakes

## By Lucretia Wright

This recipe is my Dad's. He didn't measure anything, so you will find no amounts on the ingredients list. This is where your chef skills shine...Good Luck!

Please note: Crab is a delicate, mild meat. If too many vegetables are used, the crab is lost! Be cautious with everything, but the crab meat. It should be the star in this recipe! There should be more crab than anything else when you are finished mixing all the ingredients. The veggies should look like tiny confetti next to the whiteness of the crab.

**Ingredients:**

Crab meat, picked clean and double checked for tiny pieces of shell

Red bell pepper          Green or yellow bell pepper

Purple onion             Eggs                    Rolled oats

Heavy cream              Saltine crackers        Old Bay seasoning

Sea salt                 Pepper                  Griddle cooking surface

Oil for frying

**Directions:**

Place rolled oats and enough cream to cover them in a small bowl to soften while you mix other ingredients. Place roughly chopped veggies in a food processor. The vegetables must be very tiny because the only cooking time they will have is in the cake itself. Pulse until all are uniform in size and quite small.

Place saltines in a zipper style bag and roll with a rolling pin. This should produce cracker meal, like the texture of cornmeal. This step should also help lessen stress! Keep rolling and flipping the bag and rolling and flipping the bag and rolling...well, you get it...Set aside.

In a large mixing bowl, mix together the cleaned crab meat, the processed veggies, the soaked oats and the seasoning. Taste at this time. You should taste crab first, then the veggies, and last the filler. At this point, the mixture will be crumbly and will not hold together well as "cakes", which takes us to the next step.

Add eggs and small amounts of cracker meal until a palm full of mixture holds nicely together when gently squeezed in the palm of your hand. The mixture should not be soupy, wet or dripping. It should only be damp enough to stay together to form your "patty" or "cake".

To get uniform sized crab cakes, I use my handy ice cream scoops. I have a tiny one for mini cakes, bite size for great appetizers, and a regular size ice cream scoop for a good size portion.

On a sheet of wax paper, drop scoops of the crab mixture. Once scooped into the correct portion size, just take each scoop in your hands and form a "cake" to the thickness you desire. Be consistent in the size and thickness of each one. Gently pat the crab cake in the leftover cracker meal to coat the outside of the crab cake. Place on hot griddle type surface, or skillet, with a little oil. Cook on medium high for approximately 2-3 minutes per side, depending on the size of the crab cake. The outside should be crispy and golden, while the inside is tender and almost creamy.

Serve these with a spicy mayo sauce with a wedge of lime or lemon! Enjoy!

Another favorite enjoyed by History Center guests is Simple Potato Stacks.

## Simple Potato Stacks

| | |
|---|---|
| 1 potato per person | Parmesan Cheese |
| Olive Oil | Cheddar Cheese |
| Salt & pepper | |

Consistently slice each potato as thin as possible using a mandolin slicer. They need to cook evenly. Toss potato slices in olive oil, salt, pepper and grated Parmesan cheese.

Spray a cupcake tin with non-stick spray. Stack potato slices on top of each other (7 or 8). Then place stack in cup of cupcake tin and sprinkle with grated cheddar cheese.

Bake at 375 for 30-40 minutes until tender. Cooking time depends on the thickness of each slice.

### WONDERFUL SIDE DISH FOR SEAFOOD

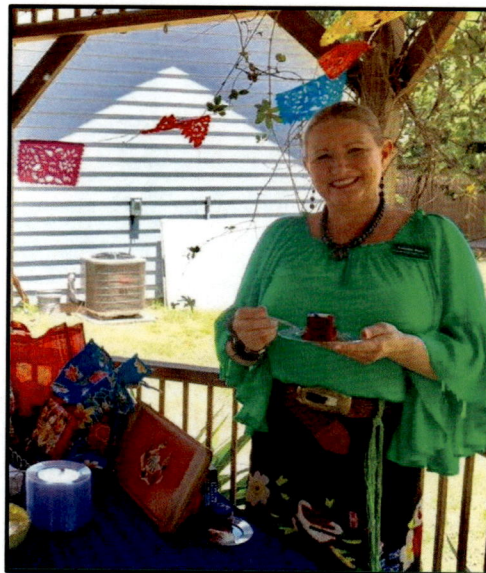

Lucretia Wright

# Growing up on the Island

## By Steve Russell

"Mom and Dad stayed in this little house on the North end of St. Joe Island…We had some wonderful meals there. On one Thanksgiving, Dad and I caught a good mess of Black Drum off the Gulf beach. We fixed them up for our holiday meal that was plenty good.

A couple of friends lived on Shell Ridge. Most of my summers as a pre-teen were spent crabbing, fishing and swimming with them in a little harbor that had been dredged there on the beach.

On summer mornings, our mother would take my brothers and me down to the bay from which we would extract crabs. We had wash tubs with line attached to them so we could pull them behind us as we waded in the shallow flats with gigs looking for crabs. The sea grasses hid these pesky crabs until they were disturbed by us and made a run for it. This is when we would gig them and place them in the tubs…"

## Surprise!

### By Melissa Cosby Pina

When Charles "Popo" Cosby was about 11 years old, he saved his money from chores to buy a special Mother's Day present. He went to Lichenstein's, a very nice department store in Corpus Christi, and purchased a Betty Crocker, the rage in the 1950s. His mom had been talking about it incessantly. Upon opening the gift, she was so excited and couldn't wait to try the recipes.

## Drunk Fruit

### By Vickie Vermillion Merchant

In the mid-1980s and 90s, Johnnie Vermillion had a large, wide bottomed, glass decanter sitting on the kitchen windowsill filled with colorful fruit. A friend had given her a "starter". Every week on the same day of the week, she would add another cup of fruit and stir it. In about three months, something had to be done with the fruit. The jar would be full. Of course, she could give someone else a "starter", but that had limited results. The longer the fruit sat, the further it would ferment. However, her fruitcakes and cobblers were AMAZING!

# Entertaining

As the holidays rolled around, local families hosted an open house in which those invited would come by, visit, have some punch and cookies and then retire to their homes. Articles noting the event were found in *The Rockport Pilot*.

## Open House Notes Holiday

ROCKPORT (Sp) — Mrs. Fred A. Bracht and Miss Mary Jo Bracht held open house last week. A lighted Christmas tree was in the living room and arrangements of poinsettias were on either end of the mantle.

Mrs. Joe Caldwell registered the guests as they entered.

The tea table was laid with a Viennese lace cloth over red, with a centerpiece of poinsettias around a large white candle. Mrs. Travis Bailey and Mrs. Jimmy Reid Simmons alternated at the silver tea and coffee service and Miss Mabel Bracht and Mrs. James C. Bracht poured eggnog. Other members of the house party included Miss Genevieve Bracht, Mrs. D. R. Simmons, Mrs. Jack Keller and Mrs. S. F. Jackson.

Music was given by Mrs. Bill Clark at organ and Mrs. Charlene Hunt at the piano. Seventy-five called during the receiving hours.

One memorable occasion was on June 27, 1947 when the Rockport Chamber of Commerce invited Governor Beuford H. Jester, Former Governor Coke Stevenson and over 300 guests to participate in the entertainment and meeting of the Capitol Press of Austin at the home of Mr. and Mrs. Fred A. Bracht.

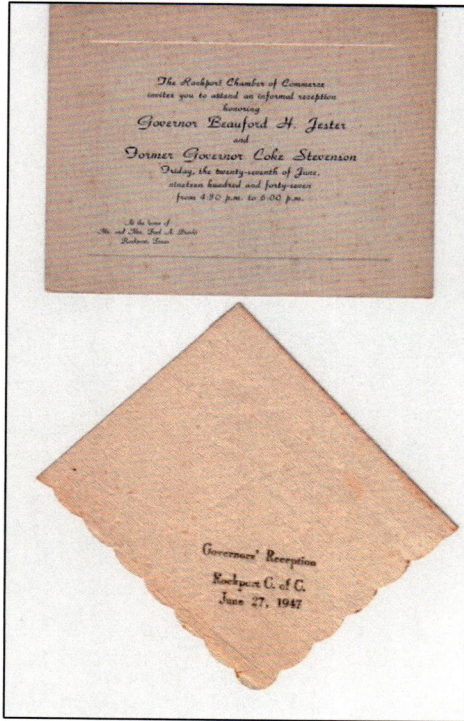

(Left to right) Ex-Governor Coke R. Stevenson, Mrs. Bracht, Governor Beauford Jester and Fred A. Bracht.

"A few 'shots' of people attending the Rockport Chamber of Commerce – a live wire organization- to welcome the Governor and his predecessor for the weekend." Mayor Albert Bruhl welcomed guests to the Third Annual Press Party. After the reception, the governor, Stevenson, their aides and the newsmen went to Rice's boathouse apartment for lodging.

From the Bracht Family Collection

The next day several boats were donated for the party to fish either in the Gulf or bay, dependent on the weather. To conclude the entertainment, Floyd Huffman, developer of Copano Village, arranged the first annual Copano Village Snipe Boat Races. Three trophies were given to the winners.

Governor Jester visits with Mrs. Jack (Connie) Hagar about old times when they were neighbors in Corsicana.

From the Bracht Family Collection

# Family Recipes

Here are some typical recipes you might find in someone's kitchen drawer, old-fashioned recipe box, or tucked inside one of their cookbooks.

## LEMON PRALINES

2½ c. sugar
2 T. grated lemon rind
1 stick butter
1 c. water
3 c. pecan halves

Put sugar, water, butter in pan and heat to boiling. Cook slowly to soft ball stage. Remove from heat; add lemon rind and pecans. Beat until creamy. Drop on waxed paper.

**Note:** This recipe came from Susie's great aunts Mabel and Bea Bracht. It is wonderfully different from a plain praline.

*Mabel and Bea Bracht were two of my Grandfather's seven sisters. They never married and lived together in the old rock house across from the ski basin.*

### Clark and Edith Herring's
### Brundrett (not Brunswick) Stew

Recipe from Anna Herring. This was a staple in the Herring family diet in the great depression. The history is more interesting than the stew. It probably came from the Brundrett family when Clark Herring was ranching on the Blackjack peninsula (Aransas Wildlife Refuge) around 1900. There were a lot of Brundretts on the peninsula at the time. This is a simple rancher's stew made from readily available staples (Yes, canned tomatoes were easily obtained 120 years ago. You did not specify what kind; you just asked for canned tomatoes.) Ingredients could be substituted or added depending on the supply. It was served with bread or grits or cornbread.

**Brundrett Stew**
as I make it from Edith Herring's directions

Saute and brown:
½ lb salt pork or thick sliced bacon, sliced into 1" bits
1 onion, diced

Parboil:
2 medium potatoes, diced (½ inch cubes)

Add:
potatoes with liquid to browned salt pork
up to 1 can diced tomatoes
a dash of Worcestershire or Tabasco sauce to taste
salt and pepper to taste

Set the potatoes to cook at the same time as you begin browning the salt pork and onions. When the pork is browned they are ready to mix.

Simmer together a few minutes.

Serve over grits or biscuits   Served 6, including 4 hungry kids

Thanks to Susie Black for letting us rummage through her treasure trove.

## Pineapple Cake — V. Shivers

2 cups Sugar
2 " Flour
2 eggs
2 tsp. soda
1 cup chopped nuts
(save ½ of nuts for Frosting)
1 20 oz. can crushed
Pineapple with juice

Mix all ingredients
-using only ½ oz
nuts -
Bake in 9×13 pan
for 30 min at
350°

over for
Frosting

− Frosting −
1 stick oleo — softened
1 8 oz pkg. cream cheese — softened
1 Box powdered Sugar
1 tsp. vanilla.
Beat until creamy. Add nuts or
save a few to sprinkle on top -
spread on warm cake -

This is a recipe from VIRGINIA SHIVERS.
SHE WAS OUR Neighbor and such a
great lady. Loved this cake of hers!

Margie McDavid

Virginia
Adolphus

### JESSE'S KARO PIE

gs
p white karo syrup
p vanilla
p granulated sugar
p brown sugar
S flour
p margarine

in order given.
in uncooked pie crust.
low oven, cook until firm.   About
hour.

Note: Jesse was a cook for my
-in-law, Charles Picton, and was

one of the best!  I tried this, but of
course I bought the pie crust.  It was
very good. RECIPE PASSED DOWN BY

MARIE JOHNSON GORDON

(TRAVIS JOHNSON'S Sister)  MARGIE

**Baked beans: no proportions!**

Bibbs Jackson (Ms. Jim Jackson)

2 cans Campbell's Pork n Beans
1 large can Ranch Style Beans
Add: small pieces of uncooked bacon, regular
mustard, ketchup, medium onion cut into smaller
pieces, honey
Mix all together.

Add strips of uncooked bacon on top.
Bake at 350 uncovered for about an hour or until good
and bubbly. They get better every day!

Courtesy of Molly Jackson McConville

Violas' Cake Salad
1 can dark sweet black cherries.
1 (no. 2) can crushed pineapple.
Drain & take syrup & bring to boil,
In this hot syrup dissolve 2 boxes
cherry jello & let chill to a heavy syrup.
Beat this until frothy - add
pineapple, cherries & 1 cup nuts and
2 small bottles coke. Chill until firm

This was a MUST for THANKSGIVING
and Christmas. My sister, Deana
Strunk, has taken this on.
Thank goodness

Margie McDavid

| BAKED BEANS FOR 100 | |
|---|---|
| 8 qt. dry beans | 4 lb. salt pork |
| 20 qt. salad | 20 doz. rolls |
| 4 lb. butter | 20 pies |
| 4 qt. cream | 2 lb. coffee |

# Recipes and Remembrances

By Susie and Clayton Black

Susie and Clayton Black have shared some of their favorite recipes. From their book, *Recipes and Remembrances,* Susie wrote, "If you are a food lover, which we both are and a lover of life (who isn't?), you understand the connection between a food, and a meal, and a memory. We both recalled childhood meals and favorite foods with our families with warm recollections. Sometimes the people we share those food memories with are no longer with us. All the more reason to keep those happy times front and center in our daily lives. We always knew we needed to gather up family recipes…It's been quite an experience going through the mountain of recipes and collecting a few favorites from both sides of our family will

---

**Horseradish Meat Loaf**

**8 Servings**

¾ cup. uncooked regular oats

2 T. prepared horseradish

2 lg. eggs, lightly beaten

2 T. spicy brown mustard

2 lbs. ground beef          ¼ cup milk

1 lg. onion, chopped                1 cup ketchup

1-1/2 t. salt                            ½ t. pepper

3 T. brown sugar

Combine beef, oats, onion, ½ cup ketchup, milk, eggs, 1 T. horseradish, salt and pepper in a large bowl. Stir well. Form mixture into a loaf and place in a 9" x 5" loaf pan. Combine ½ cup ketchup, brown sugar, 1 T. horseradish and mustard in a small bowl stirring well. Spoon mixture over the top of the meat loaf. Bake uncovered at 375° degrees for 1 hour and 30 minutes.

have these recipes to pass on and that our friends and family will enjoy them. We try and live by the motto, 'Live well, laugh often and love much'. We wish all of these for you." The following are a few of their favorites.

---

**Susie's Version of Reese's Cookies**
**10-12 dozen cookies.**

| | | |
|---|---|---|
| 4 cup flour | 2 teaspoon baking soda | 3 sticks butter |
| 2 cup sugar | 1 cup light brown sugar | 4 eggs |

2 teaspoon vanilla1 (10 oz. pkg.) of Reese's peanut butter chips

1 (12 oz. pkg.) semi-sweet chocolate chips

¼ (12 oz. pkg.) white chocolate chips

¼ (12 oz. pkg. dark chocolate chips

1 (10 oz. pkg.) pecan chips or cookie pieces

Heat oven to 350° degrees. Stir together flour and baking soda and set aside. In a large mixing bowl, beat butter, granulated sugar, brown sugar and vanilla until creamy. Add eggs; beat well. Gradually add flour mixture, beating well. Stir in chips and pecans. Drop by rounded teaspoons onto a lightly greased cookie sheet. Bake 8-10 minutes or until lightly browned. Cool slightly; remove from cookie sheet to wire rack.

## Key Lime Quail

2 servings

| | |
|---|---|
| 6 quail | salt and pepper to taste |
| ½ stick butter | 3 tablespoon flour |
| 2 cup chicken broth | Juice of 2 key limes |

1 teaspoon Worcestershire sauce

4 key limes cut into halves

1 medium onion, cut into 8 wedges

Season the quail inside and out with salt and pepper. Heat the butter in an ovenproof skillet. Brown the quail on all sides in butter. Remove the quail to a platter using slotted spoon reserving the pan drippings. Add the flour to the reserved drippings and mix well. Stir in broth, key lime juice and Worcestershire sauce. Cook until blended and slightly thickened, stirring constantly. Return the quail to the skillet. Arrange the onion and lime halves around the quail. Bake covered at 325° degrees for 45 minutes.

214

CABBAGE SALAD FOR 175:

20 lb. cabbage

2 bunches carrots

4 large cans crushed pineapple

1 ½ qt. Miracle Whip

# Baked Crab Cakes with Basil Tartar Sauce

| | | |
|---|---|---|
| 1 egg plus 1 egg yolk | 1 teaspoon lemon juice | 4 ½ teaspoon heavy cream |
| ½ teaspoon salt | ½ teaspoon ground red pepper | |
| ¼ teaspoon black pepper | ½ teaspoon Worcestershire sauce | |
| 2 tablespoons parsley | 2 tablespoons chopped green onion | |
| 2 tablespoons melted butter | ¼ cup dry bread crumbs | cracker crumbs |
| 1 lb. lump crabmeat | | |

In a medium bowl, whisk eggs and the next eight ingredients. Add green onions, parsley, cracker crumbs and crabmeat; mix well.

Divide the mixture into 8 equal portions. Shape into patties. The mixture will be crumbly. Sprinkle bread crumbs on both sides. Place on greased cookie sheet. Drizzle butter on top. Cover and refrigerate 1 hour. Preheat oven to 475 degrees. Bake crab cakes with oven rack in highest position 10 minutes or until lightly browned. Serve warm.

## Basil Tartar Sauce
Makes ½ Cup

| | | |
|---|---|---|
| ½ cup packed basil leaves | 1 t. lemon juice | ½ cup mayonnaise |
| 1 t. minced garlic | 1 T. sour cream | 1/8 t. salt |
| 1 dash ground pepper | 1 dash red pepper sauce | |

Rinse basil under very hot water; pat dry. In food processor, puree all ingredients until smooth.

# Aransas County Cookbooks

| Date | Title | Organization/Individual |
|------|-------|------------------------|
| 1927 | Queens in the Kitchen | Rockport P.T.A. |
| 1947 | Rockport Cemetery Association Cookbook | Rockport Cemetery Association |
| 1964 | Square Dancers and Friends Cookbook | Paws & Taws Square Dance Club |
| n. d. | Kitchen Treats from the Toast of the Coast | Rockport, Texas Fireman's Auxiliary |
| 1976 | Oceans of Cooking | Barbara Wells |
| 1982 | Opulent Oyster | Annette Hegen (Sea Grant) |
| 1984 | A Taste of the Coast | AC Medical Services, Inc (ACMSI) |
| 1984 | Gulf Coast Cookbook | Rockport-Fulton American Legion Aux. |
| 1986 | Rockport Collection | Rockport Art Association |
| 1987 | Teacher's Treasures | Live Oak Elementary |
| 1988 | Texas Fish: Light and Lean Recipes | Annette Hegen (Sea Grant) |

# Aransas County Cookbooks

| Date | Title | Organization/Individual |
| --- | --- | --- |
| 1988 | Love and Heirlooms Cookbook | Shirley Jocelyn Farley |
| 1988 | Rockport BP & WC Cookbook | Rockport BP & W Club |
| n.d. | Yachts of Recipes | Rockport Yacht Club |
| 1990 | Cookbook of Champions | Rockport Elementary |
| 1990 | Another Taste of the Coast | ACMSI |
| 1993 | Unique, Low-Fat & Diabetic Recipes | Woman's Club of Aransas County |
| 1993 | Gifts of Love | St. Peter's Episcopal Church |
| 1995 | Heavenly Dishes | First Methodist Youth Fellowship |
| 1999 | Harriet's Kitchen | Docents & Friends of the Fulton Mansion |
| 2000 | Favorite Recipes | Circle W RV Ranch |
| 2003 | Marithyme Treasures | Texas Maritime Museum |

# Aransas County Cookbooks

| Date | Title | Organization/Individual |
|------|-------|-------------------------|
| 2003 | Cooking with Friends | Palm Harbor RV Park |
| 2003 | Recipes from the Heart | Sacred Heart Catholic School |
| 2005 | A Patchwork of Recipes | Piecemakers by the Bay Quilting Guild |
| 2006 | A Taste of the Coast | ACMSI |
| 2007 | Hooked on Seafood | Annette Hegen (Sea Grant) |
| 2008 | Nanaw's Kitchen | Charles "Popo" Cosby |
| 2008 | Picton Family Favorites | Sally Wise Hilliard |
| 2009 | Order of the Eastern Star History & Cookbook (1909 Reprint) | Order of the Eastern Star |
| 2009 | Recipes & Remembrances | Susie & Clayton Black |
| 2012 | GLOW: Tastes from a Tiny Boathouse | Karey (Johnson) Swartwout |
| 2014 | Ingredients for Success | Rockport Rotary Club |
| 2015 | Service from the Heart | Rockport Rotary Club |

# Aransas County Cookbooks and the Culinary History of Aransas County

Dedicated volunteers in Aransas County have compiled dozens of community cookbooks since 1927 to raise funds for a variety of causes including our schools and churches, the cemetery, medical services, clubs, museums, and the art center. If something needed to be done, the "church ladies" pitched in, producing many informative and well-crafted cookbooks, often illustrated by local artists. Individual cooks and families have also written books with recipes,

**Queens in the Kitchen**

**TESTED RECIPES**

FROM

**ROCKPORT HOUSEKEEPERS**

COMPILED BY

**The Parent Teacher Association**

"Let me cook the dinners of a nation, and I shall not care who makes the laws"

**1927**
**ROCKPORT, TEXAS**

photographs and reminiscences. These books provide a historical account of everyday cooking and community life, detailing what residents cooked for their families and friends, for holidays and celebrations, to serve at baby or wedding showers, or for the next Bridge or Women's Club gathering.

The first local cookbook is considered to be the 1927 *Queens in the Kitchen – Tested Recipes from Rockport Housekeepers compiled by the Parent Teacher Association*. The motto on the cover was "Let me cook the dinners of a nation, and I shall not care who makes the laws." The book

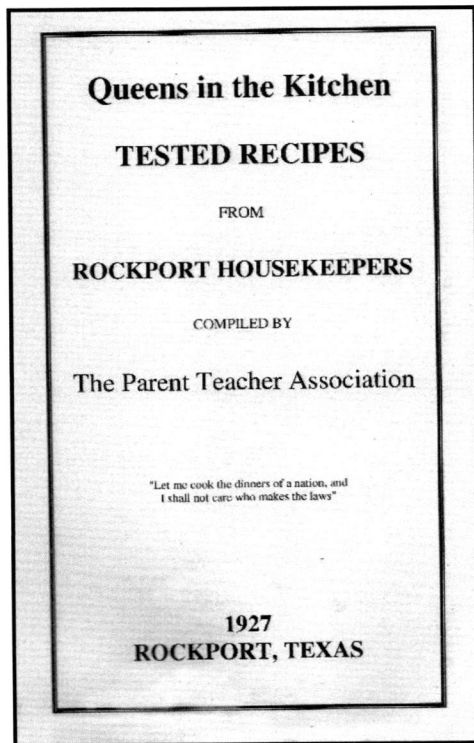

was dedicated to Mrs. S. F. Jackson, the organizer and first President of the P. T. A. in Rockport. Contributors to the book included the names of many well-known families, including Adolphus, Bracht, Bruhl, Brundrett, Casterline, Clingman, Close, Hagar, Jackson, Little, Norvell, Mills, and Sorensen.

The recipes are in old-style, narrative form, with very simple lists of ingredients, often without exact measurements, and with limited instructions, and included ingredients like sweet milk, lard and canned English peas. Here are a few examples:

"Salmon croquettes: Take crackers and moisten with milk, then crumble up and add a can of salmon and mix well together, then form in balls and fry in deep fat."

"Fried Shrimp. Beat two eggs, add salt and pepper; into this dip raw shrimp, then roll in meal. Drop them in boiling grease and fry until a nice brown."

The book noted that the "recipes are not only peculiarly suited to our climate but come from each household thoroughly tested." There are many recipes for sweets, such as vinegar pie, queen of lemon pie, Edna's prize fruit cake, Sallie's white cake, Minnehaha cake, sweet pickle figs, and carrot marmalade. Numerous Mexican recipes are included, including tamale loaf, hot tamale pie, Spanish rice, chili-con-carne, chili and eggs, and Mexican Candy. Other multi-cultural offerings included Brundrett Stew, Goulash, Spaghetti for a Spaghetti Supper, New Orleans crab gumbo and Louisiana shrimp gumbo. Recipes for entertaining are also included, such as delicate tea sandwiches with olives, dates and nuts and fruit punches.

The ads in the book are often as interesting as the recipes, as businesses helped underwrite the book, as they do today with many worthwhile non-profit projects. The Rockport Mercantile Company, Telephone 19, touted it was "as near you as your telephone". The Vaux Tea Room advertised home cooked goodies and delicatessen foods. H.T. Bailey sold fresh meats and "never met a stranger."

---

### H.T. Bailey

**Fresh Meats**

**NEVER MET A STRANGER**

---

Jackson Seafood Company advertised as shippers of fish, shrimp, oysters and crab meat. S. B. Sorenson, Sr. & Sons marketed groceries, hardware and grain. And the Community Theatre said that it had the "very best Pictures, including Westerns; Show every night except Sunday; Admission 10¢ and 25¢." Rockport Public Service Co. offered ice, light and power. Dr. H. A. Dow, expert optometrist and watch-maker, noted that "all prices in keeping with the time." "Quality Counts" and "Get your milk and cream from Spark's Diary" are in the ads for a fondly-remembered business. Hooper Brothers were dealers in fancy and staple groceries, feed, ammunition, tinware and queensware. Mrs. E. H. Norvell advertised lessons in piano and voice.

## Preface

The Aransas County Historical Society reproduced in 2011 the "Queens in the Kitchen" cookbook. The cookbook was compiled in 1927 by the Parent Teacher Association of Rockport, Texas. Photographs of many of the women who submitted recipes for the 1927 cookbook are included in this reproduction. There is an additional section in the back of recipes submitted by the ACHS board of trustees. Special thanks go to Kam and Scott Wagert for matching the original fonts and retyping the original cookbook in a format ready to reprint. The cookbook committee was Dolly Hart Close (chair) who came up with the idea to reprint the 1927 cookbook; Janet Haseman Taylor, Norinne Holman, Jo Ann Morgan and Kam Wagert.

This rare book was reprinted in 2011 by the Aransas County Historical Society with photographs by many of the women who contributed. Copies can sometimes be found at garage sales or in resale shops such as Castaways.

Many other groups have used cookbooks to raise funds since 1927. In 1964, the Paws and Taws Square Dance Club produced *Square Dancers and Friends Cookbook* to help build the original Paws and Taws Square Dance Building in Fulton. The Aransas County Medical Services (ACMSI) wrote several versions of *A Taste of the Coast* to fund the County's first ambulances. The Rockport Art Association produced the *Rockport Collection* in 1986, illustrated by artists including Al Barnes, Herb Booth and Jack Cowan. The out-of-print book contains seafood and game recipes. The Docents and Friends of the Fulton Mansion wrote *Harriet's Kitchen* in 1999 with historical information about George Fulton's wife and recipes of the time.

In 2003, the Texas Maritime Museum created *Marithyme Treasures* with local artwork and is still available at the Museum. Other cookbooks have been written by the Rockport Rotary Club, St. Peter's Episcopal Church, the Order of the Eastern Star, the Piecemakers by the Bay Quilt Guild, the Palm Harbor RV Park Winter Visitors, the Circle W RV Ranch, the First United Methodist Youth Fellowship, the Woman's Club of Aransas County, St. Peter's Episcopal Church, Rockport Elementary, the Rockport Yacht Club, the Business and Professional Women's Club, Live Oak Elementary, and numerous others.

Aransas County cooks have always liked to cook and entertain; the Appetizer sections in many of the books are large, full of mousses with seafood, seafood-stuffed mushrooms, crab dips with cream cheese, and filled Pepperidge Farm patty shells. Often more exotic selections like dove breast hors d'oeuvres with jalapeno, water chestnuts and bacon slices pop up next to cereal snacks.

---

## DEER MEAT MAGIC

Deer steaks
1 can cream of mushroom soup

Salt and pepper

Salt and pepper deer steak. Place in cast iron skillet. Pour one can of cream of mushroom soup and one can of water over the steak. Cover with foil, seal tightly. Bake at 350° for 2 hours. Steak and gravy will be ready to eat.

---

Many books have game sections replete with selections like pickled alligator gar, shark fillets, duck pate, venison salami, squirrels, woodcock, grouse, and rabbit. There are many recipes for chicken fried proteins, such as turtle, duck breast, blue or snow goose, and venison backstrap as well as for beef.

Our cookbooks have also tracked the trends and fads in cuisine over the years. Lard and bacon grease changed to Oleo and Crisco and then margarine, next butter, and more recently olive and other oils. Miracle Whip gave way to mayonnaise and then aioli. Different substances coat fried seafood. Over the years, cracker meal, crumbled saltine crackers, and cornmeal give way to Italian bread crumbs and panko. Shortcuts like using canned mushroom soup, onion soup mix, and other quick additions appear, particularly in the ubiquitous King Ranch Casserole with Velveeta, Cheez Whiz, jarred processed cheddar cheese spread, and American cheese being replaced by gruyere and parmesan.

Residents often had lived in larger, more sophisticated cities like Houston and San Antonio and brought to their part-time or retirement lifestyles influences from big city restaurants. Some had also lived around the world and traveled to famous gastronomic cities such as New Orleans. Recipes in our cookbooks reflect this with recipes like Sakowitz Shrimp Salad with Remoulade sauce, Crab Bisque from Newick's in Portland, Maine, Maryland Eastern Shore Crab Cakes from Longfellow's Restaurant, Spinach Pudding from the Menger Hotel in San Antonio, Corn Bread a

La Waldorf Astoria, Hush Puppies from the Old Stage Coach Inn in Salado, and Driskill Hotel's Cheese Soup.

A unique part of Aransas County cookbooks is the inclusion of art from local members of the art colony. For example, St. Peter's *Cooking with Love and Joy* has images by Joan and Lynn Lee, Mary Frazier, Kay Barnebey, Lisa Baer, and Bonnie Prouty.

Live Oak's *Teachers' Treasures* is illustrated with students' artwork.

Local history was also sometimes included in the cookbooks. *Gifts of Love* from St. Peter's, for example, included the story of Sea Captain C. L. Deane, a dedicated Episcopalian, who brought the lumber from Galveston to build many of the homes and businesses of Rockport. He donated the materials to build the first altar and altar rail for St. Peter's. This book also notes other food history:

"In the early days of Rockport, there were no game limits. Thousands of hunters and fishermen came and stayed at the four large hotels. They would hire guides to take them hunting and fishing. These people would often have their catch shipped home by rail. Live crabs were shipped in fresh seaweed sprinkled with cornmeal so that the crabs would have food on the trip to the table far away. Oysters were shipped in large wooden barrels already packed in ice and prepaid because the railroad would not add ice, and ice was imperative. Wild game, such as deer and javelina, were shipped whole. They were killed and bled and taken to the local ice house to be kept until ready for shipping.

At shipping time, they would be stuffed with hay and wrapped in gunny sacks so that they could be shipped safely for several days. Hotels and restaurants in Chicago and New York used the service of the rails for the largesse from Rockport."

Often you will find humorous additions in the cookbooks: *Aunt Frankie's Corn Bread:* "This is just the way she told me to do it."; "I stir gumbo with long spatula and I wear an oven glove on my hand while making roux – that stuff can get

---

### Sandy Booth's Easy Quail or Pheasant in Mushroom Sauce

1 pheasant, disjointed, back removed*
1 can cream of mushroom soup
1/3 c. dry sherry

1 t. dried thyme
1 can golden mushroom soup
½ t. pepper

Heat oven to 325 degrees. Clean birds well. Combine soups in large pot and bring to a boil. Add the sherry, thyme and pepper. Slowly add the birds. Cover and bake in a 325-degree oven for about 3 hours for pheasant and 2 ½ hours for the quail. The meat should be just starting to pull away from the bone. *May also use 6-8 quail. The birds can be whole or separated from the legs, but include the legs if you have them.

HOT!"; or this recipe for *Chicken and Rice Soup* "Open can. Put soup in pan. Heat it. Eat it."

Local resident Annette Hegen wrote several cookbooks through the Sea Grant program at Texas A & M University to promote Texas seafood. Many people still remember her seafood recipe cards distributed by numerous seafood markets and grocery chains. You often see these, and other recipes torn from the backs of packages in recipe boxes in local kitchens, along with recipes jotted down by friends or family or pulled from popular magazines such as *Southern Living* or *Better Homes and Gardens*.

## ELEPHANT STEW

*Dr. Livingston, I Presume*

1 elephant                    2 rabbits (opt.)
Salt and pepper

Cut elephant into bite-sized pieces. This should take about 2 months. Add enough brown gravy to cover. Cook over kerosene fire for about

4 weeks at 465°. This will serve 3,800 people. If more are expected, 2 rabbits may be added, but only do this if necessary, as most people do not like to find hare in their stew.

# History of Aprons

Contributed by Sandy Garrison

*Mom's or Grandma's apron was used:*

•to protect the dress underneath; After all, ladies only had a few. It was easier to wash aprons than dresses.

•as a potholder for removing hot pans from the oven.

•to dry children's tears.

•for cleaning out dirty ears.

•to carry eggs, fussy chicks, or half-hatched eggs to a warming oven.

•as a shy child's hiding place.

•as a wrap when the weather was cold.

•as a rag to wipe a perspiring brow bent over a hot wooden stove.

•to bring in kindling wood.

•to carry vegetables from the garden.

•to carry hulls after peas had been shelled.

•to bring in apples that had fallen from the trees.

•to dust furniture when unexpected company drive up the road.

•to use as a flag to wave the men folk in from the fields at dinner time

# Stir It Up

By Katy Jones-Gulsby

My love of historical cooking and food preparation can probably be traced to reading the *Little House* books as a child. Laura Ingalls Wilder had an incredible knack for describing the food preparation and cooking practiced by her parents and the people in pioneer communities –it was so different from the cooking my mother did growing up in the 1980s Houston.

I was fascinated by the old recipes my grandmother used, recipes she had memorized and made with quick precision and skill, while listening to her talk about watching her own mother cook and prepare food in their farm kitchen during World War II and the immediate post war period. I am extremely lucky to have my great grandmother still with us at 99 years of age, and still able to talk to us about growing up during the Great Depression.

She became a wife at sixteen and left home to create a homestead with my great grandfather miles away from family and her support system. She had to be industrious and thrifty and fearless as she cooked food for her husband and children as they eked out a living in Arkansas. Hearing her talk about fully sustainable food preparation – growing, harvesting, preserving, preparing and

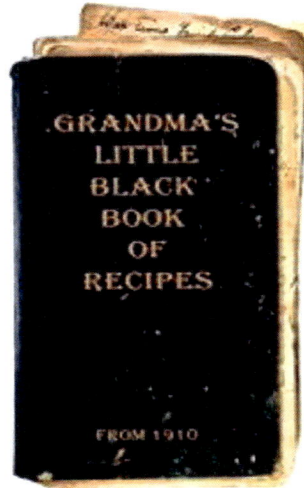

storing – stoked my imagination and led me to an interest in heritage food pathways. As a history nerd, this inevitably led me to using cookbooks and food history as a research path to learning all I could about a society or culture.

I began picking up cookbooks at estate sales and garage sales as I hunted for stock for my vintage store. I have been selling vintage clothing and home décor items for over a decade and have amassed quite the collection of vintage books in the process. I can't pass them up – I love the design, the craftsmanship, the smell of the old paper. With my interest in food history combined with my love of old books, it was only a matter of time before I started collecting vintage cookbooks.

I am not a serious collector, by any means – I don't collect based on any sense of monetary value and I don't actively seek out the cookbooks in my collection. My small collection grows organically, as I stumble across volumes or they fall into my lap. The condition never bothers me and I am not specific to a theme. In general, I prefer

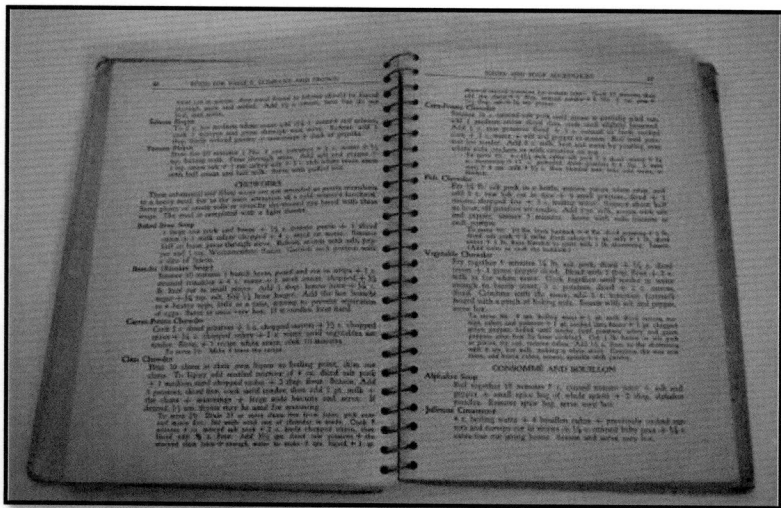

cookbooks from the first half of the 20th century, but I have been known to break that tenuous rule.

My collection doesn't really have any connecting threads other than they are all cookbooks – like the rest of my interests, they are diverse. There is a slender thread of Texana running through, but mostly because that is one of my largest interests in historical terms – I am a seventh-generation Texan from a family with an original land grant from Stephen F. Austin; its's sort of in my blood.

One of the rarest and most collectible form of vintage cookbooks are those written by African American cooks before the post-war period. This is probably one of the only specific types of cookbooks I keep an eye out for. So much of our rich American Foodway is influenced by these pioneering and industrious cooks working in homes, hotels and local restaurants. I have yet to come across one of these important cookbooks in the wild, but a wonderful source is the 2016 book, *The Jemima Code: Two Centuries of African American Cooking* by Toni Tipton-Martin. She uses original early African American cookbooks to trace the history of black influence on American cuisine and it is fascinating.

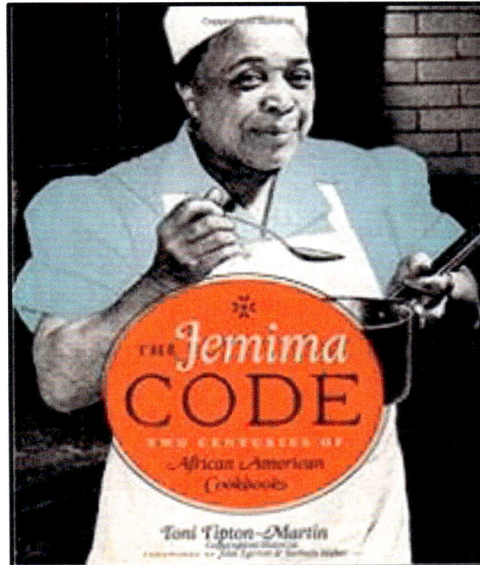

*"Next to eating good dinners, a healthy man, with a benevolent turn of mind, must like, I think, to read about them."*

-William Makepeace Thackeray

This is true today since cookbooks make up a sizeable portion of the publishing industry and cookbook authors become celebrities in their own right; but it was also true historically. Cookbooks have been kicking around since Antiquity, but American cookbooks have been published almost as long as there has been an America.

Amelia Simmons' cookbook, the verbosely titled, *American Cookery: The Art of Dressing Viands, Fish, Poultry and Vegetables*, *The*

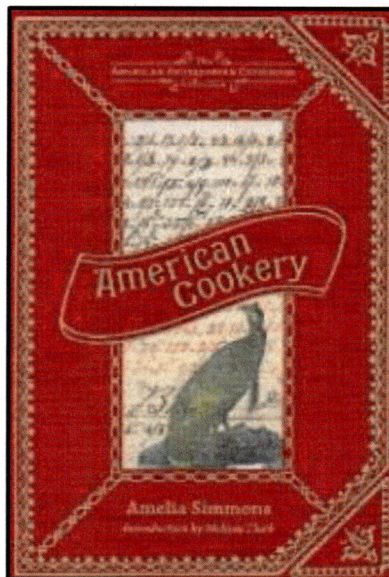

*Best Modes of Making Pastes, Puffs, Pies, Tarts, Puddings, Custards and Preserves*, and *All Kinds of Cakes from the Imperial Plumb to Plain Cake.*

*Adapted to This Country and All Grades of Life* by Amelia Simmons, an American Orphan, was first published in 1796 and, as far as we know, is the first real American cookbook. Before Simmons published her work, we relied on English cookbooks from the old country.

But Simmons introduced cooking with native ingredients and techniques. Her book was such a hit that it went through multiple printings and sparked a new industry of household cooking manuals.

Up until around World War II, most cookbooks published in this country were general cooking manuals, covering a wide range of foods, techniques and household tips. Similar in score to that classic red and white gingham Better Homes & Garden cookbook, that everyone owns.

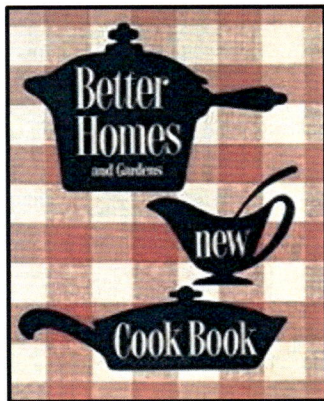

These tomes were full of recipes on how to cook meats, vegetables, pastries, cakes and all manner of dishes. The recipes were basic, with no assumptions of fancy kitchen utensils – they were written for women, who managed kitchens of all kinds; and therefore, only the most universal tools were assumed available – a source of wood-fired heat, some bowls, and a spoon. The ingredients were easy to obtain, mostly being grown by the household or produced by their livestock. Seasonality was important and cold stores not incredibly reliable, so recipes changed with the seasons and became traditional for seasonal holidays like Christmas or summer picnics.

Recipes in these older cookbooks are not written for one-upmanship. They are not fancy to impress your friends and neighbors – they were practical, often instructing the home cook on how to use ingredients that might be "going bad". What modern cookbook will tell you what to do with a slab of meat that might be close to "turning", or a bunch of "halfway rotten vegetables"? These cookbooks were written in a time when waste, as we know it, wasn't "waste". The directions can be somewhat vague to our understanding – "cook until done on a hot stove". But most heat sources were wood-fired and the art of using them to prepare food was just that – An Art. Women became very familiar with their stoves and fireplaces and knew intimately how to manipulate them to prepare meals. Every heat source was different and, therefore, recipes had to be universally vague. Equally vague were the amounts of ingredients needed. Cooking was by taste and feel and smell and touch, a full range of "sensory activity" and women were trained from childhood. Measurements could be arbitrary and by personal preference. One of my favorite quotes from Amelia Simmon's 1796 Cookbook is her recipe for a syullabub, a sweet frothy drink. "Sweeten a quart of cyder with double refined sugar, grate nutmeg into it, then milk your cow into your liquor." You wouldn't find that in a cookbook by Rachel Ray.

It wasn't until Fannie Farmer, at the turn of the 20th century, wrote her first cookbook, *The Boston Cooking School Cookbook*, that standardized measurements were introduced. Known as the "mother of level measuring", Farmer introduced a more scientific form of cooking.

If you are interested in cooking and its history, I am sure you have heard of Fannie Farmer. She is often cited as one of the most important cooks in American history, and while her introduction of standardized measurement and her contemporary popularity with over 4 million of her books were sold during her lifetime, I find her smug and slightly obscure or nitpicking. She was as interested in wholesome nutrition as she was in the science of cooking, and, therefore, her recipes tend to be rather bland and lacking spice. While I appreciate her, I don't collect her. And besides, her book, now known as *Fannie Farmer's Cookbook*, is still in print. I prefer the cookbooks, mostly

published from the turn of the century until around mid-century (20th century), written by lesser known, but equally as important cooks and communities.

The dawn of global travel being available, not just to the ultra-rich and the influx of immigrants into America in the first half of the 20th century, created an incredible diaspora of food and taste and spice. The traditional American and English recipes are still there, but they are mixed in with radical new ideas and ingredients and culture.

One of my favorite types of cookbooks is the community cookbook. Local, charity cookbooks will often have an ethnic blend reflecting the demographics of a region. Recipes are often a little more flavorful and interesting that the "kitchen

Bibles" previously popular. The community cookbooks popular in the 1940s and 1950s, often compiled by church groups or utility cooperatives, are so fascinating to look at. They present a snapshot of a community and what is important to them. The recipes are often a mix of farm kitchen staples passed down through generations and a healthy heaping of ethnic dishes specific to the demographics of the region. Take, for example, this early 1950s cookbook from the United Lutheran Ladies Aid of Grand Forks, North

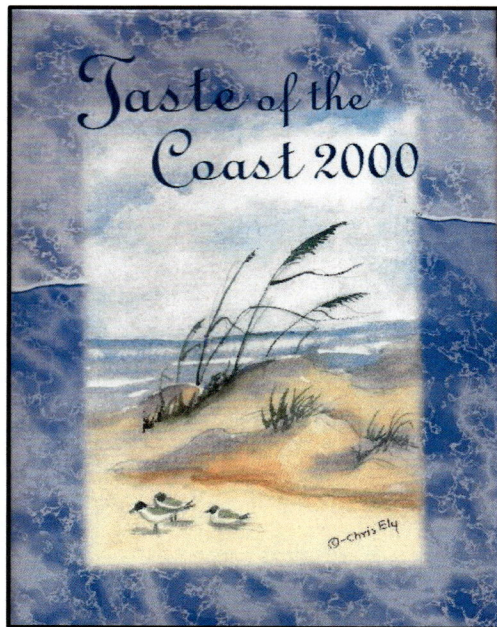

Dakota. There are apple pies, suet puddings, sponge cakes and barbeque chicken and all the recipes you would expect in a church cookbook of its age, but there is also a chapter on Scandinavian delicacies like blood dumplings and fish soup. Scandinavian-themed recipes are scattered throughout the cookbook – lutefisk next to meatloaf. Also, being a more urban community, there are recipes with a slightly global blend – chop suey and chow mein appear, probably because there was a Chinese population in Grand Forks, who possibly ran Chinese restaurants. While not authentic in any way, just their appearance in a church cookbook from 1952 means the community was interested in what others were cooking.

At the other end of the spectrum is a cookbook from the Lighthouse Electric Cooperative in Floydada, Texas, a rural community in the Panhandle. It is also from1952, but it paints a different picture of a community. The recipes are more homogeneous, though no less interesting. I love cookbooks like this because the recipes are almost guaranteed to be older than the cookbook. This is from a farming community that was fairly isolated at this time and the recipes shared are simple, classic and undeniably American. There is a nod toward Mexico, as would be expected in a Texas

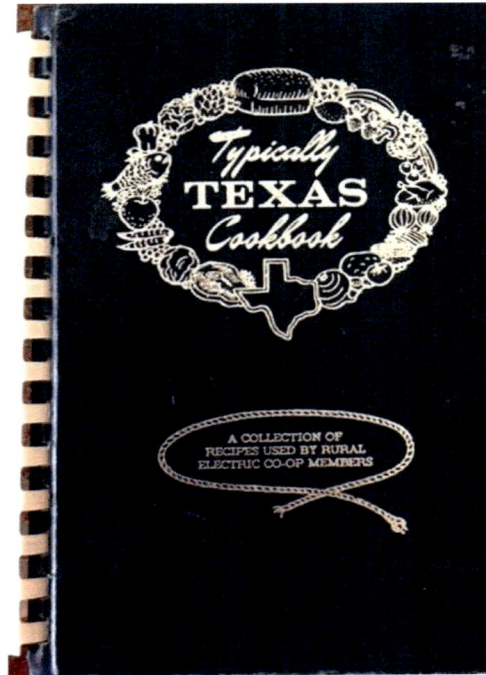

cookbook, but even those recipes are filtered through the lens of a white, rural community. It shows a continuation of ingredients, ideas, and traditions with little influence from the outside world. Even though my family isn't from this area, I imagine these were the sorts of recipes my ancestors used because the last names of the contributors are English and Scotch-Irish. I recognize some of them – Mrs. David S. Battey's recipe for Rich Giblet Gravy is almost identical to the gravy I look forward to every Thanksgiving and which only my grandmother can duplicate.

Another very American type of cookbook is the product cookbook, or manufacturer's cookbook. We've all seen the stacks of flimsy pamphlets in thrift stores, put out by some microwave's manufacturer or the head of the ketchup dynasty. But before those hilariously, badly photographed cooked dishes were compiled into a cookbook, came *The Watkins Cook Book* form the J. R. Watkins Company, a catalog sales company of baking goods and canned foods as well as other household necessities. Even though this book is in terrible shape, I wanted to share that even though book collecting can be based on condition, in cookbook collecting, it's often these tattered old books that have the most worth. While I will never see a dime for this thing and no sane vintage bookseller would buy it, the evidence of use you find inside and out is invaluable. The covers are cracked in such a way that they can only have been damaged from holding it in a certain way. There are corrections and handwritten notes and even additions – the woman, who owned this book, was opinionated and knew what she liked. She obviously didn't like J. R. Watkin's idea of a crisp, flaky pie crust because she pasted cut-out newspaper recipes for other pies and wrote in her own above the text. The cookbook itself is fascinating because it has entire sections on kitchen economies and ways to make ingredients stretch. This section on "Stretching Meat" is particularly interesting – how to make meat pie for six people from one pound of lean, raw meat, what grains to use to extend the meat, and how to use ground meat to make various dishes for large families. All the while, being seasoned with Watkins Seasonings, of course.

The next tattered specimen is one of my favorites of my collection – produced in 1930 by Manischewitz Company, a maker of "fine matzo bakers". *Tempting Kosher Dishes* is printed half in English and half in Hebrew. The illustrations are delightfully Art Deco and the recipes are a grab bag of American, Jewish, and ethnically diverse ones across the Jewish diaspora. There are multiple recipes for knoedels, or boiled dumplings, that can be made savory or sweet. The woman, who owned this cookbook, underlined her favorite recipe, *Knoedel No. 1*, a savory dumpling made with chicken fat and onion juice. She wrote, "This" emphatically in the margin. As I first flipped through the book, I noticed that this was her style – recipes she enjoyed, she simply wrote the word "This" next to Mock Oatmeal Cookies, Carrot Torte – her straightforward endorsements made

me want to try the recipes, even if the sound of Carrot Torte doesn't make my mouth water.

She also wrote "Try" next to a recipe entitled *Matzon Eier-Kuchen,* a pancake made with Manischewitz's Matzo Meal – I wonder if she ever got to try it.

The notion of celebrity chefs is not a new one – Fannie Farmer could be considered a celebrity in her day and, over the pond in England,

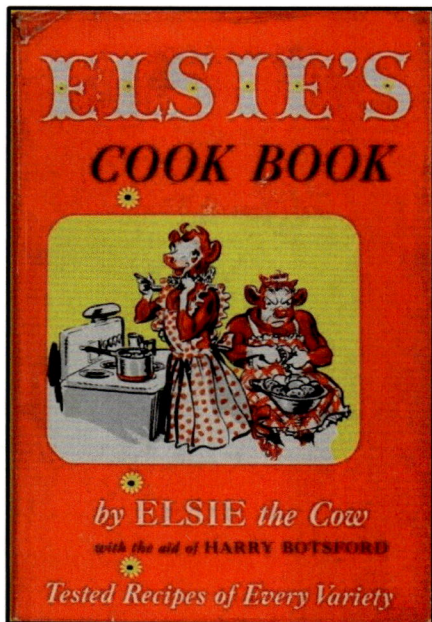

Mrs. Beeton and her *Cookery Book* reigned supreme.

I have a soft spot for Texana cookbooks and books by Helen Corbitt sit proudly in a special place in my kitchen. I love her playful, humorous style – the anecdotes she weaves into the narratives of her cookbooks are wonderful, despite being famous for being the Director of Food Services for Neiman

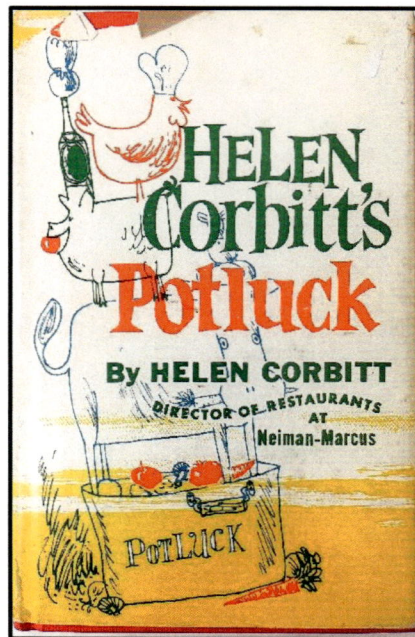

Marcus and having her recipes eaten by the "great and the good", she never takes herself too seriously. In her first cookbook, she declares that Uncle Ben's Rice is her favorite. She wrote many cookbooks based on her experiences at Neiman's, the Driskill Hotel in Austin, and the Houston Country Club. These are wonderful for parties and gatherings - as expected, the appetizers and cocktail hour hors d'oeuvres are excellent.

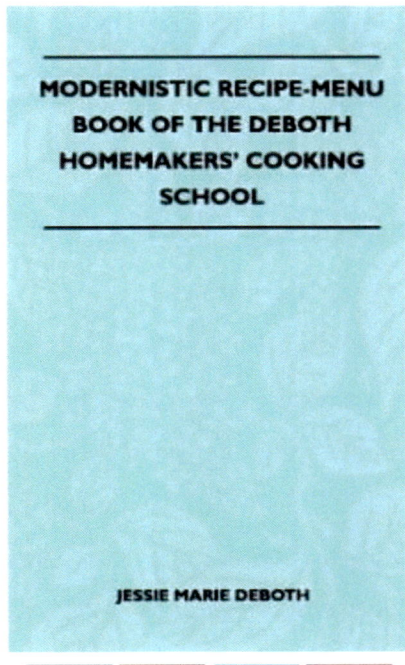

My favorite cookbook in my collection is the unassuming *The Modernistic Recipe – Menu Book* by De Both Homemakers Cooking School published in 1929. A syndicated food columnist in Chicago, Jessie Marie Deboth was a household name in the 1930s-1960s. She was a much a celebrity chef then as Rachel Ray or Emeril are today.

Newspapers, in which her column was syndicated, would sponsor vaudevillian cooking shows – much like our beloved television cooking shows today. A full kitchen was set up on stage, and Jessie, beautifully turned out in a fashionable outfit, hat and, occasionally, furs, would burst from the wings waving a sifter and calling, "Yo ho!". This four-day program included giveaways,

**MODERNISTIC RECIPE-MENU BOOK OF THE DEBOTH HOMEMAKERS' COOKING SCHOOL**

**JESSIE MARIE DEBOTH**

amateur shows, sing-alongs and musical performances by groups, such as the Gypsy Barons' Orchestra.

I love this cookbook because of the format. Instead of being arranged by food type and with recipes in sections like Meat, Dessert, Appetizers, etc., it is arranged by menu divided into three sections – Everyday Menus, Entertaining, and

Courtesy of Laura and James Fox

Miscellaneous. So much can be learned about a society by these full menus – how mealtimes were structured, how socializing fit into food consumption and, most interestingly, the varied situations involving food that they found important. The Miscellaneous section includes portion on Outdoor Cooking, Meatless Menus, Invalid Cookery, Reducing or Weight loss Menus and a Constipation Diet. The information is all very practical.

A favorite section of menus is the Refrigerator Menus. Since mechanical refrigerators were a new novelty, people threw "refrigerator parties" where all courses would be kept chilled and ready in the "frig". Having one was a status symbol and an occasion to celebrate. This section includes menus for entertaining and everyday menus, all centered around the refrigerator, such as a first course of Jellied Chicken and Egg Salad, then Orange Honey Biscuits, Baked Alaska with Meringue and finish with a bracing hot tea, as De Both always recommended that one item even in the refrigerator menu should be warm.

But the icing on the cake from this cookbook was the ephemera found tucked away in its pages – newspaper clippings of articles and recipes, handwritten menus and recipe notations, notes on the backs of city budget fliers and advertisements. Also found was a recipe for medicated shampoo on fancy hotel stationary and several typewritten menus for a Mrs. Tenney's Dining Room, who owned the book. I can only imagine that she used this cookbook to build her menus and fare. One of her lunch menus had a bowl of vegetable soup for 10 cents and a full lunch with steak or chicken legs included mashed squash, potatoes, and molded salad for 35 cents. You could even purchase a piece of custard pie, cake or ice cream for 10 cents. Drinks were extra with black coffee being 5 cents.

When I am looking for vintage cookbooks for my collection, I keep several factors in mind. I am drawn to graphic design and illustrations, so that is the first thing that catches my eye. As I flip through the pages, looking for ephemera or hand-written notes, stains from food and evidence of use, I look beyond the monetary value and instead purchase for the historical value—the way the cookbook paints a picture of a society or culture These are the things that might turn off a serious collector, one who collects because of scarcity or value. Good cookbooks can be read like a novel, or a history book – the recipes and anecdotes and accompanying bits and bobs create a narrative of a time and place. Food has always been central to our humanity, as sustenance, as entertainment, as an art. Our current food-obsessed world of cooking blogs, television shows, and celebrity chefs is nothing new. We've always been fascinated by the story's food can tell. Clifton Fadiman, an American intellectual, once said, "A good book about food informs us of matters with which we are to be concerned all our lives. Sight and hearing lose their edge; the muscles soften; even the most gallant of our glands at last surrenders, but the palate may persist in glory almost to the very end".

**Katy Jones-Gulsby** began selling vintage and antique goods more than a decade ago and has since created a following and a brand for her curated collections. Born and raised in Houston, TX with stints as an "oil brat" in Europe, Katy studied Fashion Journalism at the University of the Arts in London, England and Creative

Writing at the University of Houston. She started her vintage business to supplement her income, while she worked as a freelance writer and educator, but it quickly became her passion. Now she runs *Shell & Pine*, providing beautiful vintage and antiques to the Coastal Bend community and beyond.

# EATING ESTABLISHMENTS

From the collection of Jim Moloney

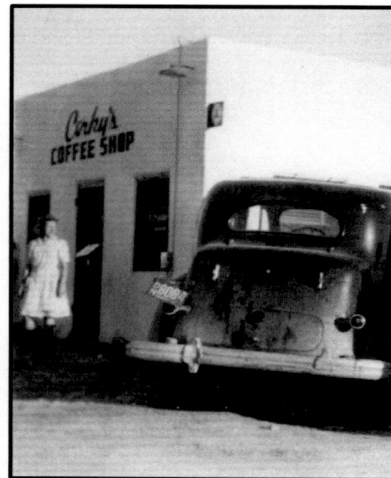

Courtesy of the Agler Family

# Early Food-Related Businesses in Aransas County

Successive waves of hard-working and inventive small business men and women have settled in Aransas County over the years, building a vibrant community around the bounty of nature. Ranchers, truck farmers, boat builders, net makers, packery workers, shrimpers, oyster and fisher men, hotel cooks and waiters, café and dinner staff, dairy workers, dry goods and grocery store workers – all built a hard-

**ROCKPORT** THE SEATTLE OF THE
THE NEW YORK OF THE **SOUTH**

This is what Rockport will be.

There is no harbor anywhere in the world without an accompanying harbor city. Our harbor—Port Aransas—is where nature has planted a bulwark in the shape of St. Joseph and Mustang Island, with Harbor Island in front of it. IT IS THE PLACE OF LEAST RESISTANCE, WHERE RAIL AND WATER MEET TO HANDLE THE COMMERCE OF THE NEW TEXAS EMPIRE.

Cheap fuel and cheap water and rail transportation, with products and raw material at our door, will make Rockport the largest manufacturing city in the South. Look at the map! Mexico within a stone's throw, and the nearest port to the Panama Canal. Have you business judgment enough to know what that means? If so, you should know that there is no place on earth AT THE PRESENT TIME where you could invest a small amount of money which would give you greater returns than in Rockport, Texas.

Briefly: A double land-locked harbor. Eighty square miles of deep water, or six times more than Galveston. Large enough to harbor the entire American fleet. Six hundred miles nearer Panama than any other naval base.

Rockport stands without the shadow of a rival, and is destined to become the largest city in the South. The question of her future is settled for all time to come.

This new harbor will be open to the commerce of the world by August, 1912. Railroads are now fighting for positions, and four or five more will hit the harbor in time to handle this year's products, as the second largest steamship company in the world has closed negotiations to ply between Rockport and European ports.

Rockport is today a city backed by all the potent factors of commerce and finance that are essential to metropolitan growth. What will she be tomorrow?

FOR FURTHER INFORMATION ADDRESS

**ROCKPORT COMMERCIAL CLUB   -   ROCKPORT, TEXAS**

working, food-loving, neighbor-helping-neighbor culture that we still enjoy today.

Food sources were first discovered by early Spanish Explorers, who learned that the Karankawa Indians had been living off the land and sea since 7000-4000 BC and took advantage of native plants and sustenance from the sea.

Many early settlers were lured to the area in the 1900s by extravagant land promotions that promised them riches from farming and agriculture.

After the Civil War, ranchers rounded up the wild longhorns on the coastal plains and built processing plants and ports to ship them. Some of the beef was kept and sold to the large area hotels. In 1873, Mary Ellen Wilkinson Close

McHugh decided to open up an "eating house" near the packeries to support herself, a widow, and her children. The workers could walk to her home and grab a quick meal.

Before the 1890s, Aransas Bay had one of the largest concentrations of migrating green sea turtles in the Gulf of Mexico. Turtle meat was canned and sent to New Orleans among other ports. At this time, turtle meat was cheap, ordinary and found in abundance here.

The San Antonio and Aransas Pass Railway (SA-AP Rail) arrived after George Fulton and others worked to advance their cattle markets.

At the 50th Anniversary of George and Harriet Fulton on March 12, 1890, guests from all over Texas were brought to the mansion via the SA-AP Rail to celebrate their Golden Anniversary. The Fulton's hosted a sumptuous dinner for their guests. When the evening had concluded, people were escorted to the Mansion where even more food was presented. This lovely gathering introduced the guests to the bounty of nature found here and possibilities of creating eating establishments (Allen & Hastings – Taylor, 1997).

Through the railroad, Aransas County was introduced to San Antonio and other cities. Tourists arrived by train to enjoy the bay waters and stay at large hotels, such as The Del Mar and La Playa.

These hotels with impressive dining rooms served elaborate meals in the Victorian tradition with fancy chandeliers, white tablecloths and, no doubt, turtle soup. The offerings also included turtle steaks on the daily menu, Taft Ranch beef from the Coleman-Fulton Packery, and oyster

Hotel Del Mar
1889 - 1914

cocktails. The bakery next door provided cakes and tasty pastries. An orchestra played nightly for the diners' enjoyment and dancing. Tourists could also attend a Grand Ball each Saturday.

According to Allen and Hastings-Taylor (1997), Professor Attwater used the train to advertise Aransas by exhibiting fruits and vegetables grown by local farmers in a special rail car.

"Rockport Oysters" began to appear on San Antonio, Dallas, New Orleans and Chicago menus

Courtesy of Jerry Brundrett.

after being packed in ice and shipped inland in barrels by rail.

Other small businesses were opened by enterprising families – meat markets, fish houses, truck farms, dairies, dry goods, grocery stores,

hunting and fishing camps. Each sold their harvests to local eateries.

The following are descriptions of the local eating establishments founded to meet the needs of the community and the tourists:

•When ships were built here during World War I, workers would walk to the Lathrop house on Church Street where Mattie Lou would fix them a meal.

•Hunters came by rail to St. Charles Hunting Club and enjoyed gizzard stew on the evenings of

CLEAN WATER, HARD SAND BEACH. FINEST ON TEXAS COAST    ROCKPORT, TEXAS

Courtesy of Gordon Stanley

their hunts during the 1920s.

•In the 1940s, the locals and visitors would dine, swim and dance at Rockport Pavilion. It was located near today's Aransas County Navigation District office.

•In the mid-1940s, Lester Simpson built The Beach Club, or Harbor Patio, a great place for young people to meet, eat, dance and view the bay. According to the Aransas County Historical Society, Buddy

Left photo: (L to R) George Lee Brundrett, Chester Johnson, Peg Leg Jim at Peg Leg's
Courtesy of Janet Taylor

Holly and the School Swing Band provided music there. The band played to earn enough gas money to get to Houston.

•The Triangle Service Station, located at the corner of Business Highway 35 South and Church Street, later added sandwiches and cold drinks. This became a popular dance hall and bar during the 1940s.

•Before Schrenkeisens and Benchwarmers, "Peg Leg's" was found on the corner of Broadway and Fulton Beach Road. It was an interesting hangout for locals.

**At the Triangle Cafe**
(L to R) Marvin Davis, Frank Holzhouser, Evelyn, Unknown
Courtesy of Janet Taylor

•Pepe's enchiladas were very tasty, and it was in the small storefront across from today's Winery by the Bay.

•Mrs. Helen Nava's Tamales were mouth-watering. People always came back for more.

•Big Fisherman located on FM 188 near Business Highway 35 South was known to the connoisseurs as the "Restaurant of 500 Parakeets". Bill Stevens, the owner, loved birds. Each dining room had a different theme from nautical, bird habitats to working bee-hives.  The seafood was not local, but the fried chicken was amazing as was the chicken fried steak.  The lentil soup was also popular (Caller-Times).

•Little Bay Club on Fulton Beach Road could be found in front of today's Bent Oaks Rookery. Locals often worked there to put themselves through college.  The kitchen was said to be the cleanest, most professional kitchen and was state of the art back then.  Only the finest ingredients were used for the 5 Star food demanded by Norman Scott, the owner.  On the weekend, a virtual list of Rockport elites dined there.

•Running Bear was located north of Lamar on Business Highway 35 near a wide spot in the highway.

According to *The Caller Times*, Bill Knox, a genial bear of a fellow, served hamburgers memorable for their prodigious amounts of lettuce, tomato and other trappings.  His onion rings were the item to order, a mountain of sweet, messy, eccentrically cut circles. Listening bonus: a jukebox featuring Johnny Preston's *Running Bear* and Hank Thompson's *Wild Side of Life* played. Many recalled they couldn't finish all the food ordered.

According to locals, "They had the best burgers.  The chicken-fried steak covered the whole plate and the fries had to go on another plate" and "That was the best place! I remember going there when we first moved to Rockport. Broke my heart when they closed down!"

•Fish fries and barbeques continue to be held to raise money for charitable causes.

### Little Bay Club Seafood Au Gratin

4 T butter      1 1/3 C. whipping cream      4 oz. Finely chopped onion

1 T. Cornstarch      ½ lb. shelled, deveined shrimp, cut into ½" pieces

¼ C. Milk      1 C. grated cheddar cheese

½ lb. firm fish fillets (like red snapper)      12 T. Grated parmesan cheese,

½ lb. crab meat, divided into half      ¾ C white wine

4 T. cracker meal      2/3 C. fish stock from fish trimmings or water

Salt, pepper, dash of powdered clove & thyme

Butter a shallow skillet and sprinkle with chopped onion. Lay the seafood on top and pour in the white wine and fish stock. Sprinkle with a little salt, pepper, powdered thyme and powdered clove. Cover and bring to a boil over high heat. Turn down the heat and simmer until cooked. Remove the seafood from the pan with a slotted spoon. Turn up heat and reduce the cooking liquid by two-thirds. Add the cream and simmer until sauce reduces a little more. Dissolve cornstarch in milk and whisk into the sauce. Bring to a boil, whisking continually. Return the seafood to the pan and turn off heat. Stir in grated cheddar cheese and 6 T. Parmesan. Continue stirring until melted. Place in a casserole dish or four individual dishes and sprinkle with remaining cheese and cracker meal. Bake in a very hot oven under broiler until golden brown. Serve with rice or green vegetables.

As the area developed, so did the number of restaurants and their offerings. Those restaurants, which could be remembered and documented, follow.

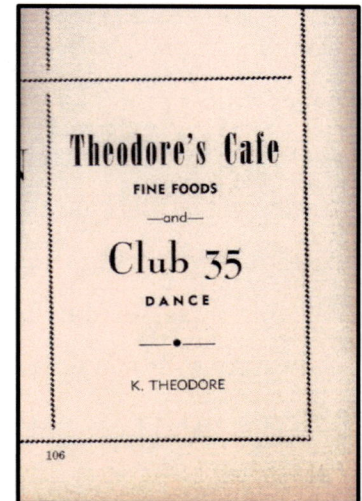

**Theodore's Cafe**
FINE FOODS
—and—
**Club 35**
DANCE

•

K. THEODORE

106

At the Foodways Exhibit, this lady (L) was
proud to have worked at both Corky's and Kline's.

IT'S A . . . . .

**WISE OWL**

. . . . . . *THAT KNOWS WHERE TO*
*FIND GOOD FOOD*

All The "Owls" Come To . . . . . .

**KANE'S CAFE**

—Seafood Dinners a Specialty—

Mrs. Arthur Kane     -:-     -:-     Proprietor

# Boiling Pot

By Karey Swartwout

Dot and her Boiling Pot Restaurant have been a legend in Rockport for decades.  Last week Dot passed away after a courageous battle with cancer. Ever her stoic self, not many folks around knew of her fight. But what is most amazing is that she has built something that carries on her legacy. Counting the dozens and dozens of times I have been to Boiling Pot, it has always been consistent.

Whether or not Dot is there, her crew exudes her attitude and belief system.

You must be passionate about what you do. You must care about people and give them the attention they deserve for walking into the establishment. You must deliver their order quickly. Make them want to come back for more. And smile, smile, smile!

Her steamed seafood always had a bit of a spicy kick. This version is milder, but still embodies the *Boiling Pot Spirit*. For local influence, I have added a bit of smoked wild boar sausage and Sriracha garlic butter for dipping the juicy crawfish and shrimp. For the full Boiling Pot experience, serve this on sheets of butcher paper alongside little plastic cups filled with lemon wedges and water for sticky fingers.

We will miss you, Dot.

**Sriracha Garlic Butter**
2 sticks of butter
2 tablespoons chopped garlic
1 tablespoon sriracha hot sauce
Squeeze of lime juice

Combine all ingredients into a small pot. Cook over medium heat until butter starts to foam. Reduce heat and keep on low heat for about 2 more minutes. Add lime juice to taste and serve immediately. Makes 1 cup.

**Seafood Boil Seasoning**

4 tablespoons mustard seeds
2 tablespoons whole allspice
1 teaspoon whole cloves
8 bay leaves

3 tablespoons coriander seeds
2 tablespoons dill seeds
1 tablespoon crushed red pepper flakes
6 cloves garlic

Combine all ingredients well, crushing slightly. Place all on a cheesecloth square, and tie securely into a bundle. Add the seasoning bundle to a large pot of boiling water along with about 4 tablespoons salt. Let it boil for about 5 minutes before adding the seafood.

### Boiled Shrimp and Crab with Wild Boar Sausage, Potatoes and Corn
Serves 12

5 lbs. baby red potatoes          3 lbs. wild boar sausage, cut into 1 inch pieces
8 ears fresh corn, shucked        5 lbs. whole crab, broken into pieces
4 lbs. fresh shrimp (or crawfish if in season)
1 tablespoon seafood seasoning
(See recipe below or you can use Old Bay Seasoning), or to taste

Heat a large pot of water over or medium-high heat. Add seasoning to taste and bring to a boil. Add potatoes, and sausage, and cook for about 10 minutes. Add the corn and crab and cook for another 5 minutes. Add the shrimp and cook for another 3 or 4 minutes. Drain off the water and pour the contents out onto a table covered with paper. Grab a beer and start peeling!

# Campus Drive In

Mr. and Mrs. Carlton owned the Campus Drive In. Steve and Priscilla, their children, both worked there. Located at the present-day Whataburger (Highway 35 and Buc Drive), Campus Drive In was near and dear to the hearts of all high school kids. Within a block of the school, favorites included fried chicken and onion rings. Mrs. Carlton, Steve's mom, had a special recipe for these delectable favorites.

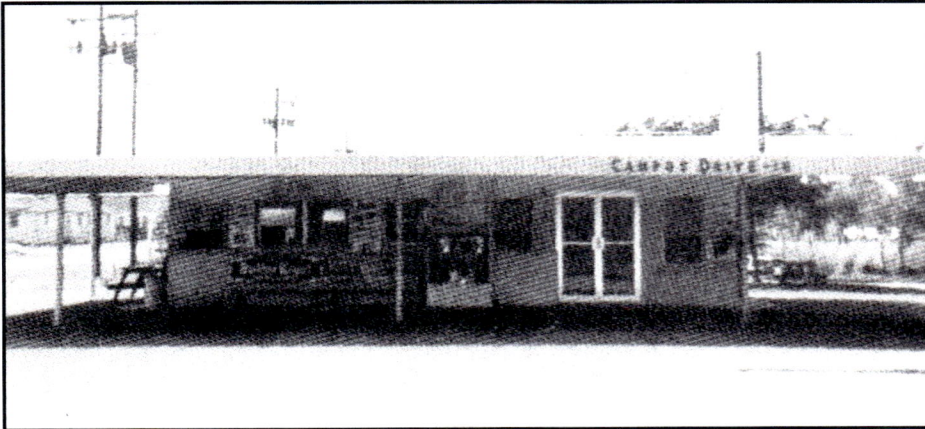

Campus Drive In for Greasy Gravy Drenched French Fries

## Campus Drive-In Batter for Onion Rings or Chicken

Ice cream (Melerine) powder

Eggs    Flour    Cream or milk

Make a batter and dip in onion rings or chicken. Fry until crispy.

262

# Charlotte Plummer's Seafare Restaurant

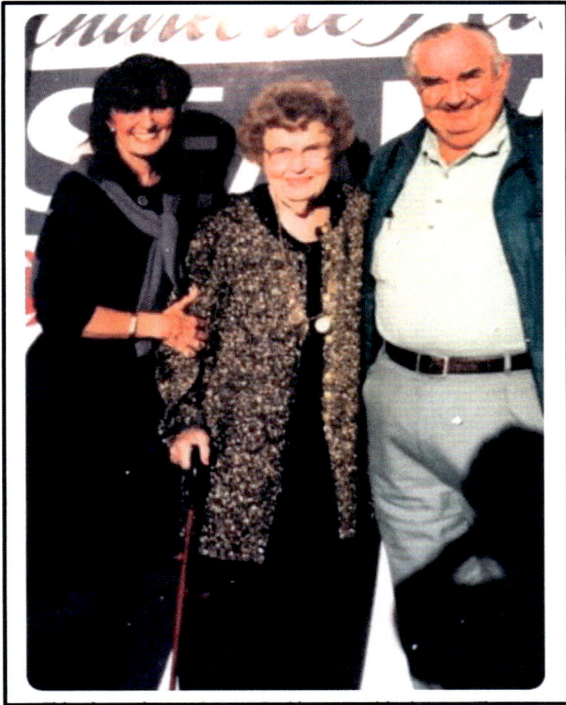

Tina, Charlotte and Al Plummer, Jr.
Courtesy of Junie Plummer

Several restaurants have been located at the site of Charlotte Plummer's (Fulton Beach Road and Cactus St. in Fulton) since the turn of the century including the Yacht Haven Cafe. Charlotte Plummer's Seafare Restaurant opened in the mid-1970s. At that time, the restaurant consisted of only the front section of the main floor and a screened porch.

According to her granddaughter, Junie, on Charlotte's bucket list included living on the coast and owning a restaurant. Charlotte Marie Heinen Plummer was from a family in Kerrville, who owned funeral homes. At the funeral home, she oversaw flowers and hair. She was a mother to three children. She lived on Key Allegro and owned a liquor store. She loved living in Rockport and taking care of people.

Customers loved her dishes of fresh seafood, and waiting lines stretched around the block so a dining room was added to the back in the late 1970s.

On a trip to Disney World pulling an RV, Grandpa Al, was driving and Grandmother Charlotte was in the trailer reading magazines and "eating bon bons". Junie looked out the back window and she exclaimed, "Grandma's going the wrong way!" Sure enough, the trailer had come unhitched. When they got back to the trailer that had landed in a field, she was outside with "stuff" all over her face and exclaimed, "Al, Sr., are you trying to kill me?"

In 1983, Charlotte sold the restaurant to Bob Lily of the Dallas Cowboys. In 1995, Craig Griffin purchased the restaurant. Since then, the upstairs dining room, deck, bar and waiting room have been added. Lines of diners are still seen waiting to order their favorite seafood dish.

Courtesy of Maria Nesbit

Charlotte Plummer's

RESTAURANT ON FULTON HARBOR

YOU'LL LOVE OUR FRESH SEAFOOD

# Cheez's

In 1988, Charles Cosby along with his daughters, Melissa and Patricia, opened a small café, specializing in home cooking, in their home in Fulton, Texas. The restaurant was called *Cheez's* because that was Charles' nickname. His "real down home" recipes were taken from family ones as well as those Charles concocted. Patrons, usually the working class, conversed while the daily offerings were prepared just like "home".

Every morning Charlie made hot biscuits the size of saucers. The local

**CHEEZ'S CAFE**

-"Cheez" Cosby with daughter Melissa-

**St. Patrick's Day Seafood Platter Special**

Your choice of Seafood combination, choose from:
Jumbo Shrimp, Popcorn Shrimp, Fried Flounder,
Softshell Crab & Fried Oysters.
Served with French Fries, Cole Slaw, Drink and Peach Cobbler for dessert...

**$6.95**

Courtesy of Melissa Cosby Pina

workers arrived daily for lunch. Specials, often determined by the patrons, might include pork

---

**PoPo's Chicken & Dumplings**

| | |
|---|---|
| 1 whole chicken | 1 cup Crisco |
| 1 medium onion, chopped | |
| 3 cup Flour | 1 carrot, diced |
| Salt & Pepper | 2 stalks celery, diced |

Put chicken in stock pot and cover with water. Add onion, carrot, celery and salt & pepper. Bring to a boil and reduce heat and simmer till tender. Remove chicken from pot; set aside to cool. Bone chicken remove skin and shred. Reduce stock in pot and bring to a boil. Make a slurry from 1 T flour and cold water. Pour into the stock to thicken. Add 1 cup of milk and stir. Drop the dumplings into the stock a few at a time and stir gently. When all have been added to stock, add the shredded chicken, stir, cover and remove from heat. Let stand for 15 minutes before serving.

*Dumplings:* Blend together 3 cup flour, 1 cup Crisco, 1 t salt. Add small amounts of cold water until the dough forms. Roll out on a floured board 1/8 to ¼ inch thick. Cut into 1 ½ inch strips. Then cut each strip into 2-inch lengths. Add slowly to stock pot.

---

chops and fried cabbage, chicken and dumplings, country fried steak with gravy, pot roast and veggies or whatever Cheez felt like cooking that day. "Seconds" were served from the kitchen. If a patron needed a refill, he had to refill other patrons' cups too, Just Like Home.

At Cheez's, diners could see wall-sized historical scenes of Aransas County including the 1889 Courthouse, Del Mar Hotel and the Fulton Mansion painted by Charles and B. J. Redfern. As a painting contractor, he worked on landmarks like the Sea Gun and Racquet Club until his retirement in 1994 due to his health. After a critical illness, Melissa, his daughter, gave him a set of watercolor paints and paper. He became a self-taught artist specializing in historical buildings and lighthouses along the Texas Coast.

## Corky's

Cora Robb, A WAVE, received her honorable discharge in 1943 at the Corpus Christ Naval Base as a AMMI 3rd class (Aviation Machinist Mate – Instruments). She was stationed at the Naval Air Station in Corpus Christi where she repaired the gyrocompass for the automatic pilot in Navy aircraft. As soon as her recently discharged fiancé, Denver Agler, could join her, they were married in 1943 and moved to Rockport. They opened a small café in 1947 adjacent to the Rockport Boat Basin (Sea Shell Shoppe) and named it after Cora's nickname – Corky's. The restaurant was built by GIs after being discharged.

Denver and Corky moved from one Rockport location to another to meet the needs of their customers, building bigger and better. Finally, they had a

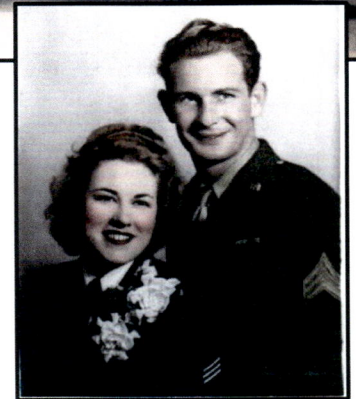

large restaurant on the west side of Austin Street, a little north of Market. Corky's Restaurant was an Aransas County institution for many years.

Her restaurant evolved into a well-known family restaurant specializing in seafood and a "Tasty Meal with Appeal."

"Corky" was a nurturing woman, sensitive to the needs of others. Community, school, and church organizations knew they could count on Corky to help with any "food service" needs in Rockport. Kam Wagert, Veronica Camehl, and Junie Ledbetter worked for Corky in the summers. When someone ordered a beer, they had to get an older waitress to serve it due to their age.

Veronica recalls that while working at Corky's, she had the pleasure of waiting on Connie Hagar and her companion Dr. Leonard Goldman, local dentist and dashing man around town. The more experienced waitresses had told her about them, so Veronica was prepared for their "routine". They perused the menu for several minutes, but the order was always the same. He always ordered for

---

**Corky's Green Onion Salad Dressing**

| | |
|---|---|
| 2 c. white vinegar | 1 c. vegetable oil |
| 2 bunches green onions | 1/8 t. garlic salt |
| 1 T. celery seed | ½ t. salt |
| ½ t. pepper | ½ t. seasoned salt |

Combine all and refrigerate at least 24 hours. Courtesy of Kam Wagert, who watched the cook make it while working there.

---

her...."Mrs. Hagar will have a grilled cheese sandwich with a slice of tomato and I would like a cup of the seafood gumbo. She would also like a beer in a regular mug, not chilled please." This had been going on for many years of Sundays and it was such a treat to see two people, who obviously enjoyed each other's company have this long-standing "date". Every Sunday, same time, same table...not sure how long this lasted as Veronica went on to bigger and better things at Johnson's Drug Store next door.

### Sandwiches

| | |
|---|---|
| Hamburger | .20 |
| Cheeseburger | .30 |
| Roast Beef | .30 |
| Bacon, Tomato | .30 |
| Grilled Cheese | .25 |
| Egg Salad | .25 |
| Tuna Fish Salad | .35 |
| Tongue | .25 |
| Ham | .40 |
| Steak | .50 |
| Combination Bacon, Egg, Tomato, three decker with French Fries | .50 |

### Steaks

| | |
|---|---|
| T-Bone | 1.25 up |
| Rib | 1.25 |
| Sirloin | 2.00 up |
| Round Steak | 1.00 |
| Hamburger French Fries, Salad | .75 |
| Order French Fries | .20 |

### Desserts

| | |
|---|---|
| Cake, slice | .10 |

### Drinks

| | | | |
|---|---|---|---|
| Coffee | .05 | Soft Drinks | .05 |
| Tea (Pot) | .10 | Milk | .10 |
| Iced Tea | .10 | Buttermilk | .10 |
| Lemonade | .10 | Hot Chocolate | .10 |
| Jumbo Lemonade | .15 | | |

### Breakfast

| | |
|---|---|
| Ham, Eggs, Coffee | .75 |
| Half Order Ham, Eggs, Coffee | .60 |
| Bacon, Eggs, Coffee | .65 |
| Half Order Bacon, Eggs, Coffee | .50 |
| Steak, Eggs, Coffee | .75 |
| Two Eggs, Toast, Coffee | .35 |
| Each extra Egg | .15 |
| Buttered Toast | .15 |
| Cereal, Milk | .25 |
| Cereal, Cream | .40 |
| Donuts | .05 |

### Soups

| | | | |
|---|---|---|---|
| Fish Chowder | .25 | Tomato | .25 |
| Crab Gumbo | .25 | Chicken Noodle | .25 |
| Vegetable | .25 | Cream of Pea | .25 |

### Cold Plate Luncheon

Salad (Ask)           Cheese
Young Roast Beef
Egg, Lettuce and Tomato Salad
Iced Tea or Lemonade
.75

### Salads

| | |
|---|---|
| Combination | .40 |

### Cocktails

| | |
|---|---|
| Shrimp | .75 |

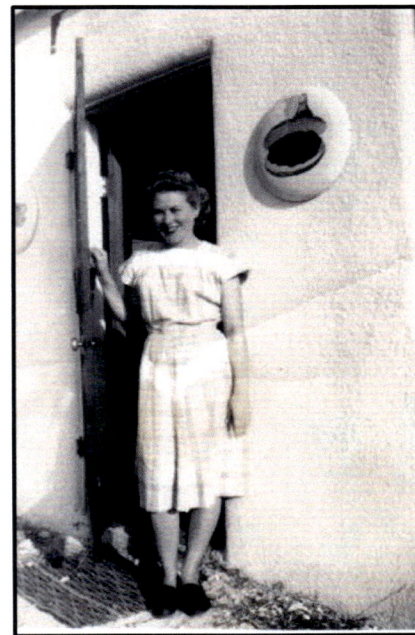

Photos from the Collection of the Agler Family

Corky (left) in the Surf Room of her restaurant on Austin Street. Estelle Stair painted the 12-foot mural shown behind her.

"A Tasty Meal == with Appeal!"

SEAFOOD OUR SPECIALTY
LUNCHEON SPECIALS DAILY
Also serving Steaks, Enchiladas
and other all-time favorites!

DOWNTOWN ROCKPORT

Winter hours 6 a.m. to 9 p.m.
Summer hours 6 a.m. to 10 p.m.
Closed Tuesday.

DELUXE SALAD BAR
DRAFT BEER & WINES
WE CATER TO WINTER
& SUMMER TEXANS

*Corky's* RESTAURANT

729-5161

513 S. AUSTIN          "Since 1947"          ROCKPORT

# 'Corky' honored at GreyFest

**By KAY GATHRIGHT**
*Features editor*

Cora Agler, known to many as "Corky" as owner-manager of Corky's Restaurant in downtown Rockport, was chosen as Outstanding Senior Citizen of Aransas County for 1985 during the third annual GreyFest held in Corpus Christi July 20-21.

Cora was awarded a plaque by Leonard Specht, representing Aransas County, at Memorial Coliseum on July 20, following a luncheon held at Trinity Towers to honor the outstanding senior citizens from each county in the Coastal Bend. "Uncle John" Leslie of Rockport was honorary master of ceremonies for the event.

To qualify for the honor, entrants were required to be 50 years of age or older, residents of South Texas and outstanding in the fields of work, community and organizational involvement, creativity and honors received.

Cora started her business in 1947 in the building currently housing the Sea Shell Shoppe by the Rockport boat basin, later moving to the present location of the Moonshell, and finally, to her current location on South Austin.

According to the application submitted on her behalf by the county offices, she not only works 12 to 16 hours a day, six days a week, but often works on her one day off, and has been very much involved in working with her employees. The application further stated that she does not ask any employee to do anything that she would not do herself.

Through her business and any other resources she can find, she has given jobs to "down and out" people, found them places to live and assisted in getting food stamps and other help for the needy, according to the application.

Cora has also regularly visited people in hospitals and nursing and convalescent centers and has taken care of many elderly people by performing such services as cleaning their homes, providing transportation for their doctor's appointments and taking them meals. When problems occur or tragedies strike, the application continued, she has been close at hand for many with a listening ear and moral support.

Her support has extended to Youth For Christ through the use of her restaurant equipment and to Lighthouse Christian School by supplying services and facilities for fundraising.

Cora has received awards of appreciation from the Order of the Eastern Star Chapter 479 of Rockport and various student organizations for her contributions.

Locally, she is a member of and contributes to the First United Methodist Church, the AARP (American Association of Retired Persons), the Order of the Eastern Star, the Rockport Art Assn., the Rockport-Fulton Area Chamber of Commerce and the VFW Auxiliary. She is also a member of the Texas Restaurant Assn., the National Federation of Independent Businesses and the Texas National Guard Auxiliary.

See CORKY, Page 3A

*Cora "Corky" Agler*

*Rockport Pilot Wednesday, July 24, 1985*

"At Corky's, order the all meat crab cakes, browned and lightly seasoned, the closest thing to genuine Maryland crab cakes the Texas coast has".

*Dividend:* Ask and ye shall receive vegetables from the daily plate-lunch specials – the turnips with greens are spectacular. Be sure and see the shag-carpeted pillars, a local motif. From the *Caller-Times*:

273

A few of Corky's staff:  Ginger (above);

Picture on right- Veronica (left), Junie (right)

# Dairy Whip

James "Jimmy" Henry Silberisen owned Dairy Whip and Jimmie's Hunting Club. Donna White Schott, Jimmy's granddaughter, shared that Dairy Whip was located at the corner of Liberty (Business Highway 35) and Live Oak Street, now an empty lot next to The Bakery. Jimmy's sister, Martha Jane Tanner, managed the business during the 1960s. After closing the business, the land was sold to Felix Solis, owner of Los Amigos, in the early 1970s.

**DAIRY WHIP**
DRIVE-IN

OUR SPECIALTY
MALTS - SUNDAES
HAMBURGERS - CHEESEBURGERS - BAR-B-QUE
FRENCH FRIES - ROOT BEER - SOFT DRINKS
CRAB-BURGERS & FISH BURGERS
CALL AHEAD YOUR ORDER

816
Liberty
Hwy 35

SO 4-2702

Food To
Go

If You Are Riding Around, Just A
Looking, Stop By & See What's
Cooking — Thank You

Photo courtesy of Donna White Schott

# Del Mar Grill

The Del Mar Grill offered "Dorothy's Famous Crab Cakes" and was the first home of the famous big blue crab, which overlooked the intersection of Austin and Main Street. It was a favorite restaurant of locals and tourists alike. Dorothy and Sal Silverman operated the restaurant from 1957 until it closed in 1965. As noted in the photo, it was in downtown Rockport next to Sorenson's Store later known as Estelle Stair Gallery.

Photo courtesy of Ruth Torres Hoese

## Dorothy's Famous Crab Cakes

1 small white onion finely chopped 2 eggs

2 T. butter divided        1 t. salt

1 t. Old Bay seasoning        2 t. lemon pepper

1/4 cup whole milk        1 lb. fresh crabmeat

1 T. spicy Dijon mustard        1/2 t. white vinegar

1 1/2 cup panko        pecans

1/2 cup finely chopped (Japanese bread crumbs)

For Spicer Cakes:

Add 1/8 to 1/4 tsp. cayenne pepper to egg/milk mixture

Sauté chopped onions with 1 T butter over medium heat until barely limp, about one minute. Transfer to a small bowl to cool. In medium bowl whisk milk, eggs, vinegar, Old Bay seasoning, salt and mustard until well blended. Add 1/2 cup bread crumbs, onions, and crabmeat and mix thoroughly. In a shallow bowl or pan mix, the remaining 1 cup bread crumbs, pecans and lemon pepper. Divide crab mixture into 8 equal piles and form cakes or use a measuring cup filling until almost full. Pack down into cup to form patties, dump and then flatten them lightly into the cakes. Cover the cakes in the bread crumb mixture. Place cakes on a large baking sheet covered with parchment paper, cover pan with plastic wrap and chill 2 to 4 hours. Preheat oven to 400° degrees Fahrenheit. Put about 1/2 teaspoon butter on each crab cake and bake around 20 minutes.

*from Dorothy Smith Krenek*

DEVILED CRAB BAKING SHELLS
SET OF SIX
BAKE
SERVE
STORE

*Guaranteed* HEAT RESISTING

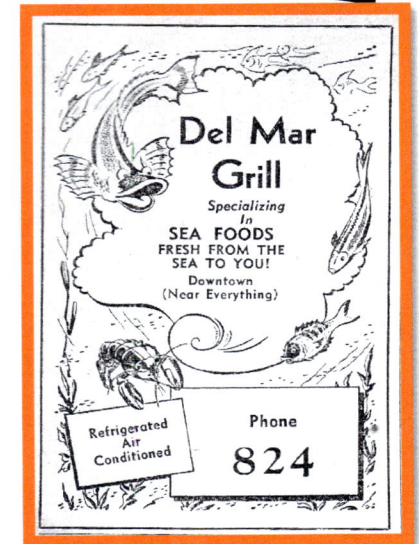

Del Mar Grill

Specializing In
SEA FOODS
FRESH FROM THE
SEA TO YOU!
Downtown
(Near Everything)

Refrigerated Air Conditioned

Phone
824

# The Story of the Big Blue Crab

The first home of the infamous Big Blue Crab once sat on top of Dorothy's Del Mar Grill. After the restaurant closed, the crab was sold to the R-F Chamber of Commerce in 1966 and moved to the Rockport Harbor. Many people had their pictures taken while standing beside it including Etta Sue Jenkins (next page). The crab survived Hurricanes Beulah in 1967 and Carla in 1970. By the late 1970s the crab had deteriorated and was laid to rest.

Photos courtesy of Jim Moloney

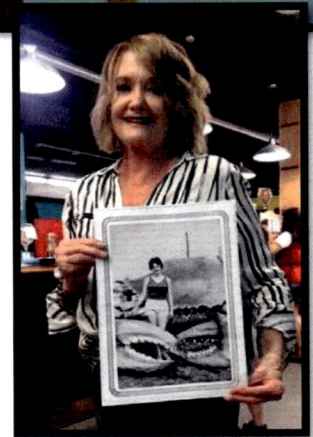

In 2005, residents revived the idea of replacing the big clue crab. A group of people raised more than $11,000 to have a crab rebuilt. This covered the materials and the labor was donated. In 2012, the 25-foot by 27-foot structure was constructed of fiberglass and aluminum and sat at the west end of the ski basin.

However, on August 25, 2017, when Hurricane Harvey stormed into the Rockport area, the beloved, big, blue crab didn't survive.

# Duck Inn

Opened in April 1946 by Charlie and Velma Ayers Duck, Duck Inn began as a hamburger and malt shop. Picnic tables were set up on an oyster shell foundation and palm fronds supplied the shade. As Mrs. Duck began expanding the menu to include seafood dishes. Mr. Duck enlarged the building. Vendors, known to Mr. Duck, supplied all the fresh seafood.

The restaurant was opened for seven months a year. The other five months, the Ducks spent in Mexico. Burt Mills, a subsequent owner, once asked Mr. Duck how he was able to close the restaurant for five months of the year. Mr. Duck replied, "We don't have children".

In 1960, Herb and Melba Mills along with Ed and Maurine Barnard purchased the restaurant.

With Ed's passing in 1968, Maurine continued to manage the restaurant until 1971.

Upon his discharge from the US Air Force and returning to Rockport, Burt and Penny Mills

Courtesy of the Corpus Christi Public Libraries

joined his parents and began learning the restaurant business with the help of seasoned employees.

Before hosting and managing, the Mills had to learn to bus tables and wash dishes before moving to work at the salad table. Then came the prep table and the cook's position to master before heading to the front door to greet guests.

Burt once asked Mr. Duck, "How do I run this restaurant and be successful like you were?" Mr. Duck replied, "All you have to do is serve the good quality food that Duck Inn is known for at a reasonable price and everything will work out fine."

Using those words of guidance, Penny and Burt operated the restaurant for the next 38 years. They

DUCK INN
Restaurant
701 Broadway (Hwy. 35)
Across From Ski Basin
Rockport, Texas
729-6663

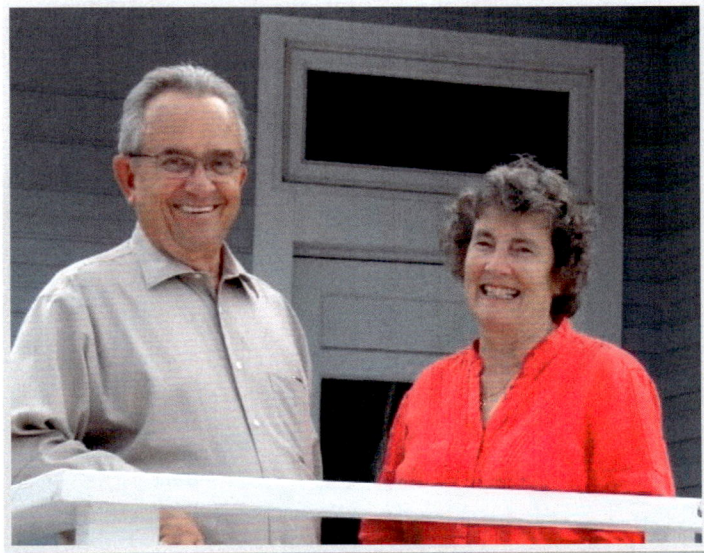

Burt and Penny Mills

closed the restaurant in 2007, while it still had a large patronage including Dan Rather, George Strait and the owners of Rudy's Barbeque.

---

### Duck Inn's Crab Meat Casserole

| | |
|---|---|
| 3 oz. crab meat | Paprika |
| 2 oz. melted butter | Garlic powder |
| 1 tablespoon fresh lemon juice | |

Use an individual crab shell or oven-ready dish. Mix crab, butter and lemon juice, and place in casserole dish. Sprinkle lightly with paprika and garlic powder. Broil until butter bubbles and crab browns. Serves 1.

---

Duck Inn was a fun place with great fried shrimp and Burt's Black Bean Soup. Never did figure out that recipe. .....And he wouldn't tell.

# Fulton Mansion Restaurant

In 1952, J. C. and Evelyn May of El Campo purchased the Fulton Mansion. During this time, the Mansion was painted a *perky pink*. They had very ambitious plans: a restaurant in the basement, hotel rooms on the second and third floors, a cluster of period guest cottages on the grounds. Most of the grand design never materialized. The arc of palm trees they planted was visible until 2017 when Hurricane Harvey destroyed them as well as many oak trees.

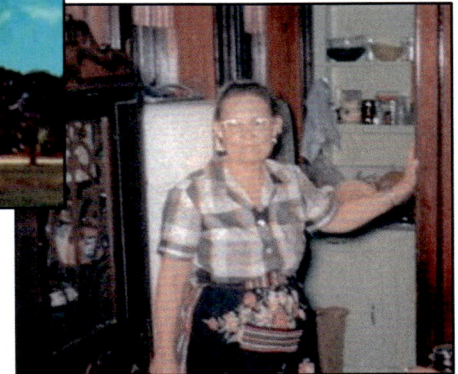

THE HOME OF FINE FOODS AND SOUTHERN HOSPITALITY

**FULTON MANSION RESTAURANT**

—SEAFOOD OUR SPECIALTY—

OWNED AND OPERATED BY
MR. AND MRS. J. C. MAY
FULTON, TEXAS

PHONE 6170          P. O. BOX 93

From the collection of Jim Moloney

**Evelyn May**

Photos Courtesy of The Fulton Mansion

## LAST CHANCE CHOCOLATE PIE
### (A Fulton Family Recipe)

Rich crust or crumb crust made with chocolate wafers

| | |
|---|---|
| 1 oz. melted baking chocolate | ¼ lb. butter |
| 1 tsp. vanilla | 3/4 cup sugar |
| 2 eggs | Whipped cream |

   All ingredients must be at room temperature. Use stationary mixer and cream butter very thoroughly and add the sugar, one tablespoon at a time. Beat 3 to 4 minutes when all the sugar has been added. Add eggs separately, beating 3 minutes after each addition. Continue beating the mixture until the sugar has dissolved and mixture does not feel grainy. Stir in chocolate and flavorings. Pour into the prepared shell. Chill at least 3 ours. Top with flavored whipped cream and shaved chocolate.

   This may not be an original recipe, but it is one Wilfreda Fulton Hoopes Foss made on special occasions and her friends who always begged for the recipe.

Linda Foss

According to Gary Merchant, the restaurant's tables were in the parlor, the room on the right upon entering. One of the clocks wasn't working so his dad, whose hobby was repairing clocks, repaired it. He also remembers the chocolate pie being delicious.

# Key Allegro Islander Club

On June 22-23, 1963, The Key Allegro Islander Club opened on the second floor of The Key Allegro Hotel. It had an exotic Polynesian theme.

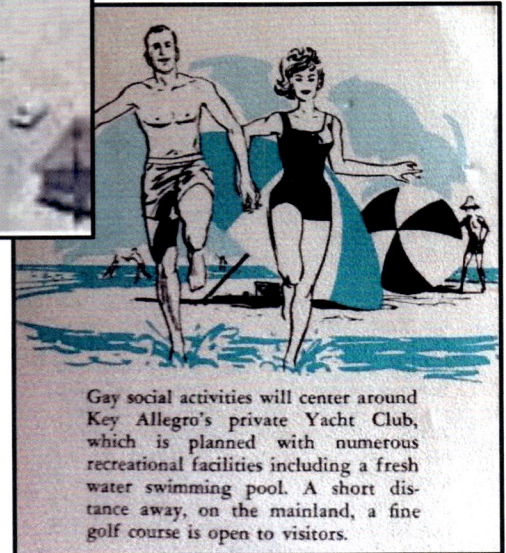

Gay social activities will center around Key Allegro's private Yacht Club, which is planned with numerous recreational facilities including a fresh water swimming pool. A short distance away, on the mainland, a fine golf course is open to visitors.

A favorite hors d' oeuvre at the Key Allegro Islander Club in the 60s was Angels on Horseback. The Club was upstairs, which slowed down the service, but somehow, they seemed to get those out fast. There surely must have been one of those angels on a young man's shoulder one evening when he plunged off the deck, fully clothed, into the bay water below. He survived and ordered another round - of oysters, that is!

---

**Angels on Horseback**

**Courtesy of Key Allegro Yacht Club**

| | |
|---|---|
| 1 ½ cup fresh oysters | ½ teaspoon salt |
| 8 slices bacon, cut into thirds | 2 tablespoon parsley |
| Dash of Paprika & Pepper | |

Drain oysters. Place an oyster on a piece of bacon. Sprinkle on parsley and seasonings. Wrap bacon around oyster and secure with toothpick. Place "angels" on broiler rack and broil about 4 inches from heat source for 5 to 10 minutes. Turn carefully. Broil another 4-5 minutes until bacon is crisp and oysters begin to curl at edges.

---

The Key Allegro Islanders Club

**Baked Oysters Mosca – Key Allegro Yacht Club**

The breadcrumb mixture is an Italian-flavored combination from Louisiana where the Mosca name is **lege**ndary in the epicurean world.

| | |
|---|---|
| 2 cup bread crumbs | ¾ cup olive oil |
| 1 cup Parmesan cheese | 2 lemons, juiced |
| 1 T. red pepper | 1 clove garlic |
| 3 T. parsley | 1 Quart oysters, drained |
| Salt and pepper to taste | |

Combine all ingredients except the oysters. Place oysters in a baking dish, ramekins, or shells. Top with breadcrumb mixture. Bake at 350° degrees until oyster's curl and the topping is slightly brown. If necessary, place under the broiler briefly until light brown. Be careful not to overcook.

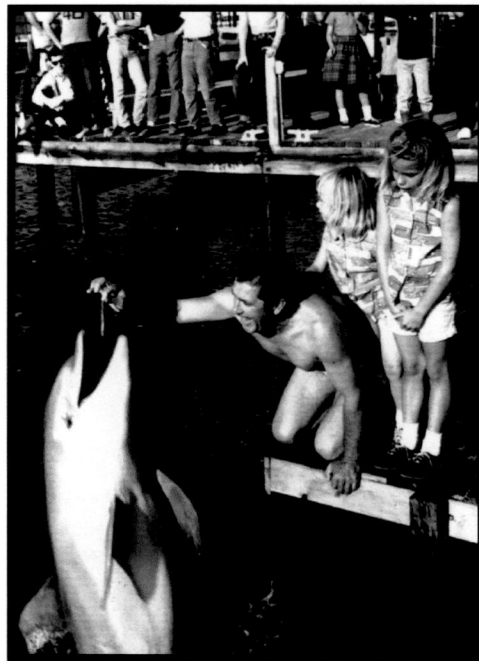

Carla Krueger (l)
Linda Krueger (r)
Courtesy of the Corpus Christi Libraries

## Baked Escargots by Key Allegro Yacht Club

Snail baking plates

Hot fresh bread for dipping

3 dozen canned snails   ½ cup olive oil

1 clove garlic, peeled and crushed

1 T. minced parsley      1 T. lemon juice

2 T. Parmesan cheese   ¼ cup garlic butter

1 ½ cup bread crumbs

Mix together breadcrumbs, lemon juice, parsley, olive oil, and garlic Drain the snails and pat dry. Place the snails in the snail baking plates with the breadcrumbs. Dot each with garlic butter. Bake at 350° degrees for about 10 minutes. Serves 4 to 6.

Courtesy of the Corpus Christi Public Libraries

Whether you dine in the snackbar, the motel dining room or the country club atmosphere of the beautiful **ISLANDER CLUB** ... every meal will be an exciting dining experience featuring excellent cuisine ... delightful service. Gay social activities center around the **ISLANDER CLUB** and fresh water swimming pool, and membership is available to property owners and motel guests.

The intriguing **TONGA SHOP**, on the motel grounds, offers colorful resort clothes, unusual gifts and various items for the forgetful traveler.

HANNAU COLOR PRODUCTIONS INC.
HOUSTON, TEX. AND MIAMI BEACH, FLA.
ROBINSONS COLOR PROCESS
PRINTED IN U.S.A.

290

ROCKPORT, TEXAS

**Your life's a holiday on**

**Key Allegro**
.ISLAND ESTATES

KEY ALLEGRO
ROCKPORT

**HOTEL**
**MARINA**
**ISLANDER CLUB**

Capt. Davis' Drive In

# Brocato's

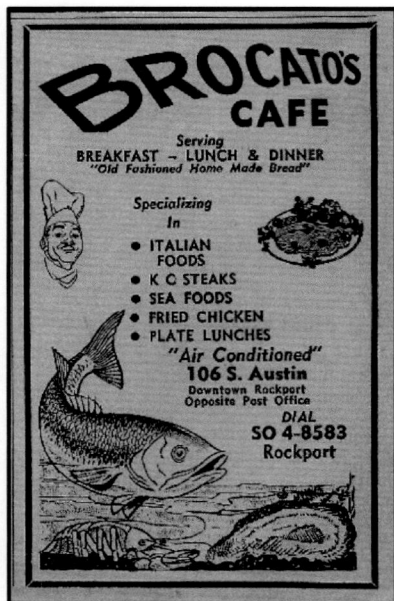

BROCATO'S CAFE
Serving
BREAKFAST → LUNCH & DINNER
"Old Fashioned Home Made Bread"

Specializing
In
● ITALIAN FOODS
● K C STEAKS
● SEA FOODS
● FRIED CHICKEN
● PLATE LUNCHES
"Air Conditioned"
106 S. Austin
Downtown Rockport
Opposite Post Office
DIAL
SO 4-8583
Rockport

A favorite eating spot since the 1930s, this café has been owned by several families. This eating establishment was founded by three Davis brothers. During the 1920s and 1930s, Marvin Davis established a coffee shop on Austin Street. He later added sandwiches. When liquor licenses were available, Marvin purchased one. According to Allen and Hasting-Taylor (1997), he owned the only liquor license in town except for the bootleggers.

Later Jack and Pearl Davis, Marvin's brother, took over the restaurant. They added a grill and sold hamburgers. After a while, Jack sold the establishment to Charlie and Molly Davis, another brother. The restaurant was then converted to a drive-in with car-hop service and it was called "Capt. Davis Drive-in"

A fire destroyed the building one night. Mrs. Molly Davis, the Captain's wife, asked A. O. Freeman, a former bridge builder, to rebuild the building. Freeman scoured the area and finally located a stockpile of shell crete building blocks. He used these in the reconstruction to withstand future harsh conditions. Today, the white stucco structure has survived as an example of art deco architecture on Austin Street. Later it was named Brocato's Café and later Kline's.

In 1963, H. R. "Shorty" Kline first leased the building from Mrs. Davis. Until his retirement in 1970, Shorty would arrive at the restaurant at 5:00 a.m., get the restaurant ready, and then drive to Seadrift where he worked as a pipefitter for Union Carbide. During this time, Gloria, his wife, would come in around 7:00 a.m. and work all day. After work, Shorty showered and went back to the café and closed the restaurant at 9:00 each night.

Kline's

Courtesy of Phyllis Kline

Kline's was a favorite morning gathering place for local businessmen for coffee and Mrs. Rinche's homemade pie. Daily noon specials were on the menu. The café was constantly busy. When asked about his favorite dish, Shorty replied, "Mexican Steak", a hamburger patty topped with onions, tomatoes and jalapenos", created by Pete, the head cook. Lights surrounding the top of the outside of the building often served as a landmark for fishermen and shrimpers as they worked during the night.

Shorty and Gloria Kline

*From a review in the Corpus Christi Caller-Times:*
"To experience the 'real', as opposed to the touristy, breakfast, go to Kline's, a great looking little place with curvaceous glass-block sides. Kline's is definitely a *social organism*. The tables fill up willy-nilly and gossipy buzz prevails. Coffee's good, as it must be in such an institution. The eggs over easy are faultless and the unorthodox *huevos rancheros* will knock your waders off. Fisherman's breakfast begins at five-thirty".

# Cornbread Dressing - With Chicken
## By Gloria Kline
### Courtesy of Phyllis Kline

**Ahead of time:**
- Cornbread – Bake a 11 x 13 pan of regular cornbread and crumble when cool.
- White Bread – Let ½ loaf of thin sliced white bread get stale and tear into very small pieces. (Fast way to get stale – lay slices on paper towel on counter for it to dry out.)
- 2 whole roasting chickens – remove giblets from inside chickens—boil whole chicken and giblets in lightly salted water until done.  Save water and add 2 chicken bouillon cubes.  If hens are skinny, add 2 or 3 Tablespoons butter or margarine to hot water and stir.
- Giblets – Finely chop and set aside (for gravy)
- 7 Eggs – Boil until hard.  Peel and chop--3 eggs in one bowl and 4 in another.
- 1 med. Onion chopped fine
- 4 or 5 stalks of celery chopped fine
- Salt and Pepper to taste

**Dressing:**
- In very large bowl or pan, mix together: crumbled cornbread, stale white bread pieces, chopped onion, chopped celery, 4 of the chopped hard-boiled eggs; add salt and pepper to taste (remember bouillon is salty)
- Slowly add chicken drippings water and continuously mix until entire mixture is evenly moist, but not wet.
- Put 2 chickens in large baking pan.  Surround chickens with dressing mixture. Rub a pat of butter or margarine on chickens.   If any leftover dressing, put in a separate shallow baking pan and bake together with chicken pan.
- Bake in 350 degree until dressing is done – dressing will be brown and crusty on top. Check frequently, but should take approximately 40-45 min.

**Gravy:**
- Heat Chicken drippings water over medium heat.  If not enough chicken drippings water, make bouillon water with 2 or 3 bouillon cubes.
- Add: 3 Finely chopped eggs, chopped Giblets, Salt and Pepper to Taste
- Use flour to thicken gravy.  (Remove cup of gravy, add 3-4 Tablespoons of flour, whisk to remove lumps, then stir slowly into large pot of gravy.)

Add small amount of yellow food coloring.

# Mary's Malt

Mary's Malt, originally operated as Dairy Malt in the 1940s-50s, was sold to Mary Kresta, who changed the name to Mary's Malts. Georgia Anne and Danny, her children, helped her make yummy burgers and unforgettable sweet treats. Many of the locals found themselves working there during the summers.

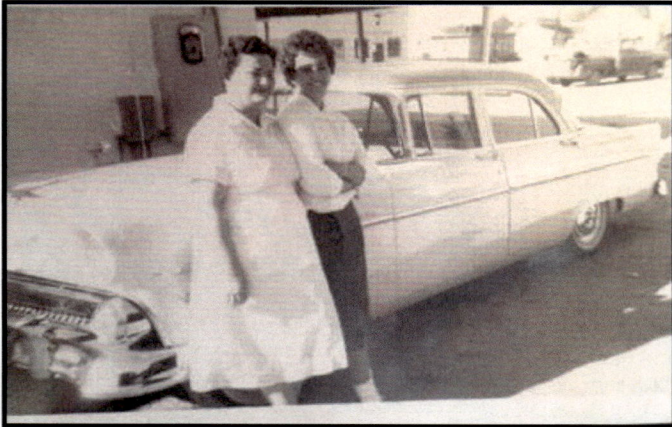

Mary Kresta and daughter, Georgia

Courtesy of Ruth Torres Hoese (right)

*Mary's Malts*

MARY C. KRESTA - Owner

• HAMBURGERS - MALTS & SHAKES
• MARY'S CUSTARDS - SUNDAES
Open 9 AM Till    7 Days A Week
FOOD TO GO
SO 4-2248
204 S. AUSTIN

•"I remember going to a drive in hang out in town…they had hamburgers, etc., but I remember always ordering my vanilla coke…anyone remember the name??"

•"Definitely Mary's Malts – I worked there and just about OD'd on cherry vanilla Dr. Ps!"

Courtesy of Mike Paul

# Mexican Influences on Local Cuisine

Like most of South Texas, Aransas County has been influenced by Mexican cooking traditions throughout its history. Delicacies from many regions in Mexico have had a place in local kitchens and restaurants, including barbacoa, cabrito, carne seca, fajitas, sopa de tortillas, aquas frescas, tamales, ceviche, migas, green enchiladas, carne guisada, and salsa. A Christmas Eve or New Year's Eve dinner would not be complete in many homes without a big platter of steamed tamales.

*Queens in the Kitchen*, the first cookbook compiled in Rockport in 1927 by the Parent Teacher Association, contained recipes for tamale loaf, Spanish rice, hot tamale pie, hot tamale loaf, chili and eggs, Mexican candy, Mexican Holyoke, and several for chili. It also contains an ad for The Sea Side Café which touted "Chili, a specialty"

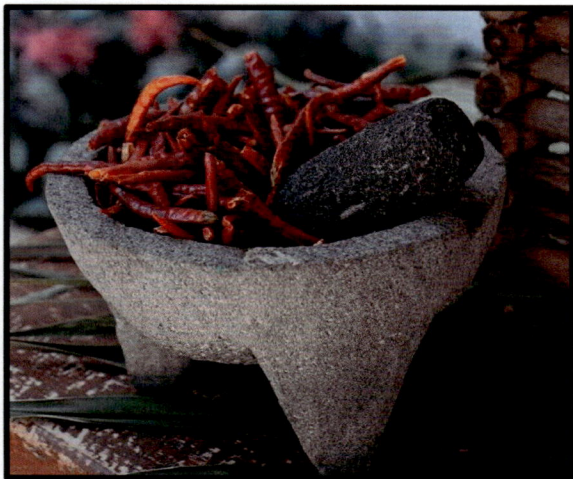

Staples in Mexican Cuisine are native foods, such as corn, beans, avocados, tomatoes, chili peppers, squash cocoa and vanilla. The Conquistadors introduced the idea of harvesting meat from domesticated animals.

with J. B. Clewis, as proprietor. Some local cookbooks contain Mexican sections such as St. Peter's Episcopal Church's, *Cooking with Love and Joy*.

Many non-Mexican restaurants also offered Mexican items on their menus such as enchiladas. Home cooks often used traditional Mexican bean pots in their kitchens.  The local Mexican community grew both healing and culinary herbs and vegetables like calabaza squash. They often made specialized preserves like pyracantha, prickly pear, mesquite or jalapeno jelly and then shared these with the rest of the community.

Early Hispanic families came up the coast from Brownsville and Port Isabel to make and repair fishing nets and built boats. Some would later transition to cooking in and opening restaurants of their own.

Katherine Sanchez shares her tamale-making skills with Steve Russell.  From the collection of the Abe Sanchez Family.

# Carne Guisada

## by Monica Burdette

| | |
|---|---|
| 3 lbs. boneless chuck roast or steaks | ½ teaspoon cumin |
| 4 tablespoon vegetable oil, divided | 1 teaspoon salt |
| 1 onion, chopped | ½ teaspoon pepper |
| ¼ cup green pepper, diced | 1 – (8 oz.) tomato sauce |
| 2 cloves garlic, peeled, smashed, minced | water to cover |
| 2 cups diced potatoes | ½ cup all-purpose flour |
| 1 cup cool water | |

Cut roast or steak into 3/4" cubes; set aside. Heat 2 Tablespoons of oil in Dutch oven over medium-high heat. Add onion and bell pepper; sauté until onion is translucent for approximately 5 minutes. Add garlic and sauté 1 minute. Remove onion, bell pepper, and garlic from pan; set aside. Heat remaining oil in Dutch oven and braise prepared meat in hot oil. Return onion and garlic to meat. Add cumin, salt, pepper and tomato sauce to pan. Cover over medium-high heat, stirring often until tomato sauce cooks down and caramelizes.

Add water to just cover the meat. Bring to a boil; lower heat, cover and simmer for about an hour or until meat is tender. Stir in diced potatoes and cook approximately 20 minutes, or until potatoes are tender. Thicken gravy by placing flour in a small bowl and whisking in water. Bring contents of Dutch oven to a low boil and slowly stir in flour and water mixture; cook just until thickened. Makes about 8 servings. Serve as main dish.

# Mexican Rice

In an iron skillet, saute 1 c. long grain rice in vegetable oil until brown. Chop ½ onion, 1 tomato and ½ green pepper. When rice is brown, add vegetables. Cook mixture until liquid form the vegetables have evaporated. Add garlic, cumin, salt & pepper to taste. Stir. Add 2 c. water, salsa and bring to a boil. When boiling, add lid to cover skillet. Turn heat to medium. Do not remove lid for 20 minutes. After 20 minutes, see if liquid gone. If not, cook longer. Fluff rice with fork.

Mary Molina

## Los Amigos

Felix and Candelaria Solis opened the Los Amigos Restaurant in 1969. This establishment brings back fond memories for many locals. Felix began working in the restaurant business when he was 11 years old washing dishes at the Del Mar Grill and was a cook and baker at Corky's before he opened his own place.

Almost every item on the menu, including the bread, was homemade. Los Amigos was especially well-known for the homemade chili and enchiladas as well as the chicken fried steak.

Photos courtesy of the Solis Family

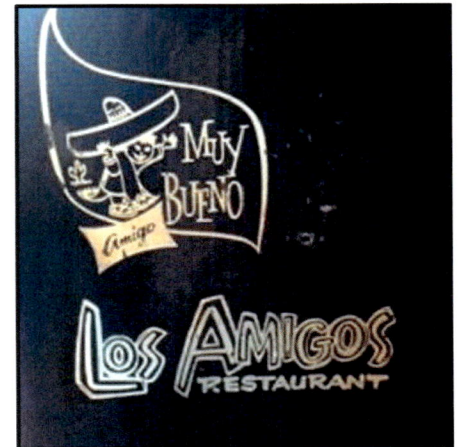

## Where I'm From

By Yvette Munoz Webb, Grandniece of Felix Solis

I am from flip flops, from Coca-Cola and pure cane sugar;

I am from flat roofs and tile floors smelling of Lysol on wash day;

I am from sea shells, live oak trees -windswept and gnarled;

I am from barbecues and long fingers, from Adelina and Amalia from Nava and Solis.

I am from laughter and cooking meals for everyone;

From "Don't slam the door" and "I'll give you something to cry about",

I am from incense and kneelers from Midnight Mass and Easter dresses.

I am from Texas and Mexico and Spain, tamales and BBQ ribs.

From the shrimp boats and oyster beds worked by uncles with the always ready shucking knives and hand tools of my grandfather.

I am from the cedar chest given to my mother, the first born, on her 18th birthday and all the photo albums kept by my grandmother keeping memories alive firmly tying us all together.

Una familia.

## Sylvia's Homemade Enchilada Sauce

By Sylvia Chavez

| 2 T vegetable oil | ½ t salt |
| 1/3 C flour | about 1 C water |
| 1 T chili powder | |

In a medium frying pan, heat oil over medium heat. Add flour, chili powder, and salt; stir to mix. Press down on flour mixture with back of spoon to break up; whisk in water, a little at a time until desired consistency. Let it come to a boil, simmer about 10 minutes, adding water as needed or chili powder as desired. Makes about 1 cup.

# Tony's

Tony Dominguez's family came up the coast from Port Isabel to make and repair fishing nets and build skiffs and boats. Tony remembers helping build the shrimp boat shown below.

From the Collection of Jim Moloney

Alicia and Tony Dominguez

From childhood, Tony remembers seafood soup, including fish head as an ingredient. When times were tough, his mother would fry fish eggs, or caviar.

After serving in the US Army, Tony began a cooking career in Rockport. Tony has served as many as 800 guests at one event including Washington dignitaries. John Sharp once dined at Tony's Restaurant in Rockport.

His cooking has raised money for scholarships or to pay medical bills for someone in need. In a cook off, his special recipe of cabrito, beef and chicken won the top prize. In the 1980s, many high school students remember having lunch at Key Allegro Marina where they often ordered Tony's Enchiladas. When ordering, they would be asked "with or without grass (lettuce on top)?"

Harold Phenix, artist
Courtesy of Carla Krueger Rinche

# Panjo's

For over 30 years, Panjo's has been an established gathering eatery in the area.  Originally, Panjo's was in the strip mall near today's Rockport Mail Center, the location of the movie theatre (1919 Highway 35 North). It was also associated with the Panjo's in Corpus Christi, which had a piano player, much like Shakey's at that time.

When Paul and Phyllis Fair, the original owners, sold the Rockport Panjo's to Jimmy Mac (McCorquodale), the recipes were also included. The menu hasn't changed much in 30 years.  Any changes have been due to not being able to access the necessary ingredients. For the most part, the menu's offerings have stayed the same. Only Linguine with Clam Sauce and Smoked Oysters have been replaced with Chicken Pasta Salad, Chicken Teriyaki, Chicken or Beef Kabob and the Loafer Sub.

Panjo's is the longest tenant in Harbor Oaks Shopping Center. In 1987, Panjo's doubled in size from 11 tables in 1500 square feet to today's 3,000 square foot restaurant. The restaurant stayed open throughout the renovation. Due to Harvey, Panjo's recently went under another.

The original dough roller is the same one used for that "one of a kind" pizza dough. Many part- and full-time residents as well as tourists find time in their schedule to drop in for a "pie" or a dish with those home-made noodles.

Jimmy Mac's goal is not to conquer the market, but to offer consistently good food in a family-friendly environment.

And then there's the "Free Beer Tomorrow" sign and a list of items which aren't available, which speaks to a special kind of humor.

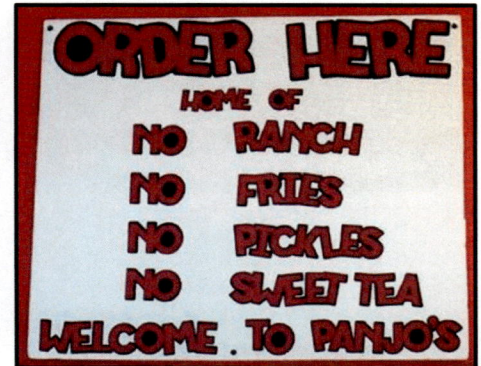

# Papa Gallo/Back 40 Restaurant

Chester "Sonny" Daniels, Jr. moved to Rockport in 1980 and began building homes in different subdivisions throughout the county. In 1985, he built the stucco building next to today's Linda S. Castro Birding Sanctuary.

During that same year, he commissioned Eduardo Jaramillo to paint murals depicting Taxco, Mexico, which accentuated the dining experience for Mexican Cuisine.

Jaramillo painted the scenes shown in the Papa Gallo Restaurant at 4061 N. Hwy 35 in Fulton. His skies, mountains, waterfalls and villages appeared three-dimensional to the viewer.

Jaramillo came to the United States in 1968 as Director of the Art Department of the Los Angeles Independent School District. Many of his murals and other paintings can be seen throughout Texas and northern Mexico.

The restaurant later evolved into The Back 40 Restaurant, which served more traditional American favorites. The diners continued to enjoy these special scenes even though the building changed hands several times over the ensuing years.

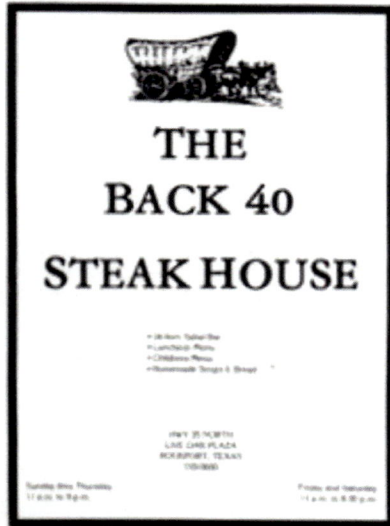

# Roaten's Drug Store

From the collection of Jim Moloney

Roaten's Drug Store was a pharmacy that also offered soda fountain treats. Local business people would frequently meet there for coffee. High school students would drop in for a quick lunch.

Shelley Roaten, pharmacist, commissioned Simon Michael, founder of the Rockport Fulton Art Colony, to have his students create a mural of local scenes. The mural hung behind the fountain.

The first location of Roaten's Drug Store was on the east side of Austin Street near Sorenson's Chandler. David Roaten, Shelley's son, shared that old comic books would be stored in a big box. Often, while reading the comics, he would fall asleep in the middle of them.

Above: Photo was taken in front of the Roaten's first location near today's Estelle Stair Gallery, the former Sorenson's Chandlery. David Roaten is standing in front of his good friend, Chris Sorenson. Courtesy of David Roaten.

*Prescriptions*

DRUGS — SUNDRIES
CANDIES — GIFTS
KODAKS & FILM

GREETING CARDS          PANGBURN'S CANDY
HELENA RUBINSTEIN        EASTMAN & REVERE
COSMETICS               MOVIE PROJECTORS

*Walgreen's* AGENCY DRUGS

Phone 3331

**ROATEN DRUG STORE**
PRESCRIPTION DELIVERY SERVICE

SHELLEY ROATEN                    ROCKPORT

While in high school, Kam Wagert (shown behind the counter) worked at the fountain as a self-proclaimed "soda jerk" at Roaten's Drug Store. If *mistakes* were made on a fountain order, then the order had to be remade and the *mistak*e had to be disposed of. Kam said that employees

Courtesy of Kam Wagert

could take home magazines and comic books, but they had to be returned in pristine condition. On the wall behind Kam, you can see part of the mural painted by Simon Michael's students. After Roaten's closed, the mural disappeared. Gail and David Roaten are still in search of it. The building now houses the Treasure Islander on Austin Street.

"We loved to go to Roaten's Drug Store. It was the only place you could pick up your prescriptions and get a chocolate shake at the soda bar. They had those nice stainless-steel stools."

"Gosh, that was the fun place to go. Get cokes and have fun with friends before or after the show that cost a dime to get in."

"Donuts with vanilla ice cream! What a treat!"

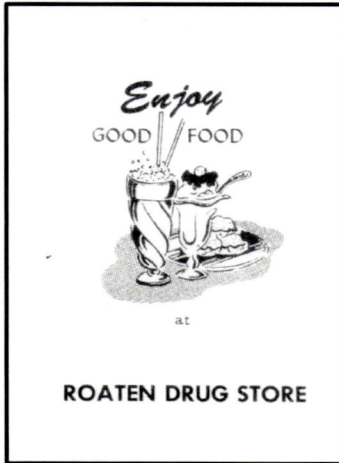

*Enjoy*
GOOD FOOD

at

**ROATEN DRUG STORE**

## Fountain Menu

Tuna Salad Sandwich
Hot Dog
Hot Dog with Chili

Milk Shakes –
Vanilla, Strawberry, Chocolate

Sundaes - Parfaits
Donuts

Peach, Lemon, or Cherry Dr. Pepper

# Sandollar Restaurant

Remembered as one of the only places for proms and class reunions, the Sandollar was where the younger set learned to tip the pianist. Inside the restaurant was a beautiful waterfall. The restaurant was located on the bluff behind the lower level motel rooms. From the restaurant, you had a beautiful view of the bay.

### Rockport Red Sauce

1 cup Chili Sauce    3 T lemon juice

1 T horseradish    3 drops Tabasco sauce

½ t. celery salt    1 t. salt

Combine all ingredients well and chill.

Makes approximately 1 cup sauce.

Courtesy of Ann Hegen

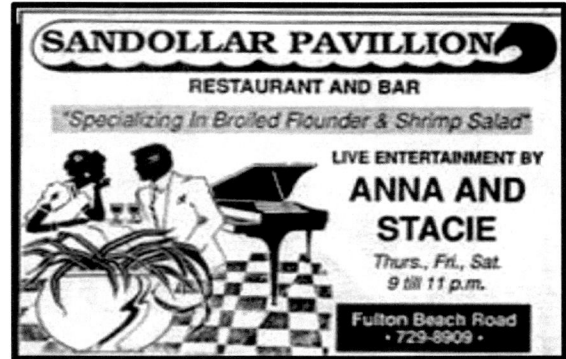

SANDOLLAR PAVILLION
RESTAURANT AND BAR
"Specializing In Broiled Flounder & Shrimp Salad"
LIVE ENTERTAINMENT BY
ANNA AND STACIE
Thurs., Fri., Sat.
9 till 11 p.m.
Fulton Beach Road
· 729-8909 ·

Sandollar Restaurant
HWY 35
ROCKPORT'S NEWEST AND FINEST
THE ULTIMATE IN DINING PLEASURE AT THE
STUDIO CLUB WITH THE EXOTIC WATERFALL
5 A.M. TO 12 P.M. WEEKDAYS
SATURDAYS TILL 1 A.M.
Banquet & Party Facilities Available
Up To 350 Guests
DIAL
SO 4-5368
FULTON BEACH

From the collection of Jim Moloney

# Schrenkeisens'

"It's too bad that Corpus Christians must travel 45 minutes up the coast to sample fine, innovative dining. Family run and reminiscent of a small country inn, Schrenkeisens' has a menu that is a shining example of what is being called the new haute American cuisine – a blend of the techniques of continental cookery and down-home ingredients. Two of the best dishes are the chicken breast and Smithfield ham in a flavorful mushroom and Swiss cheese sauce and, even more characteristic, a meltingly tender Cornish game hen braised in a casserole of fresh vegetables.

Appetizers and side dishes are equally well executed. For dessert, we tried apple crepes *flambé* topped with crème Chantilly-sort of a French version of good old American apple pie. Soft piano music played in the bar. Definitely worth the drive". Review from the *Caller Times*.

**The Schrenkeisens'** restaurant and bar

EXTENSIVE MENU INCLUDING
Fresh Delicacies from Local Waters, Prime Chicago Beef, Baby Wisconsin Veal, Colorado Lamb . . .

SOUTH TEXAS' LARGEST WINE CELLAR —
Including Some of the World's Great Vintages.

Special Sunday Brunch

LUNCH 12—3     BAR OPEN 12—12     DINNER 6:30—10
PIANO BAR
FULTON BEACH ROAD, FULTON, TEXAS
Reservations: **729-3332**

## Crab Meat Pegi

| | |
|---|---|
| 1 oz. white vermouth | 2 t. lemon juice |
| 3 oz. heavy cream | 2 T. butter |
| White pepper | 1/8 t. roux |
| ½ lb. white crab meat | Salt |

Melt the butter in a saute pan; add vermouth, heavy cream, lemon juice and heat to simmering. Add crabmeat and heat through. Add salt and pepper to taste and roux to thicken. Serve over toast rounds.

The corner of Fulton Beach Road and Broadway has been the home of Peg Legs in the 1950s, Schrenkeisens' in the 1970 and now Benchwarmers.

## Stuffed Flounder

| | |
|---|---|
| 4 large flounder | Garlic salt |
| 12 oz. fresh, cooked crab meat | 1 T. Worcestershire sauce |
| 12 oz. minced shrimp | 1 T. Tabasco sauce |
| Lemon pepper | Juice of two lemons |
| Celery salt | Butter |
| Lawry's seasoned salt | Parsley |
| Onion salt | Paprika |

Preheat oven to 325 degrees. Cut the flounder down the center on the white side. Cut under both sides with slit of ½ inch deep. Fill with cooked crab meat and minced shrimp. Sprinkle with next seven seasonings. Pour juice of 2 lemons over flounder. Dot with butter over top of fish. Sprinkle with parsley and paprika for color. Cook for 25-35 minutes.

**Sea·Gun SPORTS INN**

SPECTACULAR **OPENING TODAY** AUGUST, 11

**Sea·Gun SPORTS INN**

**For the SPORTSMAN!**
and fun loving families

**A Sportsman's Paradise in Sun, Sand, Sea Adventure.**

**FISHING** — Fishing's fun . . . double fun when you make big catches! Fishermen who know where the fishing's good . . . come to the Sea-Gun Sports Inn. Trout, redfish, flounder are thick in these parts . . . the best fishing on the Gulf Coast.

**HUNTING** — Waterfowl . . . Duck and goose hunters are lucky . . . and smart . . . in selection of the Sea-Gun as a hunting base. This is a famous waterfowl area. Complete hunting service, including blinds, boats, decoys and guides, are available at a reasonable rate.

**DEER HUNTING** — Go the Coast for deer? Sure. This is something new. Sea-Gun guests hunt deer on Matagorda Island during the season. You don't go home empty-handed. You hunt until you get a buck. Ask about deer leases and the Special Sea-Gun Deer Hunting "package."

**MILL'S WHARF & MARINA** — Mill's Wharf long ago gained recognition as the South's most prominent hunting and fishing club . . . now offering Sea-Gun guests the finest facilities and services on the coast. Bait, tackle, rental equipment, luxury cabin cruisers with experienced guides. And there's no finer marina . . . Humble offers complete marine automobile service. Here is complete marine service . . . covered stalls for all sizes boats and cruisers.

ACCOMMODATIONS:

RESTAURANT:

PRIVATE CLUB:

RATE SCHEDULE

**Your Sports Host On The Coast—SEA-GUN INN**

O. S. Brumley initially managed the 6,000-square foot restaurant and Reef Club. The structure was designed with a South Sea flavor, which blended in with the location on the bay front. The restaurant, specializing in all types of sea food and steaks, seated about 140 people. Just inside the main entrance hung a 30-foot mural of the coastline depicting Aransas, Copano, Mesquite and San Antonio and San

Courtesy of Kay Barnebey ©

Antonio Bays. The picture windows allowed the diners to view the South Seas Garden. The restaurant was open from 5 a.m. until 11 p.m. daily.

Jerry Ledbetter was the manager of Sea Gun between 1963-1965. His daughter, Parkie, remembers the wonderful summers eating at a great restaurant, going to Mills Wharf, watching summer movies on the lawn, fishing for redfish, the stagecoach that traveled from the Sea Gun to the Big Tree, and fireworks on the resort's lawn for July 4th.

Celebrities visiting the complex included Arthur Godfrey and Hoagie Carmichael. They were often found at the grand piano playing *Stardust*.

When "Flipper" was popular, dolphins were penned in between two fenced adjacent boat slips. And, it was fun to watch them.

*Memories from Parkie Ledbetter Luce*

## The REEF CLUB
### GUEST CARD

Rockport, Texas _2-10_ 19 _66_

This will introduce Mr. _Bigelow_
to whom the REEF CLUB is pleased to extend full guest privileges for a period of seven days from the above date.
Privileges to use the club's facilities was given at the request

of _____

No. _1_          Room No. _110_

Mgr

Gen-18

### it's fabulous . . .
#### Sea Gun's Sunday Gourmet Buffet
# PRIME RIB EVERY SUNDAY

Selections of Tantalizing
Seafoods—Meats
Salads · Condiments · Relish Tray
Vegetables · Homemade Pastries
Or Order From Menu

**Adults 2.50     Children 1.50**
**SUNDAY 12 NOON—8 P.M.**

## Sea Gun INN

Nine Miles North of Rockport, Texas, on Highway 35

Carmichael (r)

Godfrey (below)

Photos courtesy of Getty Photos

# Thompson's Spa

Myrtle and Benjamin Thompson founded Thompson's Spa. After the Depression, the Thompsons left Illinois and followed the Mississippi River in search of a better life. There she, her husband and son, Julian C., worked in hotels which served the upper class. In doing so, they learned culinary and presentation skills.

In 1932, Myrtle and her family prepared meals for the workers building the causeway across Copano Bay. After the causeway was completed, the Thompsons settled in Rockport and founded Thompson's Spa, or "Thompson's Oasis",

which was located at Liberty Street (Business Highway 35) and Austin Street.

According to Tommy Thompson, her grandson, Mrs. Thompson was flamboyant, which was evident in her food and presentation. Due to her training, tables were set with white tablecloths, and diners were dressed appropriately.

Thompson's SPA
*Menu*

NATIONALLY KNOWN FOR FINE FOODS

**SERVING · HOURS**

11:30 A.M. To 2:00 P.M. — 5:00 P.M. To 9:00 P.M.

SUNDAYS 11:30 A.M. To 2:30 P.M. — 5:00 P.M. To 9:00 P.M.

**CLOSED MONDAYS**

ESTABLISHED
1932
PHONE 3562
OWNED AND OPERATED BY THE THOMPSONS
**Rockport, Texas**

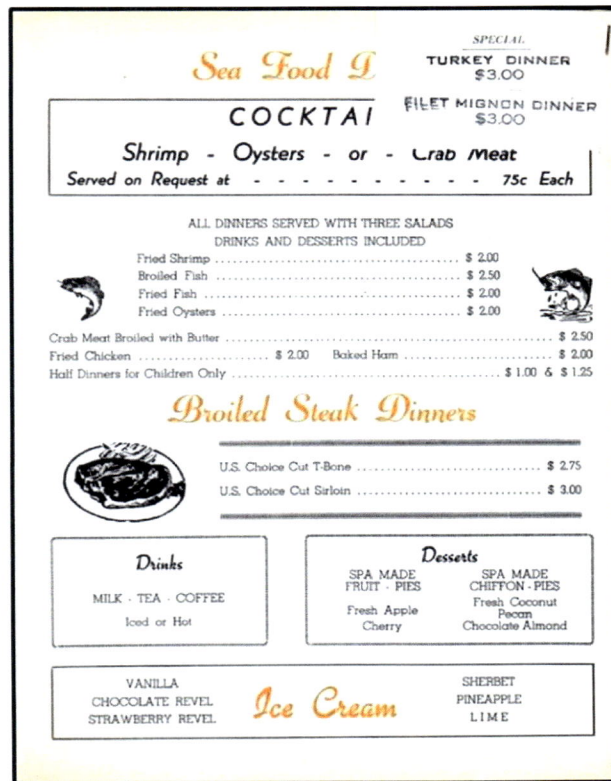

*Sea Food Q*

SPECIAL
TURKEY DINNER
$3.00

FILET MIGNON DINNER
$3.00

COCKTAI

Shrimp - Oysters - or - Crab Meat
Served on Request at - - - - - - - - - - - 75c Each

ALL DINNERS SERVED WITH THREE SALADS
DRINKS AND DESSERTS INCLUDED

| | |
|---|---|
| Fried Shrimp | $ 2.00 |
| Broiled Fish | $ 2.50 |
| Fried Fish | $ 2.00 |
| Fried Oysters | $ 2.00 |

| | | | |
|---|---|---|---|
| Crab Meat Broiled with Butter | | | $ 2.50 |
| Fried Chicken | $ 2.00 | Baked Ham | $ 2.00 |
| Half Dinners for Children Only | | | $ 1.00 & $ 1.25 |

*Broiled Steak Dinners*

| | |
|---|---|
| U.S. Choice Cut T-Bone | $ 2.75 |
| U.S. Choice Cut Sirloin | $ 3.00 |

**Drinks**

MILK · TEA · COFFEE

Iced or Hot

**Desserts**

| SPA MADE FRUIT · PIES | SPA MADE CHIFFON · PIES |
|---|---|
| Fresh Apple | Fresh Coconut |
| Cherry | Pecan |
| | Chocolate Almond |

VANILLA
CHOCOLATE REVEL
STRAWBERRY REVEL

*Ice Cream*

SHERBET
PINEAPPLE
LIME

And liquor was not allowed, except when the priest brought his wine to be served with dinner. "All you can eat was not advertised;" however, a sign stated, "Anything you want for $2.00" was posted. Instead of a cash register, a cigar box was used.

Mrs. Thompson also specialized in pickles, preserves and jellies. Her pickles went through seven solutions, were kept in 30-gallon crocks, and took a month without refrigeration to make. At one time, Heinz representatives offered her $100,000 for her pickle recipe. She declined.

John Wayne. Courtesy of Getty Photos

Her son, Julian C., "Judy," worked alongside his mother in the kitchen. Judy was a chef in his own right. He married Alice Marie Ballou from Rockport. In the early 1950s, he took his young family to Los Angeles, California where he supplied pies to famous restaurants like the Brown Derby. When a competing company began undercutting his prices, he returned to Rockport.

John Wayne brought his yacht to Rockport and docked here several days. During that time, he and his friends dined at the Spa after regular hours. Edgar G. Robinson was an annual visitor

Robinson (left), Courtesy of Getty Photos

When Ben Thompson retired, Judy bought the restaurant and continued the same traditions as his parents. His children also helped in the restaurant.

Regular customers, residing in Aransas Pass, Victoria and Corpus Christi, would drive to Rockport to eat at the restaurant. These included the Lichtensteins, the Cantwells, the Tandies, the Means, and the O'Connors.

Judy and Tom O'Connor were also great friends. Judy believed that the diners always felt welcomed because they visited the kitchen especially when he was cooking. He loved people and always made time for them.

Judy also created different types of hot sauce and cocktail sauces. During the holiday seasons, customers purchased boxes of jellies, preserves and sauces for gifts.

Judy was approached by HEB Grocers to purchase the recipe for his sauces. They wanted to put an HEB label on the jars. Judy Thompson said that if the label didn't have his name, then he wasn't interested. Thompson's Spa served diners in Rockport at the same location until the mid-1960s.

# Adventures in Good Eating

Duncan Hines, traveling salesman and future inventor of boxed cake mix, considered himself an authority on hot coffee, good food and ways to locate a tasty restaurant meal for under a dollar and a quarter. Through his search for the best restaurants across America due to his profession, he became an accidental gourmet.

Hines' appreciation for a good meal arose out of mere necessity. From the 1920s through the 1940s, he motored across the country hawking letter openers and paperclips, while subsisting on unreliable road food. Usually the names and locations of good restaurants were conveyed by word of mouth. For an out-of-town traveler, locating a decent dinner was challenging.

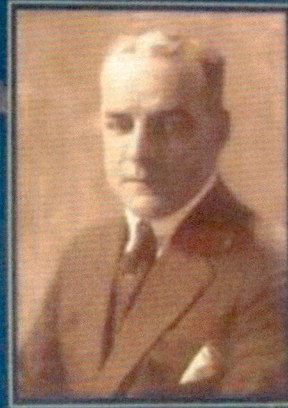

## DUNCAN'S BEGINNINGS

Based in Chicago from 1905, Duncan Hines sold printing services by traveling to clients. Going by train in the beginning, Hines purchased his first car in 1919 and enjoyed the freedom that the automobile allowed.

While on the road, Hines looked for local restaurants that "offered standout attractions in the culinary department."

Keeping notes on the restaurants he liked, Hines compiled a list of his 167 favorite restaurants. In 1935, he sent this list along with his Christmas cards, and everyone who heard about it wanted a copy. So, like any good salesman, Hines published the information in a book entitled *Adventures in Good Eating*.

Desperate for a clean place to dine, Hines became a self-made restaurant critic. He carried a tiny journal in his coat pocket, jotting down the precise locations of his favorite places. He noted the hours of operation, whether the restaurant had air conditioning, as well as the prices for breakfast, lunch, and dinner.

As word spread about his list of restaurants among his family and friends, people pleaded with him to share his list of eating establishments. His first list of recommended restaurants was mailed to family and friends in 1935 in a Christmas card. It contained 167 restaurants across 33 states.

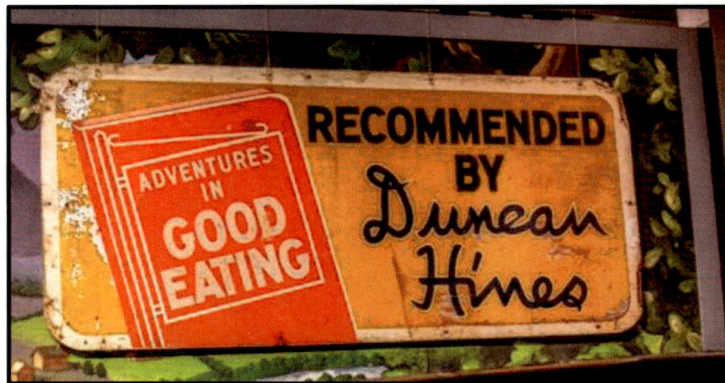

Soon salesmen and other travelers began seeking his recommendations. In 1936, Hines self-published his first edition of *Adventures in Good Eating,* selling for $1 each. At this time, the book listed the names and locations of 475 restaurants from coast to coast that had Hines' rigorous seal of approval. Because the books sold out quickly, the price was raised to $1.50.

---

**ROCKPORT, TEXAS**                    Thompson's Spa
*35—30 Mi. N. of Corpus Christi. Austin St. Open all year. 7 A.M. to 9 P.M.* Mrs. Thompson and her son do all the cooking. They specialize in sea foods, and their pies are something to write home about. Her sweet pickles are rare confections; you will want a few jars to take home. B., 50c; L., $1; D., $1.

From Adventures in Good Eating, 1941

Being "Recommended by Duncan Hines" became the gold standard in dining by the 1950s. Restaurants endorsed by Hines tacked up metal signs in their front windows.

In the Thompson's Spa advertisement, the restaurant claimed, "Nationally known for fine foods". That claim was realized as Thompson's Spa was listed in Hines' book, "Good Eating Places along the Highways of America".

---

### King Ranch Casserole

1 hen, cooked and deboned

2 c. grated American Cheese

1 dozen corn tortillas

1 onion, cut fine

1 can chicken soup

1 can cream of mushroom soup

1 can chicken broth

½ can Ro*Tel Tomatoes

Mix chicken soup, mushroom soup, chicken broth, and Ro*Tel Tomatoes together for sauce. Layer chicken, corn tortillas to line a 9 x 13 pan. Then ½ of onion and ½ cheese. Repeat for second layer with cheese on top. Bake 1 hour at 350°. Can be kept in refrigerator overnight and cooked the next day.

Vickie Merchant

---

# Vietnamese Cuisine and Customs Contributions to the Culinary Traditions of Aransas County

By Leah Oliva

During the mid-70s, Vietnamese refugees fleeing the communist regime in Vietnam were relocated to the Texas coast including Aransas

Courtesy of Leah Oliva

County. Climate and topography like Vietnam facilitated the adaptation of the new settlers, mostly Catholics. They had previously been professionals, government employees, agriculture workers, and craftsmen who became shrimpers and fishermen.

They demonstrated their strong entrepreneurial spirit by building boats, opening bait stands, and a grocery store, which still caters to the general public. Because the newcomers could not find some of the familiar ingredients of their cuisine, they began growing gardens with herbs and spices. A variety of mints, fish mint, perilla leaf plants and red chili peppers were commonly grown in addition to traditional herbs such as lemon grass.

The Vietnamese families brought a cuisine that is a sophisticated mix of French and Asian influences abundant in fresh seafood, spices, and

herbs. They also began sharing their cuisine with locals. Restaurants and food stands began selling Vietnamese platters with foods such as eggrolls as part of community celebrations such as Oysterfest and Seafair to fund activities at St. Peter's Catholic Church.

Years later their community of faith, St. Peter's Catholic Church, began hosting the annual

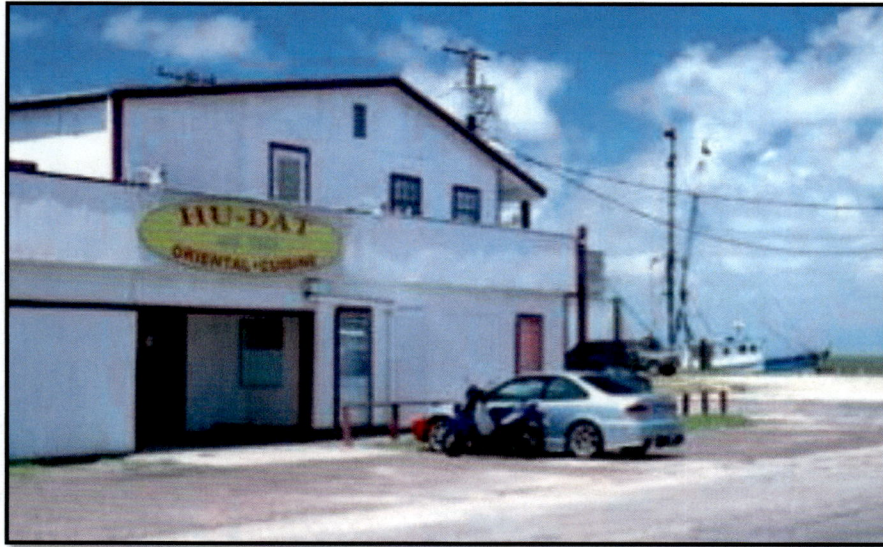

Dat Nguyen, the Texas A&M and Dallas Cowboys' football star. Dat Nguyen's family moved to the U. S. in 1975 after the fall of Saigon. After living in other parts of the U.S., the family relocated to Rockport in 1979. Dat's father and brother purchased shrimp boats and established a marine supply company. His mother would cook for the family and other shrimpers who would shop at the store, and that evolved into Hu Dat, a pun made from Dat's name.

Just as the community adopted spices and cooking methods from other cultures such as the Hispanic, locals now seek out this form of ethnic

Vietnamese New Year Celebration with samples of Vietnamese cuisine, while also celebrating the Vietnamese community's cultural heritage through dance, music and traditional clothing.

One of the first entrepreneurs opening a restaurant was the Nguyen family, which includes

cuisine. Many Vietnamese ingredients, such as rice noodles or rice paper for spring and summer rolls, are available at HEB. Vietnamese spring rolls have become as common as tamales and tacos for many celebrations in Rockport-Fulton.

Many are attracted to Vietnamese food, a mixture of French and Asian cooking, for its emphasis on healthy, fresh ingredients. Because healthy, fresh ingredients are stir-fried in small amounts of oil, vegetables are lightly cooked or served fresh. Vietnamese culinary customs, such as drying shrimp or fish in the open air on homemade wire frames, can often be observed next to local bait stands.

The Vietnamese-American emphasis on family and education has also resonated with the local community. As the Gulf Shrimping Industry has declined, many have opened businesses such as nail salons, earned degrees from higher education or pursued professional careers.

## Herbs and Spices used in Vietnamese Cuisine:

**Cilantro:** Used in salads, soups, spring rolls, and beyond. Widely used as the finishing touch garnish. Depending on your genetics, it might taste soapy.

**Mint:** Several varieties grow in Vietnam. Some are fuzzy. Some taste lemony, some spear minty, others are spicy.

**Fish Mint or Fish Leaf:** Appropriately named, this leafy herb has an awfully pungent smell and taste. Based on the smell, you'll think an actual fish is wrapped inside your spring roll. Instead it's just this sneaky leaf.

**Basil:** More popular in Thailand, but still makes an appearance in pho and on herb plates.

**Lime Leaf:** A bright, shiny green leaf; has a somewhat bitter oil.

**Lemongrass:** Tastes and smells like lemon. Used in both sweet and savory dishes.

**Green Onions and Scallions:** commonly used around the world.

**Garlic Chives:** Flat leaves with a delicate onion and garlic flavor.

**Perilla Leaf:** Green on top, purplish on the underside with a complex flavor that combines the taste of licorice, mint, and lemon in one leaf.

**Dill:** Hardly associated with Southeast Asian cuisine but used in a famous Vietnamese fish dish called Cha Ca, where it's treated more like a veggie than an herb.

**Turmeric:** Sometimes called *poor man's saffron*, it adds a vivid goldenness to fried foods and some peppery flavor.

**Ginger and Galangal:** Both knobby rhizomes; both pervasive in Vietnamese cooking.

**Saigon Cinnamon:** Indigenous to Vietnam, this cinnamon has a woody, earthy flavor and aroma and is important in pho.

**Tamarind Pulp:** The sweet-sour pulp is used in noodle soups and curries.

Chả giò Việt Nam

1 Ký thịt heo xay.
1 củ hành.
2 củ cà rốt cắt nhỏ.
1 Bó miến.
1 hột trứng gà.
1 Xấp bánh Tráng.
½ muỗng caphê muối.
½ muỗng caphê tiêu.

Cách làm:
Củ hành cắt mỏng.
Cà Rốt bào nhỏ.
Miến gầm nước nóng cho mềm, và cắt nhỏ.
Trộn tất cả lại (thịt heo, hành, cà Rốt miến, trứng, muối, Tiêu.).
Một miếng bánh tráng ♥
một muỗng thịt heo trộn, cuốn lại để chiên.

Recipe by Nghia Nguyen

333

# The Art of Food

Courtesy of Tommy Thompson

Courtesy of Elsa Mathews

# The Art of Food

The artists of the Rockport-Fulton Art Colony are connected with our culinary heritage in many ways. Its founder, Simon Michael, began the Fulton School of Painting in 1948, living and teaching at "Tortilla Flats", off Fulton Beach Road. He would often take his students out to paint the fish houses, fisherman, Mexican net makers, and shrimp and oyster boats around the harbors in Rockport, Fulton, Aransas Pass and Ingleside. Some of his favorite subjects were market scenes, especially from trips on which he would take his students to places like Mexico City and Guatemala.

Michael talked about what inspired him about local food scenes in an oral history interview: "Fulton at that time was very picturesque, and the old shrimp house and the boats, and it was so colorful. And I found that Fulton from the very

Simon Michael (Courtesy of Sandy Garrison)

first outdoor session was very, very cooperative. There was a warmth of the people, the interest on the part of the people of the community. And the owners of the shrimp house and of boats, the captains or the crew, were most cooperative, and they collaborated into any situation most generously by way of making it possible for the students to be comfortable…even to the extent of holding boats an hour later before going out so that they could get a drawing or a painting of that boat or some part of the riggings. And we would enter the fish house and as boats were being unloaded and as they were carrying on their business, we would get into various corners and were encouraged just to continue and not feel that they were thinking that we were disturbing them."

In 1950 he moved to King

Estelle Stair, second from left, in the back of the studio
Courtesy of Lisa Baer Frederick

Street in Rockport and hosted a free barbeque for hundreds of locals. He may have hoped that food would help the community accept "that artist fellow," who dressed and talked in a cultured manner and often had nude models and scores of young female students around. He also purchased "The Rambler," a 35-foot cabin cruiser, from the Morrison family and often took his students out on it to watch boats catching fish, shrimp or oysters.

Shelley Roaten commissioned Michael to paint a mural with his students for the fountain area of the drug store. This mural featured illustrations of Aransas County, dolphins,

John Dearman, Steve Russell, Kent Ulberg, Herb Booth, Harold Phenix
"Sporting Art" Exhibition
1998 September

Courtesy of Elsa Mathews

People gathered together at the home of Kit Dinger, a well-respected artist, who taught students like Steve Russell or at Estelle Stair's, an early member of the Rockport Art Association,

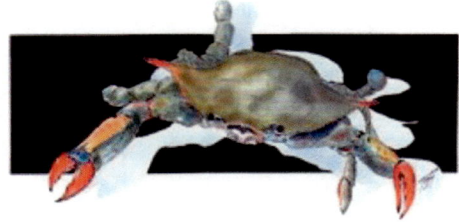

Courtesy of Melissa Cosby Pina

fish and seabirds. Michael noted that there was no church represented, so he suggested that a student add a Bible to a pelican that she was painting.

Other artists also sold paintings to decorate local restaurants including a12-foot painting of sand dunes by Estelle Stair for Corky's Restaurant.

would often cook and drink together as they dreamed of creating an art colony and later an art center. This was financed, in part, by food and beer sales at the early Rockport Art Festival, which began in 1967.

Fulton Oysterfest 2008

Local artist Steve Russell, frequently mentioned as one of the best cooks in the local county, often invited friends and area newcomers to his studio for a musical gathering, complete with grilled Barbados Sheep he'd shot himself or Paella, cooked on a pan he's forged himself. Russell, like many other artists over the years, has often painted shrimping and fishing boats, fish camps, Jackson's Seafood, ducks, and harbor scenes.

Russell joined other artists like Al Barnes, Herb Booth, Sam Caldwell, Jack Cowan and Kent Ullberg, who donated artwork to be auctioned off during fund-raising dinners to gather funds for the advocacy work of groups like Ducks Unlimited and Gulf Coast Conservation Association (GCCA),

---

**Estelle Stair's Shrimp Curry Dip**

| | |
|---|---|
| 3 lbs. shrimp | 2 T. chopped green pepper |
| 1 pint mayonnaise | 2 T. chopped green onion |
| 1 small can Pet milk | 2 T. chopped pimento |
| ¼ to ½ t. curry powder | Salt and pepper to taste |

Boil shrimp; clean and cut into bite size pieces. Mix in remaining ingredients. Add shrimp. Chill. Can also be heated in double boiler and served with rice.

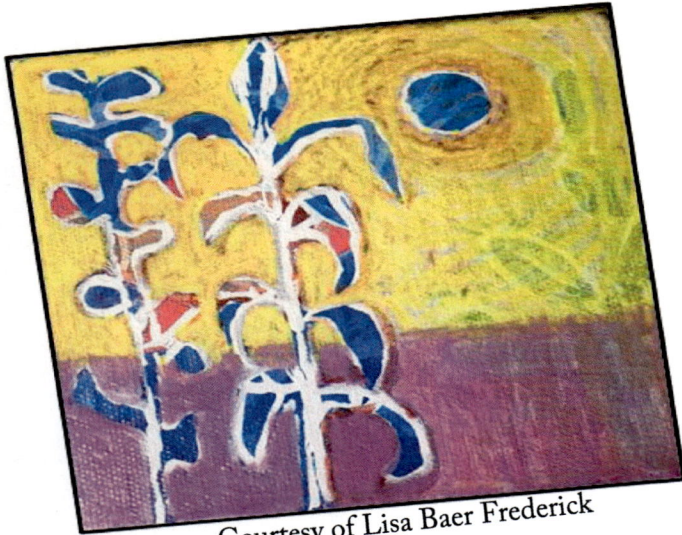
Courtesy of Lisa Baer Frederick

the forerunner of Coastal Conservation Association (CCA).

These artistic conservation efforts were instrumental in helping save and replenish local wildlife and the environment as well as fund Texas Parks and Wildlife personnel and

equipment. In 1986, "The Rockport Collection – Fish Game Fine Art," a cookbook, was published to benefit the Rockport Art Association. Al Barnes, Herb Booth, Jack Cowan, Michael Frary, Harold Phenix, and E.M. "Buck" Schiwetz contributed paintings for the book.

Charles "Popo" Cosby was a painting contractor, who opened a restaurant called Cheez's in his house on Palmetto and 5th in Fulton. He and B. J. Redfern painted a mural on one wall of the restaurant featuring landmarks like the old

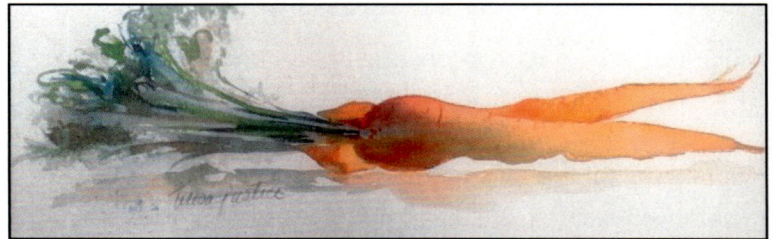
Courtesy of Teresa Justice

Moorish Courthouse, the Fulton Mansion and others.

As a self-taught artist, he learned from his mistakes as well as other artists who came by Popo's Art Studio. He was also a supporter of local charities and helping others in need by getting a barbeque or benefit together at Paws and Taws. He also sold food-related prints at Oysterfest such as this Oysterfest Poster in 2006.

Chris Ely, owner of the Little Gallery in Fulton, like numerous other artists, earned extra money by illustrating ads and menus for local restaurants and recipe books for non-profit organizations like Aransas County Medical Services, Inc.

Shirley Farley, another note-worthy artist, not only wrote a cookbook, but illustrated the cover and divider pages as well.

Artists and food were intricately woven throughout the cuisine of Aransas County.

PASTACIUTA                                    Kit Dinger

a large pkg. flat noodles          2 lb. ground beef
3 chopped onions                   2 cloves minced garlic
pinch of rosemary                  salt and pepper to taste
1 oz. red wine                     can mushrooms
can whole kernel corn

Brown 2 lb. ground beef in large skillet in olive oil. Add onions, garlic and pinch of rosemary and cook till onions are soft. Salt and pepper to taste. Add tomatoes, tomato sauce (1 can) and 1 can tomato paste. Also 1 oz. red wine if desired. Add mushrooms, corn and simmer very slowly with lid on skillet, while noodles are cooking in salted water. In large flat pan or casserole put a layer of noodles, layer of sauce and repeat. Sprinkle grated parmesan cheese on top. Bake at 350 for about 45 minutes. When done sprinkle more cheese on top and serve.

ROCKPORT-FULTON
SeaFair

Food

Festivals

22nd Annual Rockport
Festival of
Wine & Food
Join us for LIVE Music, Teflon Chef
Competition, and Shopping!

SATURDAY, MAY 26TH & SUNDAY, 27TH 2018

Taste
of Rockport & Fulton, TX
eat ✹ drink ✹ bid

Showcase of
Restaurants and Caterers

342

# Oysterfest

Several celebrations are held every year in Aransas County. Beginning on the first weekend of March, the Fulton Volunteer Fire Department and the Town of Fulton sponsor the annual Oysterfest. This four-day celebration on the first weekend in March salutes this tasty bi-valve found in our local waters through food, crafts and entertainment.

Along with carnival rides and games, with contests for oyster eating contest and oyster shucking, it provides family fun! All proceeds benefit the Fulton Volunteer Fire Department and the Town of Fulton.

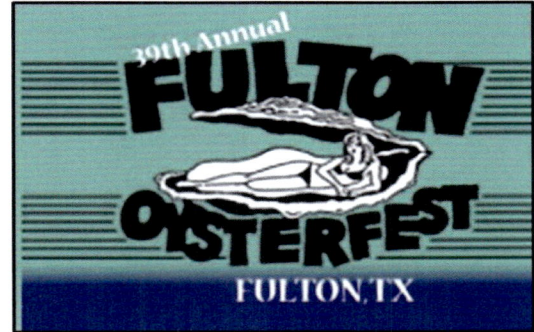

"Aw Shucks" (right) and "Raw Bar" (left) courtesy of Elsa Mathews.

# Taste of Rockport

Each spring, the Rotary Club offers diners a taste of the local restaurants on one night, at one place for one price. Along with this fund-raiser for high school scholarships, auctions, wine and entertainment are always included.

Photos courtesy of The Rotary Club.

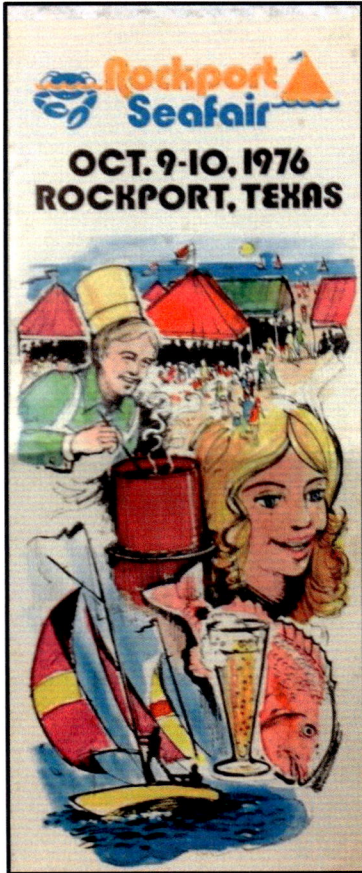

Courtesy of Turf Overturf

## Seafair Began as One Man's Idea

Over forty years ago, the idea for Seafair was the brainchild of a Rockport man, Bill Christian. He believed the area needed a celebration in the fall to fill the lull between the summer visitors and the arrival of winter tourists. Since the initial event, Seafair has been scheduled annually for the second weekend of October.

Though the event has grown since its creation, it remains very much the same as Christian envisioned it: a parade, arts and crafts, bands, water entertainment and a gumbo cook-off. These were part of the very first Seafair. Today they all remain major attractions.

During that initial year, a Board of Directors was formed, and each board member

was an integral part of planning the 4-day event. A lot of blood, sweat and tears was expended during those beginning years.

In April 2000, the Chamber agreed to take over the festival. That year, during Seafair the community experienced the coldest of cold fronts for that time period and four solid days of rain.

It was shortly after that rain out event that Bill Christian came into the office of the Chamber with a lot of encouraging words and a box full of Seafair history. The Chamber is committed to the continuing the Seafair legacy and the wonderful ideas of Bill Christian.

Courtesy of Turf Overturf

Courtesy of Harriet McCarty

Photos courtesy of the RF Chamber of Commerce

# Rockport Festival of Wine & Food

During Memorial Day weekend, the Texas Maritime Museum hosts a festival focusing on food and wine. Over 100 different wines are available for the celebration.  People from all over the nation attend annually.

Photos courtesy of the Texas Maritime Museum

Courtesy of Steve Russell

# Map of Historical Markers- Courtesy of Nancy Paulson

**Legend:**
- 🔺P Pavilion and Bridge
- ♿ ADA Accessible
- 🚻 Public Restrooms
- 🐦 Birding Sites 🔴
- 🛶 Kayak Launch Sites 🔵
- 📋 Historical/Heritage Sites 🟢
- 🚶🚴 Trails - Hike/Bike 🟡

**Websites with more information**

- www.TheHistoryCenterForAransasCounty.org
- www.AransasPathways.com
- www.Rockport-Fulton.org
- facebook.com/AransasPathways/
- facebook.com/AransasCountyHistoryCenter/
- twitter.com/RockportBirder
- info@aransaspathways.com

© Rockport Web Sites - Rockport, Texas
REV Fall 8-2017

**Discover Aransas County**

ARANSAS PATHWAYS

Birding • History • Trails • Kayaking

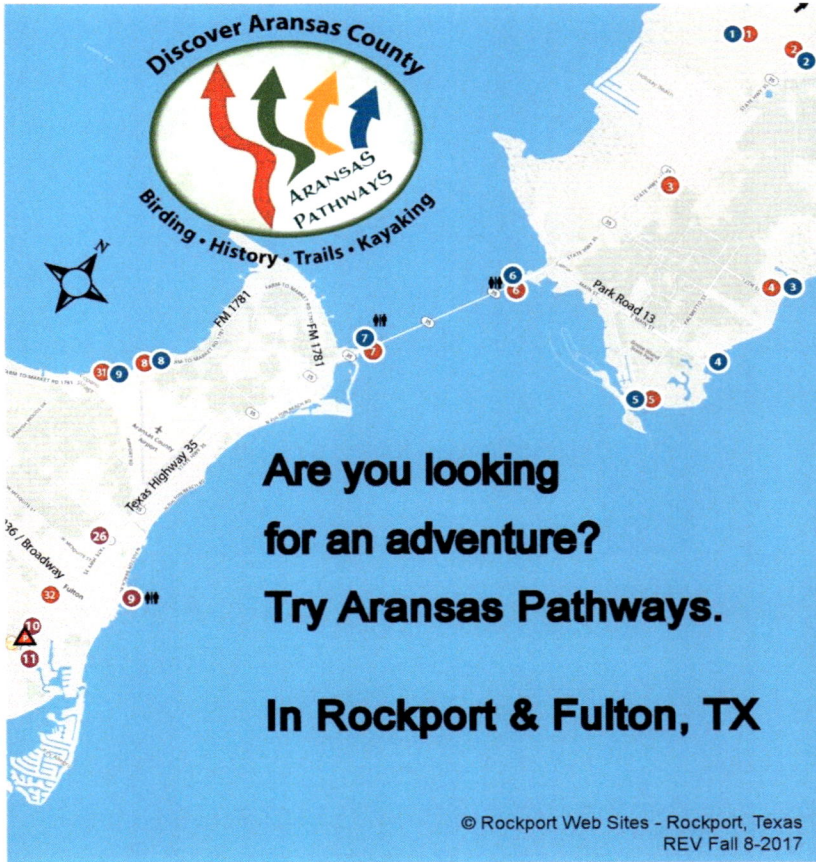

Are you looking
for an adventure?
Try Aransas Pathways.

In Rockport & Fulton, TX

© Rockport Web Sites - Rockport, Texas
REV Fall 8-2017

**Downtown Rockport**

**Downtown Fulton**

## About the Editors

Vickie Moon Merchant, History Center President, has a Doctor of Philosophy in Curriculum and Instruction from Texas A&M University – College Station with a concentration in Multicultural, Urban and International Education. Before her retirement, she was an Assistant Professor of Education, Adjunct Faculty, University Lecturer, Coordinator of The Teacher Induction Program and Researcher, as well as an ACISD elementary teacher. She has presented at numerous local, regional, national and international conferences, including for the American Association of Colleges for Teacher Education, the American Educational Research Association, the Society for Information Technology & Teacher Education, the International Mentoring Association, and the Association of Supervision and Curriculum Development. She also has publications in several national journals. Since her retirement, she has volunteered for several local non-profits in her hometown, connecting and training members. She has curated numerous exhibits at the History Center, been Secretary, Exhibit and Education Chair, and Publicity Chair. She helped edit a book, *30 Years Through the News/Lens: A History of Aransas County in News, Highlights & Photos* by Mike Probst and *Doc's Garden: A Guide to Useful Plants* by Pat Garland. She and Dr. Betz presented their research on the Rockport-Fulton Art Colony at the Annual National Conference of the American Association for State and Local History in 2017.

Kay Betz, former History Center Secretary and Development and Membership Chair, is retired from the University of Texas at Austin, where she was Director of Learning and Organizational Development. Her doctorate in adult education specialized in human resource and organizational development. She has presented at local, regional, state, national and international conferences. She was a researcher and editor for *The Aransas Pass Light Station. A History*, conducting numerous oral history interviews for the current owner, Charles Butt, for whom she worked for five years. She was the co-curator for "The Rockport Art Colony Exhibit: 1948-1984," conducting many oral history interviews with artists, gallery owners, and other members of the community. She is continuing that research and writing a book for TAMU UP about the Art Colony with Dr. Merchant. She also presented the results of her and Dr. Merchant's research on Aransas County Foodways and Culinary Traditions at the 2018 Foodways-Texas Symposium with chef and cookbook author Terry Thompson-Anderson. She was instrumental in helping obtain a Cultural Arts District designation from the Texas Commission on the Arts for the local community, helping develop a successful application. She also chaired several committees for the Rockport Art Center, including ones to develop a Strategic Plan, expand programming in other art forms, and determine a new site.

From the work of Herb Booth Studios

# Index of Recipes

| Entrees | *Beef* | |
|---|---|---|
| | Beef Kabobs | 73 |
| | Clark and Edith Herring's Brundrett (not Brunswick) Stew | 209 |
| | Horseradish Meat Loaf | 212 |
| | Pastaciuta | 341 |
| | *Chicken* | |
| | King Ranch Chicken Casserole | 327 |
| | Cornbread Dressing- with chicken | 295 |
| | Popo's Chicken & Dumplings | 268 |
| Seafood | | |
| | Little Bay Club Seafood Au Gratin | 256 |
| | Shrimp and Crab with Wild Boar Sausage, Potatoes and Corn | 260 |
| | *Crab* | |
| | Baked Crab Cakes with Basil Tartar Sauce | 215 |

## Desserts

## Miscellaneous

# References

Aransas County Medical Services, Inc. (1999). *Taste of the Coast 2000: A Collection of Recipes by the Women's Committee of the Aransas County Medical Services, Inc.* Kearney, NE: Cookbook by Marris Press.

Aransas County Medical Services, Inc. (2000). *Another Taste of the Coast,* Olathe, KS: Cookbook Publishers, Inc.

Aransas County Medical Services, Inc. (2006). Taste of the Coast: 2006. Olathe, KS: Cookbook Publishers, Inc.

Allen, W. & Hastings-Taylor, S. (1997). *Aransas: The life of a Texas coastal county.* Austin, TX: Eakin Press.

Anonymous. (1905). *Corpus Christi and Rockport: For health and recreation.* San Antonio, TX: Photos by Wheeler of Corpus Christi and Mills Printer.

Anonymous. (1919). *Gulf coast immigration company* [Brochure]. San Antonio, TX: E. J. Jackson Co. Printer.

Baughman, J. (1949). *The toast of the coast: A guide to pleasure.* [Brochure]. Rockport, TX: Rockport Chamber of Commerce.

Black S. & C. (2009). *Recipes & remembrances.* Kearny, NE: Morris Press Cookbook.

Burdette, M. (2014). *The Inn at El Canelo Cookbook: Recipes & More*. Kearney, NE: Morris Press Cookbooks.

Burdette, M. (22 July, 2017). *Historic Aransas County.* Presented at The History Center for Aransas County, Rockport, Texas.

Clark, G. (1981). *The South Coast of Texas*. On South Coast of Texas Album (CD). Location: Warner Bros. Retrieved from https://genius.com/Guy-clark-south-coast-of-texas-lyrics

Clark, G. (1983). *Homegrown Tomatoes*. On Better Days Album (CD). Location: Warner Bros. Retrieved from https://genius.com/Guy-clark-homegrown-tomatoes-lyrics

Cosby-Pina, M. (6 August, 2017). *Vintage fishing lures.* Presented at The History Center for Aransas County, Rockport, Texas.

Covey, C. (1961). *Cabeza de Vaca: Adventures in the unknown interior of America, 1542*, translated and edited by Cyclone Covey, Albuquerque, N. M.: University of New Mexico Press.

Cox. M. (2013). *Aransas Abattoir*. Retrieved from http://www.texasescapes.com/MikeCox/TexasTales/Aransas-Abattoir.htm

Ehrenberg, H. (1843). *With Milam and Fannin: Adventures of a German Boy in Texas' Revolution*. Austin, TX: Pemberton Press.

Elverson, V. (1991). *Gulf coast cooking*. Fredericksburg, Texas: Shearer Publishing.

Foster, W. (2008). *Historic native peoples of Texas*. Austin, TX: University of Texas Press.

Freeman, J. (2012). Rockport: *A childhood by the sea*. CreateSpace Independent Publishing Platform.

Garrido, D. & Walsh, R. (1998). *Nuevo Tex-Mex*. San Francisco, CA: Chronicle Books.

Gilpin, P. (1956). *A two-toned symphony: Rockport's fishbowl*. The Houston Chronicle Rotogravure Magazine. Copy in possession of The Friends of the History Center.

Hein, P. (1984). *Tastes & tales from Texas*. Austin, TX: Hein & Associates.

Herndon, W. (2010). *Texas Gulf coast stories*. Charleston, SC: The History Press.

Hines, D. (1941). *Adventures in good eating* (17th ed.). Bowling Green, KY: Adventures in Good Eating, Inc.

Jackson, J. (13 August, 2017). *The Three Generation Jackson Seafood Business.* Presented at The History Center for Aransas County, Rockport, Texas.

Johnson, K. (17 August, 2012). *Coastal flavors: Tapping the sea for salt.* Retrieved from: http://nl.newsbank.com/nl-search/we/Archives?p_action=list&p_topdoc=21

Johnson, K. (19 September, 2012). *Coastal Flavors: Sweet and smoky mesquite.* Corpus Christi Caller-Times. Retrieved from: http://nl.newsbank.com/nl-search/we/Archives?p_action=list&p_topdoc=21

Johnson, K. (22 August, 2012). *Coastal Flavors: When life gives you lemons, say thank you!* Retrieved from: http://nl.newsbank.com/nl-search/we/Archives?n.action=list&p.topdoc=21

Johnson, K. (26 September, 2012). *Coastal flavors: Snapper crudo,* Retreived from: http://nl.newsbank.com/nl-search/we/Archives?p_action=list&p_topdoc=21

Johnson, K. (6 March, 2013). *Coastal flavors: A bouquet of greens.* Retrieved from:
http://nl.newsbank.com/nl-search/we/Archives?p_action=list&p_topdoc=21

Johnson, K. (7 August, 2013). *Coastal flavors: Dot's Boiling Pot.* Retrieved from
http://nl.newsbank.com/nlsearrch/we/Archives?p_action/=list&p_topdoc=21

Johnson, K. (14 August, 2013. Coastal flavors: An oyster token of change. Retrieved
From http://nl.newsbank.com/nl-search/we/Archives?p_action=list&p_topdoc=21

Jones-Gulsby, K. (30 July, 2017). *Stir It Up.* Presented at The History Center for
Aransas County, Rockport, Texas

Kenmotsu, N. & Dial, S. (n. d.) Native peoples of the coastal prairies and marshlands
in early historic times. *Texas Beyond History* accessed June 02, 2018 from
https://www.texasbeyondhistory.net/coast/prehistory/images/intro.html

Krieger, A. (2002). *We came naked and barefoot: The journey of Cabeza de Vaca across North America.* Austin, TX:
University of Texas Press.

La Vere, D. (2004). *The Texas Indians*. College Station, TX: Texas A&M University Press.

Lipscomb, C. (2018). Karankawa Indians, *Handbook of Texas Online* accessed June 1, 2018 from
    http://www.tshaonline.org/handbook/online/ articles/bmk05

McCallister, J. (1986). *Rockport collection: Fish, game, fine art*. Austin, TX: Hart Graphics, Inc.

McKey, N. (2005). *Cooking with Texas Highways*. Austin, TX: University of Texas Press.

Mills, J. (1963). *Remembering Mills Wharf. Corpus Christi Caller-Times*. Copy in possession of Friends of the
    History Center, Rockport, Texas.

Morgan, J. (2018). *Remembrances of the Fox family*. Retrieved from https://www.facebook.com/joann.morgan.754

Pack, MM (2012). Earliest residents: Karankawa. *Oxford encyclopedia of Food & Drink in America*. Oxford,
    England: Oxford University Press.

Paws & Taws Square Dance Club. (1964). *Square Dancers and Friends Cookbook*. Kansas City, KS: North America
    Press of Kansas City, Inc.

Picton Reunion (n. d.). *The Rockport Pilot.* Copy in possession of Friends of the History Center, Rockport, Texas.

Ricklis, R. (n. d.). The Prehistory of the Texas Coastal Zone: 10,000 Years of Changing Environment and Culture, *Texas Beyond History* accessed June 2, 2018, from https://www.texasbeyondhistory.net/coast/prehistory/images/intro.html

Ricklis, R. (1996). *The Karankawa Indians of Texas: An Ecological Study of Cultural Tradition and Change.* Austin, TX: University of Texas Press.

Rockport Firemen's Auxiliary (n. d.) *Kitchen Treats from The Toast of the Coast Rockport, Texas.* Olathe, KS: Cookbook Publishers, Inc.

Russell, S. (2004). *Notes by a Texas painter.* Rockport, TX: Instantpublisher.com

Steward, C. (1991). Jackson Gulf boats sold, described as 'end of an era'. *The Rockport Pilot.* Copy in possession of the Friends of the History Center.

St. John, R. (2006). *Deep South Parties:* How to survive the southern cocktail hour without a box of French onion soup mix, a block of processed cheese, or a cocktail weenie. Westport, CT: Hyperion Press.

Teal, A. (1931). Reminiscences. *Southwestern Historical Quarterly*, XXXIV, pp. 327.

The Blackland Museum. (2018). Coleman-Fulton Pasture Company. Retrieved from https://www.facebook.com/The-Blackland-Museum-160371267332260/

The Parent Teacher Association of Rockport, Texas (1927). *Queens in the Kitchen Tested Recipes from Rockport Housekeepers.* Manuscript reproduced by the Aransas County Historical Society in 2011.

Thompson-Anderson, T. (2017, August). *Texas Gulf Coast Cuisine.* Presented at The History Center for Aransas County, Rockport, Texas.

U.S. Patent Office (1869). *Improvement in apparatus for slaughtering and curing meat, patent certificate to George Fulton.* Retrieved from https://www.thc.texas.gov/historic-sites/fulton-mansion/history/george-fulton-inventor

Visionaries in Preservations. (2009). Retrieved from https://www.aransascountytx.gov/historiccomm/heritage.php

Walsh, R. (2002). *Legends of Texas barbecue.* San Francisco, CA: Chronicle Books.

Walsh, R. (2012). *Texas eats: The new lone star heritage cookbook.* Berkeley, CA: Ten Speed Press.

Wright, L. (2017) *Helpful hints.* Presented at The History Center for Aransas County, Rockport, Texas.

Wright, L. (2017). *Red snapper run.* Presented at The History Center for Aransas County, Rockport, Texas.

Courtesy of Steve Russell

371

# Ordering your copy of *Foodways*

*Foodways* will make great gifts for birthdays, anniversaries, wedding, showers, Christmas, Mother's Day and other special occasions. To order additional copies of this book, detach and mail the order form below with a check or money order to:

The History Center for Aransas County

P.O. Box 106

Fulton, Tx 78358

Or contact us at:

361-727-9214

friends@thehistorycenterforaransacounty.org

Order from our website at www.thehistorycenterforaransascounty.org Click on "Support" and then "Gift Shop"

---

Please send me _____ copies of

Foodways: The Culinary Traditions of Aransas County, Tx

At $45.00 each plus $5.00 s/h per book

Enclosed is my check for $_____

Mail book to:

Name_____

Address_____

City_____State_____Zip_____

Phone_____Email_____

56796269R00215

Made in the USA
Columbia, SC
02 May 2019